Learning Reso

Level 2 Accounting

for OCR Level 2 Accounting Units 1 – 3

Michael Fardon

Sheila Robinson

osborne
BOOKS

Published by Osborne Books Limited
Unit 1B Everoak Estate
Bromyard Road
Worcester WR2 5HP
Tel 01905 748071
Email books@osbornebooks.co.uk
Website www.osbornebooks.co.uk

Printed and Bound in Great Britain by MPG Books Group
Cover design by Richard Holt

British Library Cataloguing in Publication Data
A catalogue record for this book is available from the British Library

ISBN 978 1905777 181

CONTENTS

ACKNOWLEDGEMENTS

The authors wish to thank the following for their help with the reading and production of this book: Mike Gilbert, Roger Petheram, and Malcolm Robinson. The publisher is also very grateful to Ruth Grant who has provided invaluable practical advice and support during the course of this project.

THE AUTHORS

Michael Fardon has extensive teaching experience of a wide range of banking, business and accountancy courses at Worcester College of Technology. He now specialises in writing financial texts and is General Editor at Osborne Books. He is also an educational consultant and has worked in the areas of vocational business curriculum development.

Sheila Robinson has extensive teaching experience as a Senior Lecturer in Accountancy at Stockport College where she taught on accountancy and management courses. She is a well-established author of accountancy text books and continues as a practising accountant. Sheila is a former Council Member and Director of the Association of Accounting Technicians.

INTRODUCTION

the textbook

Level 2 Accounting has been written as a practical guide for students studying the three units of the OCR Level 2 Certificate in Accounting. This book also builds on the skills developed by the OCR Level 1 Certificate in Bookkeeping and the associated Osborne Books text *Level 1 Bookkeeping*, (endorsed by OCR). The three Units of the Level 2 Accounting Certificate deal in turn with:

- writing up the day books from source documents, posting to the ledger accounts and drawing up a simple trial balance
- further postings to ledger accounts from day books and the cash book, balancing the accounts and drawing up control accounts
- journal entries and adjustments and the production of a revised trial balance

The text of *Level 2 Accounting* contains:

- clear and practical explanations and numerous diagrams
- three 'follow through' business Case Studies, one for each Unit
- chapter summaries and 'Exam Tips'
- practical Exercises

This text has been prepared with great care to ensure that it is fully in line with the terminology and requirements of current OCR assessment practice.

e-resources

A large part of the OCR course involves the completion of day books, ledger accounts, journals and trial balances. To help with this, Osborne Books has produced suitable blank formats, available for free download from the Resources Section of www.osbornebooks.co.uk. Answers to selected exercises (marked in the text with an asterisk) are also freely available from the website.

A *Tutor Resource CD* for this text, containing photocopiable account formats and documents, together with a practice exam and assignments (with answers) based on the OCR model, is available to teaching centres which have adopted the textbook. If you are a tutor and are interested in the *Tutor Resource CD*, please call Osborne Books Customer Services on 01905 748071 for further details.

Introduction to the Unit 1 Examination

The Unit 1 title for the OCR Level 2 in Accounting is:

Maintain Day books, Prepare Ledger Balances and Extract a Trial Balance

This Unit is compulsory and you will have to sit an external exam for your assessment. You will have two hours in which to complete the exam plus ten minutes reading time. The exam is very straightforward and involves a number of processes. You should already be familiar with some of the formats and terminology used. If they are new to you, there will be notes in this text to explain how they work.

● You will be given a number of financial documents – invoices and credit notes

  - issued to customers

  - received from suppliers

  These 'source documents' record transactions – sales and purchases – which need to be entered into the double-entry accounts of the business.

● You will enter the figures from these invoices and credit notes into summaries in table form known as 'day books'.

● From the day books you will then enter figures into the double-entry accounts of the business which are organised in a series of 'ledgers':

  - purchase ledger (supplier accounts)

  - sales ledger (customer accounts)

  - nominal ledger (all the other accounts)

● When you have entered all the figures from the day books you will then total and 'balance' the double-entry accounts.

● You will then transfer the balances of the double-entry accounts into a 'trial balance' which lists and totals all the debit account balances and all the credit account balances. If your work so far has been accurate the debit and credit totals should be the same.

These processes are summarised here in the diagram on the opposite page. Study this diagram and then work through the chapters that follow.

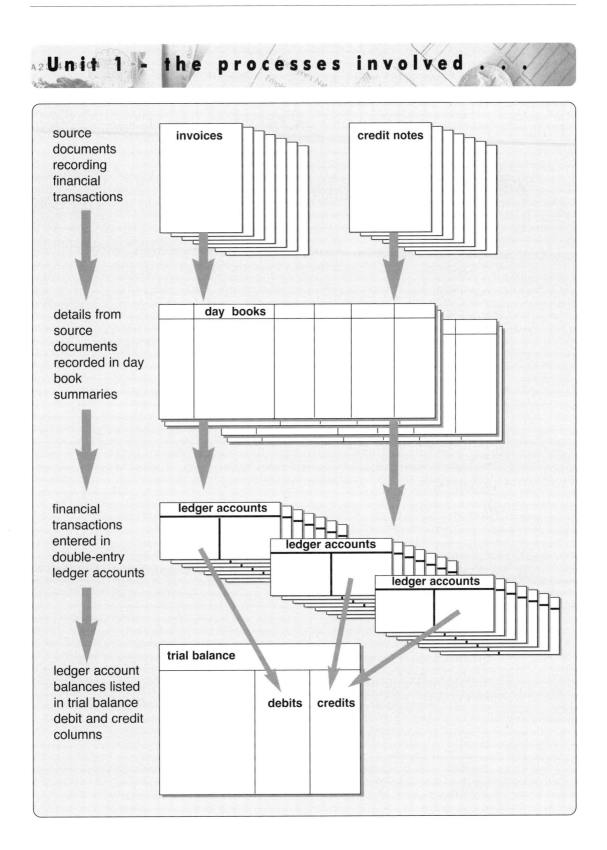

source documents recording financial transactions

invoices

credit notes

details from source documents recorded in day book summaries

day books

financial transactions entered in double-entry ledger accounts

ledger accounts

ledger accounts

ledger accounts

ledger account balances listed in trial balance debit and credit columns

trial balance

debits credits

1 Documents to day books

what this chapter covers . . .

This chapter:

- shows the ways in which information about financial transactions such as sales and purchases is shown on invoices and credit notes

- explains how VAT (Value Added Tax) is calculated on invoices and credit notes

- illustrates the way in which this financial information is transferred from invoices and credit notes into 'day book' summaries

- explains the format of day books - ie the various headings and columns, and the way in which they are written up

- shows how the day book columns are totalled

- explains how checks can be made on the accuracy of the writing up of the day books

Unit 1 Case Study – Zest Sports

Zest Sports

All the processes carried out in Unit 1 will be illustrated in this book by a Case Study of a specialist sports goods supplier 'Zest Sports'.

This business is run by Tom Hick, who supplies a number of sports shops in the UK. Tom specialises in two types of sports balls: footballs and tennis balls.

Tom obtains his stock from a wide variety of suppliers and sells his goods on credit.

He deals with a number of invoices and credit notes each week, issuing them to his customers and also receiving them from his suppliers.

INVOICE

An **invoice** is a financial document which is sent by the seller of goods or services to a customer. When an invoice is issued, normally the goods or services have been sold **on credit**. This means that the goods or services will be paid for at a later date. Two invoices are illustrated and explained in full on the next two pages. The main information an invoice contains is:

- **details** (name and address) of the seller and buyer
- the **date** of the invoice
- **details** of the goods or services that have been sold
  - how many items, a description of what they are and how much they cost
- the **price** charged and the amount due after deduction of any discount
  - a discount is a percentage reduction in the price, for example
    20% trade discount on goods costing £100 is £100 x 20/100
    = a £20 deduction in price
- **VAT** (Value Added Tax) charged on the goods
  - VAT is a government tax which is charged at a set percentage of the invoice total
  - most businesses are 'VAT registered' and have to charge VAT on their sales to their customers
- the **time period** allowed before payment has to be made
  - a period such as 30 days after invoice date is fairly common

purchase invoices and sales invoices

A **purchase invoice** is an invoice received by a business which has bought goods and services from a supplier. When you deal with a business scenario in an exam you need to think about a purchase invoice as the document which is **received by you** from someone else.

Often in the exam the supplier invoices contain two types of product and trade discount is deducted.

A **sales invoice** is an invoice issued by a business which is selling goods and services. When you deal with a business scenario in the exam, you need to think about a sales invoice as the document which is **issued by you**.

Often in the exam the seller has two types of product and there is no trade discount involved, although in practice trade discount may be deducted.

Remember that purchase and sales invoices are not different types of invoice; they just have a different description - 'purchase' and 'sales' – depending on who you are in the transaction: the purchaser or the seller.

purchase invoice – details for the purchases day book

This purchase invoice has been sent by a supplier – AB Supplies Limited – to Zest Sports for payment for two different types of balls supplied. The details explained in the boxes on the left of the invoice are the details that you need to identify when doing an exam.

Note that in this case trade discount has been deducted by the supplier.

The details in the boxes will have to be entered in the day book summary (see later in the chapter).

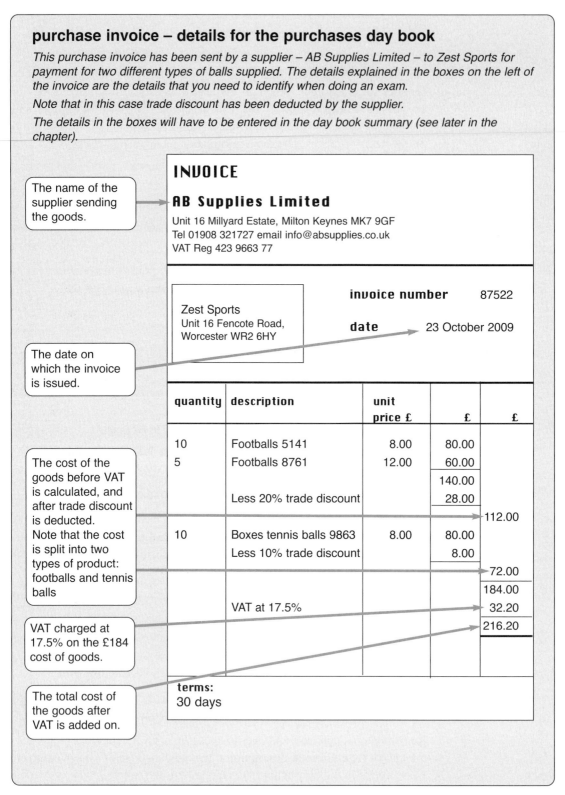

The name of the supplier sending the goods.

The date on which the invoice is issued.

The cost of the goods before VAT is calculated, and after trade discount is deducted.
Note that the cost is split into two types of product: footballs and tennis balls

VAT charged at 17.5% on the £184 cost of goods.

The total cost of the goods after VAT is added on.

INVOICE

AB Supplies Limited
Unit 16 Millyard Estate, Milton Keynes MK7 9GF
Tel 01908 321727 email info@absupplies.co.uk
VAT Reg 423 9663 77

Zest Sports
Unit 16 Fencote Road,
Worcester WR2 6HY

invoice number   87522

date   23 October 2009

quantity	description	unit price £	£	£
10	Footballs 5141	8.00	80.00	
5	Footballs 8761	12.00	60.00	
			140.00	
	Less 20% trade discount		28.00	
				112.00
10	Boxes tennis balls 9863	8.00	80.00	
	Less 10% trade discount		8.00	
				72.00
				184.00
	VAT at 17.5%			32.20
				216.20

terms:
30 days

sales invoice – details for the sales day book

This sales invoice has been issued by Zest Sports to its customer Gullwing Sports Ltd. The details explained in the boxes on the left of the invoice are the details that you will need to identify when doing an exam.

Note that there is no trade discount involved on this invoice.

The details in the boxes will have to be entered in the day book summary (see later in the chapter).

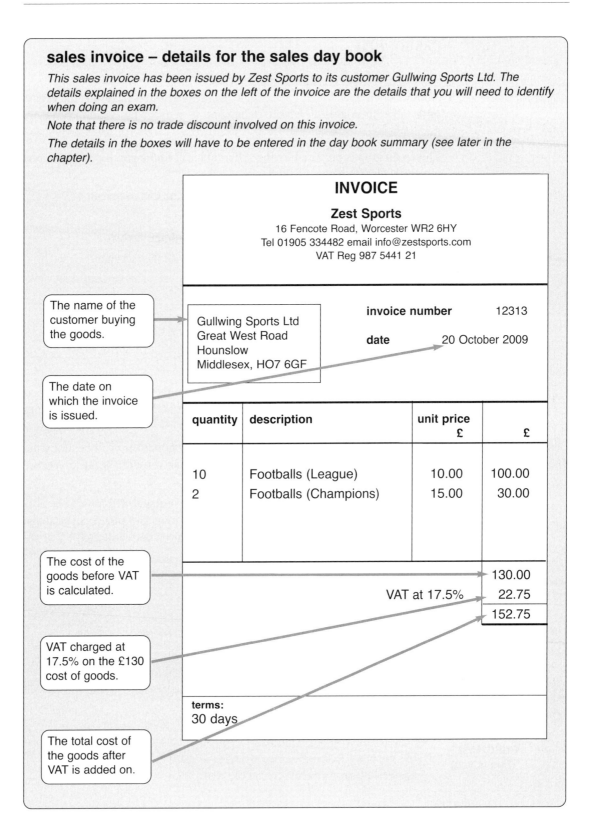

The name of the customer buying the goods.

The date on which the invoice is issued.

The cost of the goods before VAT is calculated.

VAT charged at 17.5% on the £130 cost of goods.

The total cost of the goods after VAT is added on.

INVOICE

Zest Sports
16 Fencote Road, Worcester WR2 6HY
Tel 01905 334482 email info@zestsports.com
VAT Reg 987 5441 21

Gullwing Sports Ltd
Great West Road
Hounslow
Middlesex, HO7 6GF

invoice number	12313
date	20 October 2009

quantity	description	unit price £	£
10	Footballs (League)	10.00	100.00
2	Footballs (Champions)	15.00	30.00
			130.00
		VAT at 17.5%	22.75
			152.75

terms:
30 days

CREDIT NOTE

Another document which you will have to deal with in an exam is the **credit note**. A credit note is a 'refund' document. It reduces the amount owed by the purchaser.

The credit note is prepared by the seller and sent to the purchaser. Situations where this might happen include:

• the goods may have been damaged or faulty or lost in transit

• the wrong goods may have been sent

• the quantity of goods sent does not tie up with the invoice

A credit note is illustrated and explained in full on the next page

As you will see from this illustration, the credit note has basically the same format as the invoice.

sales returns and purchase returns credit notes

As has been explained above, a credit note is issued by the seller to reduce the amount owed by the purchaser.

This happens in the case of **sales returns**. This term is easy to understand because it means that if you are the **seller**, the goods are being **returned** to you and so a credit note will have to be issued.

On the other hand if you have **purchased** faulty goods you will be doing the returning and the faulty goods become **purchase returns**, because you are **returning** them.

This is illustrated in the diagram below. In the exam you will have to be able to identify credit notes relating to both **sales returns** and **purchase returns**. To do this you will have to think about the situation and work out if you are the seller or the purchaser.

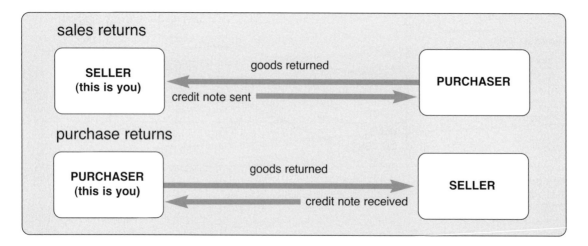

purchase returns credit note – details for the day book

This credit note has been sent by a supplier – AB Supplies Limited – to Zest Sports as a refund for two different types of balls supplied. Zest Sports has returned some of the balls because they were damaged (a purchase return). The details explained in the boxes on the left are the details that you will need to identify when doing your exam, assuming that you are Zest Sports, the seller.

Note that in this case trade discount has been deducted by the supplier.

The details in the boxes will have to be entered in the day book summary (see later in the chapter).

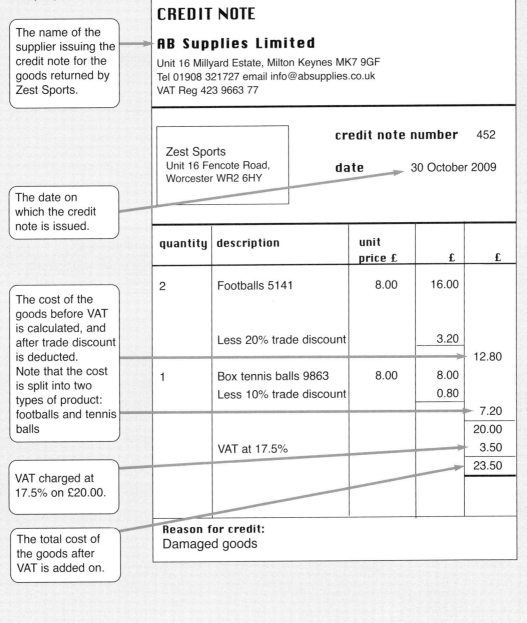

The name of the supplier issuing the credit note for the goods returned by Zest Sports.

The date on which the credit note is issued.

The cost of the goods before VAT is calculated, and after trade discount is deducted. Note that the cost is split into two types of product: footballs and tennis balls

VAT charged at 17.5% on £20.00.

The total cost of the goods after VAT is added on.

CREDIT NOTE

AB Supplies Limited

Unit 16 Millyard Estate, Milton Keynes MK7 9GF
Tel 01908 321727 email info@absupplies.co.uk
VAT Reg 423 9663 77

Zest Sports
Unit 16 Fencote Road,
Worcester WR2 6HY

credit note number   452

date   30 October 2009

quantity	description	unit price £	£	£
2	Footballs 5141	8.00	16.00	
	Less 20% trade discount		3.20	
				12.80
1	Box tennis balls 9863	8.00	8.00	
	Less 10% trade discount		0.80	
				7.20
				20.00
	VAT at 17.5%			3.50
				23.50

Reason for credit:
Damaged goods

sales returns credit note – details for the day book

This credit note has been issued by Zest Sports to its customer Gullwing Sports Ltd. The credit is a refund due for two footballs received in a damaged condition and returned by Gullwing Sports (a sales return). The details explained in the boxes on the left are the details that you will need to identify when doing your exam, assuming that you are Zest Sports, the seller.

Note that there is no trade discount involved on this credit note.

The details in the boxes to the left of the credit note will have to be entered in the sales returns day book summary (see later in the chapter).

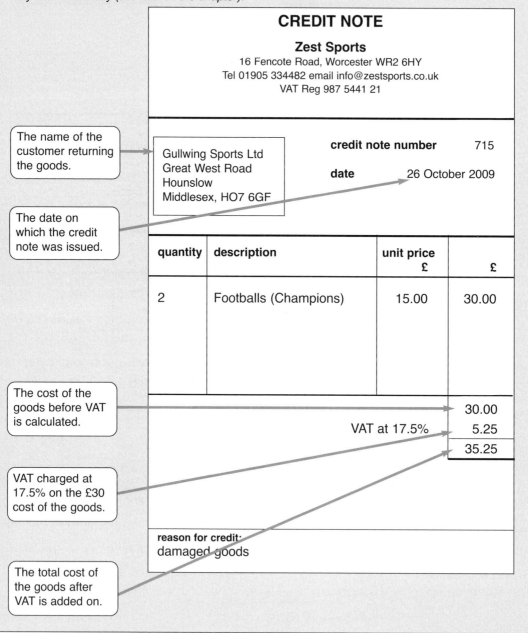

The name of the customer returning the goods.

The date on which the credit note was issued.

The cost of the goods before VAT is calculated.

VAT charged at 17.5% on the £30 cost of the goods.

The total cost of the goods after VAT is added on.

CREDIT NOTE

Zest Sports
16 Fencote Road, Worcester WR2 6HY
Tel 01905 334482 email info@zestsports.co.uk
VAT Reg 987 5441 21

		credit note number	715
Gullwing Sports Ltd Great West Road Hounslow Middlesex, HO7 6GF		date	26 October 2009

quantity	description	unit price £	£
2	Footballs (Champions)	15.00	30.00
			30.00
		VAT at 17.5%	5.25
			35.25

reason for credit:
damaged goods

WRITING UP THE DAY BOOKS

what is a day book?

A day book is a summary list of financial transactions. It is the source of information needed for entering up the ledger accounts. Study the diagram below to see how a day book fits into the accounting system.

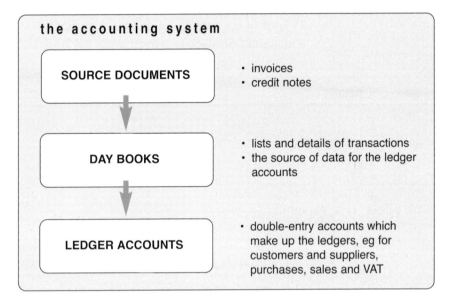

A day book therefore acts as the link between the invoices and credit notes shown in the last few pages - the **source documents** - and the accounts which are needed to record all aspects of credit purchases and credit sales.

Until the various day books are completed, all the business will have to show for its credit sales and purchases and returns will be piles of invoices and credit notes. The day books organise and summarise all this information into a manageable form.

types of day book

There are a number of different day books, each dealing with a different type of transaction. In the exam you will have to write entries in four day books:

- **purchases day book** - compiled from purchase invoices sent by suppliers

- **purchase returns day book** - compiled from credit notes received from suppliers

- **sales day book** - compiled from sales invoices sent to customers

- **sales returns day book** - compiled from credit notes issued to customers

format of a purchases day book

Day books are set out in a series of columns and it is a very simple process to enter up the necessary data from the source documents.

The purchases day book for Zest Sports is shown below, and purchase and sales invoices are shown on the next two pages. You should:

1   Study the day book format on this page and read the explanatory notes that follow.

2   Look at the invoices on the next two pages to identify the source of the information which is entered in the day book (follow the arrows).

Purchases Day Book

Date	Details	Footballs	Tennis Balls	VAT	Total
2009		£	£	£	£
23 Oct	AB Supplies	112.00	72.00	32.20	216.20

| The date is the date of the purchase invoice. | The details are the name of the supplier. | These two columns distinguish between two different types of product ordered by the business. | VAT is charged and added to the cost of goods. | this is the final total owing to the supplier. |

The day book columns are, from left to right:

Date	• the year date is shown on the first line
	• the month and day date of the invoice is entered on the lines underneath
	• you should never enter a ditto mark (") in the date column
Details	• the name of the supplier (not the goods)
Footballs	• the amount owing (excluding VAT) for a category of product (here it is footballs)
Tennis balls	• the amount owing (excluding VAT) for a second category of product (tennis balls)
VAT	• the total VAT amount on the invoice
Total	• the final total of the invoice

Note that there is a £ sign on the first line of the four money columns. The product columns (footballs, tennis balls) can be used for any category the business wants to include in the day book; the amount quoted here is the amount after deduction of any discount, but before the addition of VAT.

The format of the Sales Day Book is exactly the same (see page 14).

On this page you can see, by following the arrows, where the information for the **purchases day book** can be found on a purchase invoice.

INVOICE

AB Supplies Limited

Unit 16 Millyard Estate, Milton Keynes MK7 9GF
Tel 01908 321727 email info@absupplies.co.uk
VAT Reg 423 9663 77

| Zest Sports
Unit 16 Fencote Road,
Worcester WR2 6HY | **invoice number** | 87522 |
| | **date** | 23 October 2009 |

quantity	description	unit price £	£	£
10	Footballs 5141	8.00	80.00	
5	Footballs 8761	12.00	60.00	
			140.00	
	Less 20% trade discount		28.00	
				112.00
10	Boxes tennis balls 9863	8.00	80.00	
	Less 10% trade discount		8.00	
				72.00
				184.00
	VAT at 17.5%			32.20
				216.20

terms:
30 days

Purchases Day Book

Date	Details	Footballs	Tennis Balls	VAT	Total
2009		£	£	£	£
23 Oct	AB Supplies	112.00	72.00	32.20	216.20

On this page you can see, by following the arrows, where the information for the **sales day book** can be found on a sales invoice.

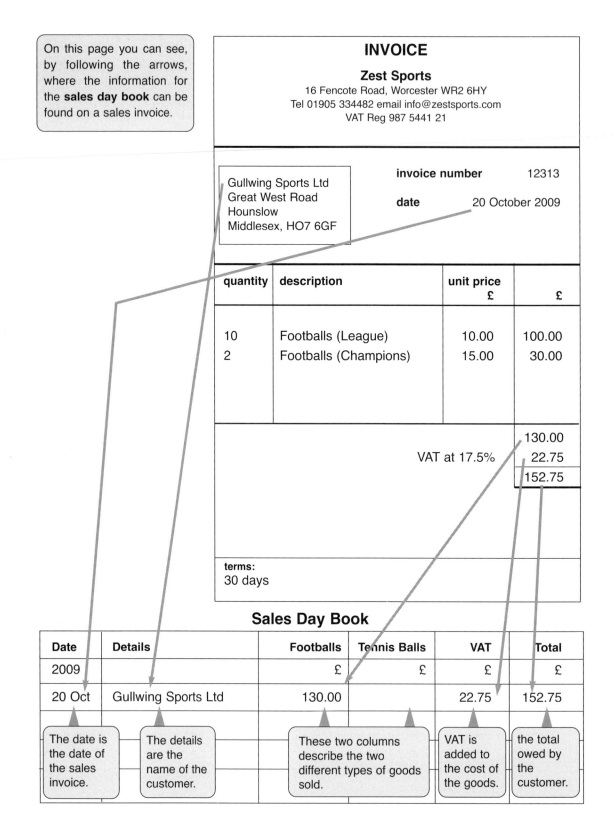

INVOICE

Zest Sports
16 Fencote Road, Worcester WR2 6HY
Tel 01905 334482 email info@zestsports.com
VAT Reg 987 5441 21

Gullwing Sports Ltd
Great West Road
Hounslow
Middlesex, HO7 6GF

invoice number 12313

date 20 October 2009

quantity	description	unit price £	£
10	Footballs (League)	10.00	100.00
2	Footballs (Champions)	15.00	30.00
			130.00
	VAT at 17.5%		22.75
			152.75

terms:
30 days

Sales Day Book

Date	Details	Footballs £	Tennis Balls £	VAT £	Total £
2009					
20 Oct	Gullwing Sports Ltd	130.00		22.75	152.75

The date is the date of the sales invoice.

The details are the name of the customer.

These two columns describe the two different types of goods sold.

VAT is added to the cost of the goods.

the total owed by the customer.

purchase returns and sales returns day books

Set out below are the formats, with entries and explanations, for the other two day books which can feature in an exam:

- **purchase returns day book** which records details from credit notes received from suppliers for goods returned

Purchase Returns Day Book

Date	Details	Footballs	Tennis Balls	VAT	Total
2009		£	£	£	£
30 Oct	AB Supplies	12.80	7.20	3.50	23.50

This day book records credit notes received from suppliers (for goods returned by Zest Sports). The information can be seen on the purchase returns credit note from AB Supplies on page 9.

- **sales returns day book** which records details from credit notes issued to customers for goods returned

Sales Returns Day Book

Date	Details	Footballs	Tennis Balls	VAT	Total
2009		£	£	£	£
26 Oct	Gullwing Sports Ltd	30.00		5.25	35.25

This day book records credit notes issued to customers (for goods returned to Zest Sports). The information can be seen on the credit note from Zest Sports to Gullwing Sports on page 10.

The day books shown here are extracts only; in reality they will have more lines and more entries. They will also need totals.

TOTALLING THE DAY BOOKS

So far in this chapter we have explained how a business such as Zest Sports takes information from its purchases and sales invoices and credit notes to write up its day books.

The next step is to **total up** the various money columns in the day book on a single 'totals' line. There is no strict rule for when this should be done: it could be daily, weekly, monthly, or whenever the business needs the figures for writing up the ledger accounts (see next chapter).

The totals should then be carefully checked by **cross casting**. This means adding up all the money totals from left to right – except the 'Total' column – and checking that this calculated figure agrees with the total of the 'Total' column. If it does not there must be an error in the figures which will have to be traced and corrected.

The totalled purchases day book for Zest Sports for the second week in October 2009 is shown below. Study the figures on the bottom line and read the notes in the boxes underneath.

Purchases Day Book

Date	Details	Footballs	Tennis Balls	VAT	Total
2009		£	£	£	£
5 Oct	AB Supplies	80.00	16.00	16.80	112.80
6 Oct	S Gerrard Limited	120.00		21.00	141.00
7 Oct	Murray Enterprises		200.00	35.00	235.00
8 Oct	Hermes Sports	60.00	160.00	38.50	258.50
9 Oct	AB Supplies	96.00	164.00	45.50	305.50
9 Oct		356.00	540.00	156.80	1,052.80

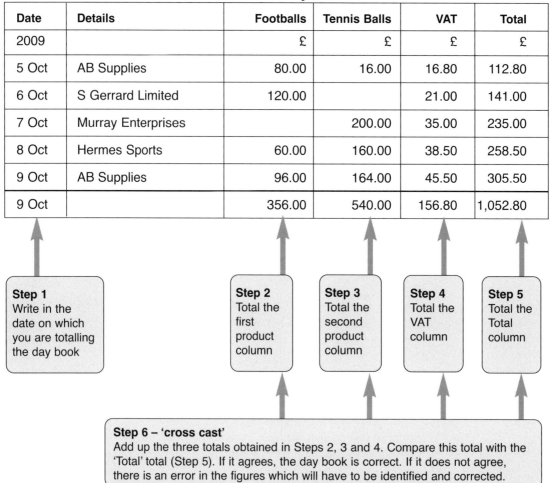

Step 1
Write in the date on which you are totalling the day book

Step 2
Total the first product column

Step 3
Total the second product column

Step 4
Total the VAT column

Step 5
Total the Total column

Step 6 – 'cross cast'
Add up the three totals obtained in Steps 2, 3 and 4. Compare this total with the 'Total' total (Step 5). If it agrees, the day book is correct. If it does not agree, there is an error in the figures which will have to be identified and corrected.

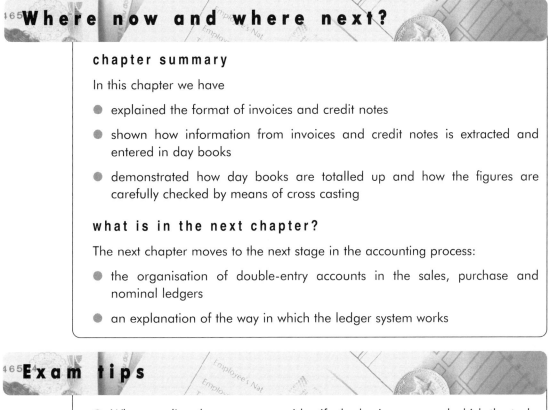

Where now and where next?

chapter summary

In this chapter we have

- explained the format of invoices and credit notes

- shown how information from invoices and credit notes is extracted and entered in day books

- demonstrated how day books are totalled up and how the figures are carefully checked by means of cross casting

what is in the next chapter?

The next chapter moves to the next stage in the accounting process:

- the organisation of double-entry accounts in the sales, purchase and nominal ledgers

- an explanation of the way in which the ledger system works

Exam tips

- When reading the exam paper, identify the business around which the tasks are based - this is effectively 'you' for the next couple of hours.

- When examining the documents given you in the exam, identify those which are issued by your business - these will be sales invoices and sales credit notes. Write 'sales invoice' or 'sales credit note' on them.

- The remaining documents will be purchase invoices and purchase credit notes. Write the words 'purchase invoice' or 'purchase credit note' on them.

- Head up your day books and day book columns clearly – remembering to identify the two products which need to be entered in separate columns.

- Enter the year date in the first day book column and a £ sign at the top of all the money columns.

- When you enter the day book information, always enter the month and day date in the first column – never use a ditto (") mark.

- Write clearly at all times. If you have to change a figure, cross through the incorrect figure and enter the correct figure above it or to the side of it.

- When totalling up the day books, always cross cast the totals to make sure you have not made a mistake.

free online resources at www.osbornebooks.co.uk
Available from the Resources page for *Level 2 Accounting*:
• blank day book pages for use in these exercises
• answers for the exercises in this book marked with an asterisk (*)

1.1* A number of invoices and credit notes were issued and received by Campbell Designs during the last week of October 2009. Campbell Designs is a wholesaler which deals with two main products: cards and calendars. The accounts assistant has already sorted the documents into date order and also by day book.

The date is 30 October 2009.

You are to enter up these transactions in the appropriate day books, total the money columns and cross cast the totals to check your accuracy. Remember to write the headings in the day books.

purchase invoices				
date	*supplier name*	*goods supplied and amount*	*VAT*	*Invoice total*
26 Oct	J Miller Ltd	Cards £80.00	£14.00	£94.00
27 Oct	Hirst Supplies	Calendars £168.00	£29.40	£197.40
28 Oct	Turner & Co	Cards £48.00	£8.40	£56.40
29 Oct	Manet Ltd	Cards £36.00, Calendars £96.00	£23.10	£155.10

purchase returns credit notes				
date	*supplier name*	*goods supplied and amount*	*VAT*	*Credit Note total*
26 Oct	J Macmillan	Cards £16.00	£2.80	£18.80
28 Oct	J Constable	Calendars £64.00	£11.20	£75.20

sales invoices				
date	*customer name*	*goods supplied and amount*	*VAT*	*Invoice total*
26 Oct	Coppola Ltd	Cards £304.00	£53.20	£357.20
28 Oct	J Mason	Calendars £88.00	£15.40	£103.40
28 Oct	Cute Shop	Cards £120.00, Calendars £96.00	£37.80	£253.80
29 Oct	P Casso	Cards £152.00	£26.60	£178.60

sales returns credit notes				
date	*customer name*	*goods supplied and amount*	*VAT*	*Credit Note total*
28 Oct	Coppola Ltd	Cards £56.00	£9.80	£65.80
29 Oct	J Steinbeck	Calendars £72.00	£12.60	£84.60

1.2* A batch of invoices and credit notes was issued and received by Campbell Designs during the first week of November 2009.

The accounts assistant has already sorted the documents into date order and also by day book.

The date is 6 November 2009.

Your job is to enter up these transactions in the appropriate day books, total the money columns and cross cast the totals to check your accuracy. Remember to write the headings in the day books. But before doing this, you need to read the following note:

important note
The accounts assistant mentions that the purchase invoices from one supplier seem to have mistakes in the calculation of VAT – which should be charged at 17.5%. You should check the purchase invoice calculations carefully and only enter the invoice figures in the day book if they are correct. If they are incorrect they cannot be entered; the invoices will have to be passed to the manager for querying with the supplier.

purchase invoices				
date	*supplier name*	*goods supplied and amount*	*VAT*	*Invoice total*
2 Nov	T M Inn Ltd	Cards £120.00	£21.00	£141.00
3 Nov	Hirst Supplies	Calendars £144.00	£28.80	£172.80
5 Nov	T M Inn Ltd	Cards £56.00, Calendars £32	£15.40	£103.40
6 Nov	Hirst Supplies	Cards £184.00,Calendars £80.00	£52.80	£316.80

purchase returns credit notes				
date	*supplier name*	*goods supplied and amount*	*VAT*	*Credit Note total*
4 Nov	J Miller	Cards £16.00	£2.80	£18.80
5 Nov	Manet Ltd	Calendars £10	£1.75	£11.75

sales invoices				
date	*customer name*	*goods supplied and amount*	*VAT*	*Invoice total*
3 Nov	R Khan	Cards £72.00	£12.60	£84.60
3 Nov	Wong Art	Calendars £128.00	£22.40	£150.40
4 Nov	Carmen Corner	Cards £220.00	£38.50	£258.50
6 Nov	R M Brandt	Cards £356.00, Calendars £96.00	£79.10	£531.10

sales returns credit notes				
date	*customer name*	*goods supplied and amount*	*VAT*	*Credit Note total*
5 Nov	P Casso	Cards £32.00	£5.60	£37.60
5 Nov	Cute Shop	Calendars £56.00	£9.80	£65.80

1.3 This exercise continues the Case Study of Zest Sports, a specialist sports goods supplier.

The date is 6 November 2009. The accounts assistant has sorted the invoices and credit notes for the first week of the month into the following four piles:
- purchase invoices
- purchase returns credit notes
- sales invoices
- sales returns credit notes

Your job is to write these transactions in the appropriate day books in date order, total the money columns and cross cast the totals to check your accuracy. The documents should be entered in date order.

INVOICE

AB Supplies Limited

Unit 16 Millyard Estate, Milton Keynes MK7 9GF
Tel 01908 321727 email info@absupplies.co.uk
VAT Reg 423 9663 77

Zest Sports Unit 16 Fencote Road, Worcester WR2 6HY	**invoice number** 87571 **date** 2 November 2009

quantity	description	unit price £	£	£
10	Footballs 5141	8.00	80.00	
10	Footballs 8761	12.00	120.00	
			200.00	
	Less 20% trade discount		40.00	
				160.00
8	Boxes tennis balls 9863	8.00	64.00	
	Less 10% trade discount		6.40	
				57.60
				217.60
	VAT at 17.5%			38.08
				255.68

terms:
30 days

INVOICE

AB Supplies Limited

Unit 16 Millyard Estate, Milton Keynes MK7 9GF
Tel 01908 321727 email info@absupplies.co.uk
VAT Reg 423 9663 77

invoice number	87579
date	4 November 2009

Zest Sports
Unit 16 Fencote Road,
Worcester WR2 6HY

quantity	description	unit price £	£	£
16	Footballs 5141	8.00	128.00	
20	Footballs 8761	12.00	240.00	
			368.00	
	Less 20% trade discount		73.60	
				294.40
8	Boxes tennis balls 8729	10.00	80.00	
	Less 10% trade discount		8.00	
				72.00
				366.40
	VAT at 17.5%			64.12
				430.52

terms:
30 days

INVOICE

N Mehta Limited

17, Market Street, Middleton MI5 6HP
Tel 01709 826421 email sales@nmehta.com
VAT Reg 723 3863 37

invoice number	7261
date	3 November 2009

Zest Sports
Unit 16 Fencote Road,
Worcester WR2 6HY

quantity	description	unit price £	£	£
24	Footballs Ref FB88	9.00	216.00	
15	Footballs Ref FB95	12.50	187.50	
			403.50	
	Less 20% trade discount		80.70	
				322.80
	VAT at 17.5%			56.49
				379.29

terms:
30 days

CREDIT NOTE
N Mehta Limited
17, Market Street, Middleton MI5 6HP
Tel 01709 826421 email sales@nmehta.com
VAT Reg 723 3863 37

credit note number   967

date   3 November 2009

Zest Sports
Unit 16 Fencote Road,
Worcester WR2 6HY

quantity	description	unit price £	£	£
4	Footballs Ref FB88	9.00	36.00	
	Less 20% trade discount		7.20	
				28.80
	VAT at 17.5%			5.04
				33.84

reason for credit:
Faulty goods

CREDIT NOTE
AB Supplies Limited
Unit 16 Millyard Estate, Milton Keynes MK7 9GF
Tel 01908 321727 email info@absupplies.co.uk
VAT Reg 423 9663 77

credit note number   454

date   2 November 2009

Zest Sports
Unit 16 Fencote Road,
Worcester WR2 6HY

quantity	description	unit price £	£	£
2	Footballs 8761	12.00	24.00	
	Less 20% trade discount		4.80	19.20
1	Box tennis balls 8729	10.00	10.00	
	Less 10% trade discount		1.00	9.00
				28.20
	VAT at 17.5%			4.93
				33.13

Reason for credit:
Cancelled order

INVOICE

Zest Sports

16 Fencote Road, Worcester WR2 6HY
Tel 01905 334482 email info@zestsports.com
VAT Reg 987 5441 21

invoice number   12332

date   3 November 2009

Kerrison Sports
44, Kilmersdon Road
Bath
BA1 5FG

quantity	description	unit price £	£
5	Practice Tennis Balls (box)	20.00	100.00
2	Centre Court Balls (box)	16.00	32.00
			132.00
	VAT at 17.5%		23.10
			155.10

terms:
30 days

INVOICE

Zest Sports

16 Fencote Road, Worcester WR2 6HY
Tel 01905 334482 email info@zestsports.com
VAT Reg 987 5441 21

invoice number   12331

date   2 November 2009

Gullwing Sports Ltd
Great West Road
Hounslow
Middlesex, HO7 6GF

quantity	description	unit price £	£
20	Footballs (League)	10.00	200.00
8	Footballs (Champions)	15.00	120.00
			320.00
	VAT at 17.5%		56.00
			376.00

terms:
30 days

INVOICE

Zest Sports

16 Fencote Road, Worcester WR2 6HY
Tel 01905 334482 email info@zestsports.com
VAT Reg 987 5441 21

invoice number	12334
date	5 November 2009

Kerrison Sports
44, Kilmersdon Road
Bath
BA1 5FG

quantity	description	unit price £	£
7	Practice Tennis Balls (box)	20.00	140.00
3	Centre Court Balls (box)	16.00	48.00
			188.00
	VAT at 17.5%		32.90
			220.90

terms:
30 days

INVOICE

Zest Sports

16 Fencote Road, Worcester WR2 6HY
Tel 01905 334482 email info@zestsports.com
VAT Reg 987 5441 21

invoice number	12333
date	4 November 2009

Gullwing Sports Ltd
Great West Road
Hounslow
Middlesex, HO7 6GF

quantity	description	unit price £	£
15	Footballs (League)	10.00	150.00
5	Footballs (Champions)	15.00	75.00
			225.00
	VAT at 17.5%		39.37
			264.37

terms:
30 days

CREDIT NOTE

Zest Sports
16 Fencote Road, Worcester WR2 6HY
Tel 01905 334482 email info@zestsports.co.uk
VAT Reg 987 5441 21

	credit note number	723
	date	3 November 2009

Gullwing Sports Ltd
Great West Road
Hounslow
Middlesex, HO7 6GF

quantity	description	unit price £	£
4	Footballs (Champions)	15.00	60.00
	VAT at 17.5%		60.00
			10.50
			70.50

reason for credit:
shortage in delivery

CREDIT NOTE

Zest Sports
16 Fencote Road, Worcester WR2 6HY
Tel 01905 334482 email info@zestsports.co.uk
VAT Reg 987 5441 21

	credit note number	724
	date	4 November 2009

Kerrison Sports
44, Kilmersdon Road
Bath
BA1 5FG

quantity	description	unit price £	£
1	Practice Tennis Balls (box)	20.00	20.00
	VAT at 17.5%		20.00
			3.50
			23.50

reason for credit:
damaged goods

2 Ledger accounts for purchase transactions

The last chapter dealt with the writing up of four day books from source documents – invoices and credit notes – for purchase and sales transactions.

In this chapter you will deal with the supplier side of the business and use figures extracted from the purchase and purchase returns day books to enter up the ledger accounts in the double-entry accounting system.

This will take one step further the process of recording financial transactions in the accounting system, as seen in the diagram below.

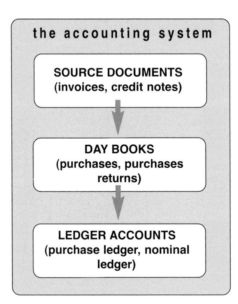

the accounting system

SOURCE DOCUMENTS
(invoices, credit notes)

DAY BOOKS
(purchases, purchases returns)

LEDGER ACCOUNTS
(purchase ledger, nominal ledger)

This chapter, in short, explains the processes of

● setting up double-entry accounts for purchase transactions in the purchase ledger and also in the nominal ledger

● transferring the appropriate figures from the day books to the double-entry accounts in the purchase ledger and the nominal ledger

INTRODUCTION TO THE LEDGER SYSTEM

A '**ledger**' is another name for a 'book' of accounts which records financial transactions such as sales, purchases and payments. It is convenient for a business to divide up all the accounts into sections according to their function – eg recording credit sales or credit purchases – and so over time a number of different ledgers have developed.

For the purpose of this exam you will deal with three different ledgers:

- **purchase ledger** – which contains the **supplier accounts**, recording the amount a business owes to each supplier; each account is a named 'personal' account, eg 'AB Supplies' in the last chapter

- **sales ledger** – which contains the **customer accounts**, recording the amount that the business is owed by each customer; as with the purchase ledger each account is a named 'personal' account, eg 'Gullwing Sports' in the last chapter

- **nominal ledger** – which contains all the other accounts, eg Purchases Account, Sales Account, Value Added Tax Account; these accounts are not in the name of a person or business and so are known as 'impersonal' accounts; they often record items such as expenses or income

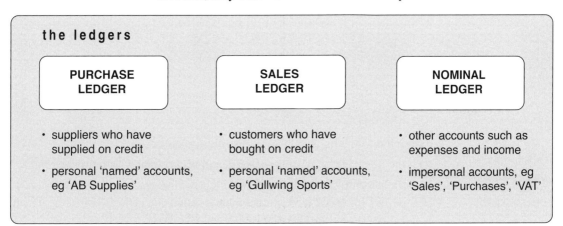

the ledgers

PURCHASE LEDGER	SALES LEDGER	NOMINAL LEDGER
• suppliers who have supplied on credit	• customers who have bought on credit	• other accounts such as expenses and income
• personal 'named' accounts, eg 'AB Supplies'	• personal 'named' accounts, eg 'Gullwing Sports'	• impersonal accounts, eg 'Sales', 'Purchases', 'VAT'

accounting for purchase transactions

In this chapter we will deal with entering up the credit purchase transactions in the **purchase ledger** and **nominal ledger** accounts.

In the next chapter we will deal with entering up the credit sales transactions in the **sales ledger** and **nominal ledger** accounts.

Before entering up the ledger accounts, however, you may need to revise your knowledge of double-entry bookkeeping.

DOUBLE-ENTRY ACCOUNTS

double-entry bookkeeping – a revision note

First of all we will give a brief explanation of the principles and workings of double-entry bookkeeping.

Double-entry bookkeeping involves entries being made in the accounts for each transaction – debit entries (on the left-hand side of the account) and credit entries (on the right-hand side).

We will first look at the layout of a double-entry account as it is likely to be required in your exam.

The illustration here shows an account of a supplier AB Supplies in the purchase ledger of Zest Sports. Goods have been bought on credit on 6 July by Zest Sports for £188.00, which will then be owing to AB Supplies.

Dr					AB Supplies Account			Cr
2009	**Details**	**£**	**p**	**2009**	**Details**	**£**	**p**
				6 Jul	**Purchases**	**188**	**00**
				▲	▲	▲	▲
				date of the trans- action	*name of the account in which the other entry is made*	*amount of the trans- action*	

Note the following from the layout of the account:
- the name of the account – 'AB Supplies Account' – is written at the top
- the account is divided into two identical halves, separated by a central double (or bold) vertical line: the left-hand side is the 'Debit' side ('Debit' is abbreviated to 'Dr'), the right-hand side is the 'Credit' ('Cr') side
  A note for UK drivers! – **Dr**ive on the left   **Cr**ash on the right
- the year date is entered in the first column on both sides of the account
- the day and month are entered in the date column against each transaction
- in the column marked 'Details' appears the name of the other account involved in the double-entry transaction; in this example it is 'Purchases' Account, which is a nominal account
- the amount of the transaction is entered in the money column – note that this column may be divided into 'pounds' and 'pence' (as here); you may also see just one column for the money amount, headed up by a £ sign

debit or credit?

The decisions faced by anyone operating the double-entry system are:

- deciding which accounts should be used for each transaction
- deciding which entry is the debit and which is the credit

Debits include

- expenses - including purchases
- items **owed to you** – eg customer accounts in the sales ledger
- assets – items owned by you

Credits include

- income items – including sales
- items **owed by you** – eg supplier accounts in the purchase ledger which you have to pay (these are also known as 'liabilities')

DAY BOOKS TO LEDGER ACCOUNTS – CREDIT PURCHASES

In your exam you are required to set up the ledger accounts from the day books you have completed. You will need to start with:

- **purchases day book** – which records purchases you have made – entered from suppliers' invoices; in this case you owe them money
- **purchase returns day book** – which record refunds you have received from suppliers' credit notes; in this case they have reduced the amount which you owe them

You will need to set up the ledger accounts in the ledgers first. Using the Case Study of Zest Sports, the first ledgers you deal with will be:

- **purchases ledger**
  - made up of individual accounts for suppliers, to be posted with purchases you have made and refunds they have made
- **nominal ledger** made up of accounts for the other aspects of the credit purchases
  - purchases accounts for each type of product, eg 'Purchases Account - Footballs' and 'Purchases Account - Tennis Balls'
  - purchase returns accounts (one each for footballs and tennis balls)
  - Value Added Tax (VAT) account to record the VAT

On the next two pages you will see how the accounts in the **purchase ledger** are written up from the day books. Study these pages and see from the arrows how the figures are transferred from the day books into the accounts.

The nominal ledger accounts are then dealt with on pages 32 to 33.

Purchases Day Book

Date	Details	Footballs	Tennis Balls	VAT	Total
2009		£	£	£	£
6 Jul	AB Supplies	64.00	32.00	16.80	112.80
7 Jul	S Gerrard Limited	160.00		28.00	188.00
9 Jul	AB Supplies		180.00	31.50	211.50
10 Jul		224.00	212.00	76.30	512.30

Purchase Returns Day Book

Date	Details	Footballs	Tennis Balls	VAT	Total
2009		£	£	£	£
9 Jul	AB Supplies		16.00	2.80	18.80
9 Jul	S Gerrard Limited	32.00		5.60	37.60
10 Jul		32.00	16.00	8.40	56.40

PURCHASE LEDGER

Dr	AB Supplies Account						Cr	
2009	Details	£	p	2009	Details	£	p	
9 Jul	Purchase returns	18	80	6 Jul	Purchases	112	80	
				9 Jul	Purchases	211	50	

Dr	S Gerrard Limited Account						Cr	
2009	Details	£	p	2009	Details	£	p	
9 Jul	Purchase returns	37	60	7 Jul	Purchases	188	00	

WRITING UP THE PURCHASE LEDGER

At the top of the previous page you will see two day books written up by Zest Sports in the second week of July:

- the **purchases day book** records details of purchase transactions made from two suppliers, AB Supplies and S Gerrard Limited
- the **purchase returns day book** contains details of returns transactions with the two suppliers, AB Supplies and S Gerrard Limited

You will also see, at the bottom of the page, an extract from the **purchase ledger** of Zest Sports with the double-entry accounts of the two suppliers.

We will take the two accounts in turn and explain the double-entry involved.

AB Supplies

There are three entries on this account. The day books have been totalled on 10 July and the entries to the ledger accounts will be made on that day

- the entries in the **Purchases Day Book** are both individually transferred from the 'Total' column - they are not added together before the transfer
- Zest Sports therefore owes AB Supplies £112.80 and £211.50
- these entries, being **items owed** by Zest Sports, are **credit entries**; note that the date is the date of the day book entry and the description is 'Purchases', the name of the day book
- the one entry for £18.80 in the **Purchase Returns Day Book** is transferred to the account from the day book 'Total' column
- Zest Sports has effectively received a refund of £18.80 from AB Supplies
- this is an **item owing** to Zest Sports and is therefore a **debit entry**

S Gerrard Limited

There are two entries on this account:

- the **credit entry** for £188.00 (an **amount owing** by Zest Sports) has been transferred from the 'Total' column of the **Purchases Day Book**, and is given the date of the day book entry and the description 'Purchases'
- the **debit entry** for £37.60 has been transferred from the 'Total' column of the **Purchases Returns Day Book**, and is given the date of the day book entry and the description 'Purchase returns' – it is a debit because it is an **amount owed to** Zest Sports

remember: purchase ledger double-entry rule!

In the account of a supplier in the purchase ledger of a business:

- amounts **owed by** a business to a supplier are **credit** entries
- amounts **owed to** a business by a supplier are **debit** entries

writing up the nominal ledger

Set out below you will see the **purchases day book** and **purchase returns day book** written up by Zest Sports in the second week of July. These are the same as the two day books shown on page 30. You will now need to use the figures on these two day books to write up the accounts in the **nominal ledger** which are shown on the opposite page.

Follow the lines and study the debit and credit entries made.

Purchases Day Book

Date	Details	Footballs	Tennis Balls	VAT	Total
2009		£	£	£	£
6 Jul	AB Supplies	64.00	32.00	16.80	112.80
7 Jul	S Gerrard Limited	160.00		28.00	188.00
9 Jul	AB Supplies		180.00	31.50	211.50
10 Jul		224.00	212.00	76.30	512.30

Purchase Returns Day Book

Date	Details	Footballs	Tennis Balls	VAT	Total
2009		£	£	£	£
9 Jul	AB Supplies		16.00	2.80	18.80
9 Jul	S Gerrard Limited	32.00		5.60	37.60
10 Jul		32.00	16.00	8.40	56.40

notes to the account entries

- there are two purchases (and purchase returns) accounts, one for each type of ball
- the date on each account entry is the same date as the total date in the day books – 10 July
- entries in the **purchases accounts** are both **debits** – they represent **expenses** to the business (expenses are always debits) - note the day book abbreviations used: PDB and PRDB
- entries in the **purchases returns accounts** are both **credits** – they represent **a refund** – a form of **income** – to the business (income items are always credits)
- Value Added Tax Account is an accounting record which works out what needs to be paid to the VAT authorities: VAT on purchases will always be a debit and VAT on purchase returns will always be a credit.

NOMINAL LEDGER

Dr	Purchases Account - footballs					Cr	
2009	**Details**	**£**	**p**	**2009**	**Details**	**£**	**p**
10 Jul	Total P D B	224	00				

Dr	Purchases Account - tennis balls					Cr	
2009	**Details**	**£**	**p**	**2009**	**Details**	**£**	**p**
10 Jul	Total P D B	212	00				

Dr	Purchase Returns Account - footballs					Cr	
2009	**Details**	**£**	**p**	**2009**	**Details**	**£**	**p**
				10 Jul	Total P R D B	32	00

Dr	Purchase Returns Account - tennis balls					Cr	
2009	**Details**	**£**	**p**	**2009**	**Details**	**£**	**p**
				10 Jul	Total P R D B	16	00

Dr	Value Added Tax Account					Cr	
2009	**Details**	**£**	**p**	**2009**	**Details**	**£**	**p**
10 Jul	Total P D B	76	30	10 Jul	Total P R D B	8	40

PURCHASES DAY BOOKS TO LEDGER ACCOUNTS – A SUMMARY

debit or credit?

The problem when entering the figures from the day books into the ledger accounts is to decide whether the entry is a debit or a credit.

The diagram below shows the two Zest Sports day books which have been explained earlier in this chapter.

The notes in the boxes show:

- the ledger to which the day book figures should be posted
- the account to which the figures from the day books should be posted
- whether the entry made is a debit or a credit.

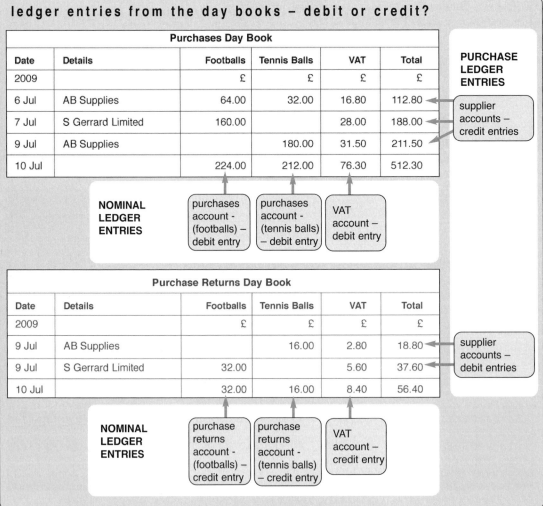

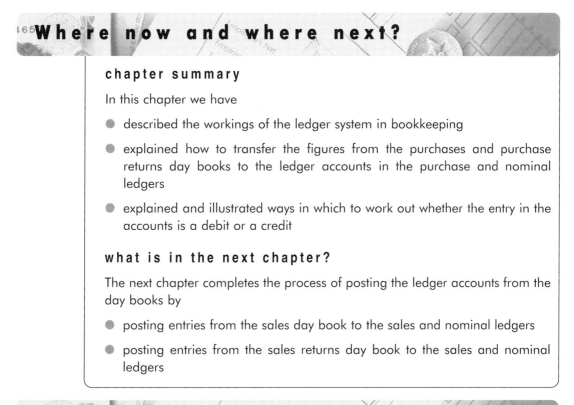

Where now and where next?

chapter summary

In this chapter we have

● described the workings of the ledger system in bookkeeping

● explained how to transfer the figures from the purchases and purchase returns day books to the ledger accounts in the purchase and nominal ledgers

● explained and illustrated ways in which to work out whether the entry in the accounts is a debit or a credit

what is in the next chapter?

The next chapter completes the process of posting the ledger accounts from the day books by

● posting entries from the sales day book to the sales and nominal ledgers

● posting entries from the sales returns day book to the sales and nominal ledgers

Exam tips

● When setting up the accounts in the ledgers, start with the supplier accounts in the purchase ledger, using the supplier names from the details columns of both day books, taking care not to duplicate any.

● When setting up the nominal ledger, get the account names from the column headings in the day books, eg 'Purchases - footballs', 'Purchases - tennis balls' 'Value Added Tax' – starting with the purchases day book and then moving to the purchase returns day book.

● Enter the Value Added Tax Account as the last account in the nominal ledger – it will be easier to find and will also be needed for the sales day books.

● Find a way of remembering whether the entries in Purchase Ledger and Nominal Ledger are debits or credits, for example:

- **P**urchase ledger accounts: **P**urchases are **C**redits and **R**eturns are **D**ebits

  Try the words '**P**arty **P**eople **C**an **R**eally **D**ance'

- **N**ominal ledger accounts: **P**urchases are **D**ebits and Returns are **C**redits

  Try the words '**N**ice **P**eople **D**rive **R**eally **C**arefully'

2.1*   It is 17 July 2009 and you have just written up the purchases day book and the purchase returns day book for the week (see below) for Fine Gems Ltd, a business which distributes high quality Italian and Spanish jewellery which it buys from importers based in the UK and sells to retail shops. Its product lines are analysed according to these two countries (Italy and Spain).

You are to set up ledger accounts in the purchase and nominal ledgers listed below. Make sure that the ledgers are headed up with the name of the ledger and are kept separate.

> **Purchase Ledger:**
>
> Personal accounts for two suppliers: Continental Importers and Gems Espana
>
> **Nominal Ledger**
>
> Purchases - Italy, Purchases - Spain, Purchase Returns - Italy, Purchase Returns - Spain, VAT

You are required to enter up the ledger accounts with the appropriate figures from the two day books.

Purchases Day Book

Date	Details	Italian gems	Spanish gems	VAT	Total
2009		£	£	£	£
14 Jul	Continental Importers	120.00	320.00	77.00	517.00
15 Jul	Gems Espana		160.00	28.00	188.00
16 Jul	Continental Importers	640.00		112.00	752.00
17 Jul		760.00	480.00	217.00	1,457.00

Purchase Returns Day Book

Date	Details	Italian gems	Spanish gems	VAT	Total
2009		£	£	£	£
15 Jul	Continental Importers	32.00		5.60	37.60
16 Jul	Gems Espana		96.00	16.80	112.80
17 Jul		32.00	96.00	22.40	150.40

2.2 Sweet Things is a business which specialises in luxury toffees and chocolates. It is 14 August. The accounts assistant has been off sick for a fortnight and the line manager has handed you the completed day books for the last two weeks. She asks you to enter them in the ledger accounts with entries for both Fridays, ie 7 August and 14 August. You will need to set up the accounts.

week 1   **Purchases Day Book**

Date	Details	Toffees	Chocolates	VAT	Total
2009		£	£	£	£
4 Aug	Buxton Confectionery	104.00	128.00	40.60	272.60
5 Aug	Toffee Galore	168.00		29.40	197.40
6 Aug	Buxton Confectionery	128.00		22.40	150.40
7 Aug		400.00	128.00	92.40	620.40

Purchase Returns Day Book

Date	Details	Toffees	Chocolates	VAT	Total
2009		£	£	£	£
5 Aug	Buxton Confectionery	56.00	12.00	11.90	79.90
6 Aug	Toffee Galore	16.00		2.80	18.80
7 Aug		72.00	12.00	14.70	98.70

week 2   **Purchases Day Book**

Date	Details	Toffees	Chocolates	VAT	Total
2009		£	£	£	£
10 Aug	Buxton Confectionery	64.00	220.00	49.70	333.70
11 Aug	Toffee Galore	232.00		40.60	272.60
12 Aug	Buxton Confectionery	640.00		112.00	752.00
14 Aug		936.00	220.00	202.30	1,358.30

Purchase Returns Day Book

Date	Details	Toffees	Chocolates	VAT	Total
2009		£	£	£	£
12 Aug	Buxton Confectionery	16.00	38.00	9.45	63.45
14 Aug	Toffee Galore	112.00		19.60	131.60
14 Aug		128.00	38.00	29.05	195.05

3 Ledger accounts for sales transactions

The last chapter dealt with the writing up of the ledger accounts for purchase transactions from the purchases and purchase returns day books.

This chapter describes very much the same processes, but this time deals with sales transactions with the customers of the business.

Again, figures will be extracted from the day books to enter up the ledger accounts in the double-entry accounting system of the business.

The diagram below shows how this works.

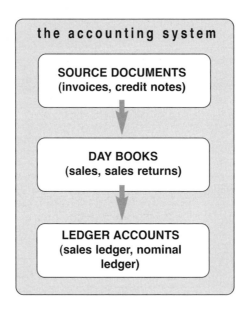

This chapter, in short, explains the processes of

- setting up double-entry accounts for sales transactions in the sales ledger and also in the nominal ledger

- transferring the appropriate figures from the day books to the double-entry accounts in the sales ledger and the nominal ledger

DAY BOOKS TO LEDGER ACCOUNTS – CREDIT SALES

In the last chapter we saw that a '**ledger**' is another name for a 'book' of accounts which records financial transactions such as sales, purchases and payments:

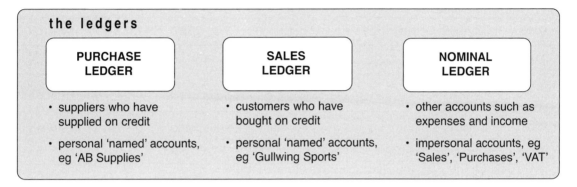

the ledgers

PURCHASE LEDGER	SALES LEDGER	NOMINAL LEDGER
• suppliers who have supplied on credit	• customers who have bought on credit	• other accounts such as expenses and income
• personal 'named' accounts, eg 'AB Supplies'	• personal 'named' accounts, eg 'Gullwing Sports'	• impersonal accounts, eg 'Sales', 'Purchases', 'VAT'

In your exam you are required to set up the ledger accounts from the day books you have completed. You will need to start with:

- **sales day book** – which records sales you have made on credit – normally entered from copies of invoices you have sent to customers who then owe the amounts stated on the invoices

- **sales returns day book** – which records refunds you have made to customers for returned or faulty goods; in this case the source documents will be credit notes you have issued – these will reduce the amount the customers owe you

Using the Case Study of Zest Sports, the accounts you will set up will be:

- **sales ledger**
  - made up of individual 'personal' accounts for customers, to be posted with sales and any refunds you have made to them

- **nominal ledger** made up of 'impersonal' accounts for the other aspects of the credit sales:
  - sales accounts for each type of sale made, eg 'Sales Account - footballs' and 'Sales Account - tennis balls'
  - sales returns accounts (one each for footballs and tennis balls)
  - Value Added Tax Account to record the VAT charged to the customers

On the next two pages you will see how the accounts in the **sales ledger** are written up from the day books. Study these pages and see from the arrows how the figures are transferred from the day books into the accounts.

The nominal ledger accounts are then dealt with on pages 42 to 43.

Sales Day Book

Date	Details	Footballs	Tennis Balls	VAT	Total
2009		£	£	£	£
6 Jul	Gullwing Sports Ltd	130.00		22.75	152.75
8 Jul	Gullwing Sports Ltd		64.00	11.20	75.20
9 Jul	Kerrison Sports	120.00	92.00	37.10	249.10
10 Jul		250.00	156.00	71.05	477.05

Sales Returns Day Book

Date	Details	Footballs	Tennis Balls	VAT	Total
2009		£	£	£	£
7 Jul	Kerrison Sports		48.00	8.40	56.40
9 Jul	Gullwing Sports	56.00		9.80	65.80
10 Jul		56.00	48.00	18.20	122.20

SALES LEDGER

Dr			Gullwing Sports Account			Cr	
2009	Details	£	p	2009	Details	£	p
6 Jul	Sales	152	75	9 Jul	Sales returns	65	80
8 Jul	Sales	75	20				

Dr			Kerrison Sports Account			Cr	
2009	Details	£	p	2009	Details	£	p
9 Jul	Sales	249	10	7 Jul	Sales returns	56	40

WRITING UP THE SALES LEDGER

At the top of the previous page you will see two day books written up by Zest Sports in the second week of July:

- the **sales day book** records details of goods sold on credit to two customers, Gullwing Sports and Kerrison Sports
- the **sales returns day book** contains details of returns transactions with the two suppliers, Gullwing Sports and Kerrison Sports

You will also see, at the bottom of the page, an extract from the **sales ledger** of Zest Sports with the double-entry accounts of the two suppliers.

We will take the two accounts in turn and explain the double-entry involved.

Gullwing Sports – sales ledger account

There are three entries on this account. The day books have been totalled on 10 July and the entries to the ledger accounts will be made on that day

- the entries in the **Sales Day Book** are both individually transferred from the 'Total' column - they are not added together before the transfer
- Gullwing Sports therefore owes Zest Sports £152.75 and £75.20
- these entries, being **items owed** to Zest Sports, are **debit entries**; note that the date is the date of the day book entry and the description is 'Sales', the name of the day book
- the entry for £65.80 for Gullwing Sports in the **Sales Returns Day Book** is transferred to the account from the day book 'Total' column
- Gullwing Sports is now owed £65.80 by Zest Sports; as this is an **item owed** to Gullwing Sports it is a **credit entry**

Kerrison Sports

There are two entries on this account:

- the **debit entry** for £249.10 (an amount **owed to** Zest Sports) has been transferred from the 'Total' column of the **Sales Day Book**, and is given the date of the day book entry and the description 'Sales'
- the **credit entry** for £56.40 has been transferred from the 'Total' column of the **Sales Returns Day Book**, and is given the date of the day book entry and the description 'Sales returns' – it is a credit because it is an **amount owed to** Kerrison Sports

remember: sales ledger double-entry rule!

In the account of a customer in the sales ledger of a business:

- amounts **owed to** a business by a customer are **debit** entries
- amounts **owed by** a business to a customer are **credit** entries

writing up the nominal ledger

Set out below you will see the **sales day book** and **sales returns day book** written up by Zest Sports in the second week of July. These are the same as the two day books shown on page 40. You will now need to use the figures on these two day books to write up the accounts in the **nominal ledger** which are shown on the opposite page.

Follow the lines and study the debit and credit entries made.

Sales Day Book

Date	Details	Footballs	Tennis Balls	VAT	Total
2009		£	£	£	£
6 Jul	Gullwing Sports Ltd	130.00		22.75	152.75
8 Jul	Gullwing Sports Ltd		64.00	11.20	75.20
9 Jul	Kerrison Sports	120.00	92.00	37.10	249.10
10 Jul		250.00	156.00	71.05	477.05

Sales Returns Day Book

Date	Details	Footballs	Tennis Balls	VAT	Total
2009		£	£	£	£
7 Jul	Kerrison Sports		48.00	8.40	56.40
9 Jul	Gullwing Sports	56.00		9.80	65.80
10 Jul		56.00	48.00	18.20	122.20

notes to the account entries

- there are two sales (and sales returns) accounts, one for each type of ball

- the date on each account entry is the same date as the total date in the day books – 10 July

- entries in the **sales accounts** are both **credits** – they represent **income** to the business (**income items** are always **credits**) - note the day book abbreviations used: SDB and SRDB

- entries in the **sales returns accounts** are both **debits** – they represent **an expense** to the business (**expense items** are always **debits**)

- Value Added Tax Account is an accounting record which works out what needs to be paid to the VAT authorities: VAT on sales will always be a **credit** (**money owing** to the VAT authorities) and VAT on sales returns will always be a **debit**.

NOMINAL LEDGER

Dr	Sales Account - footballs						Cr	
2009	**Details**	**£**	**p**	**2009**	**Details**	**£**	**p**	
				10 Jul	Total S D B	250	00	

Dr	Sales Account - tennis balls						Cr	
2009	**Details**	**£**	**p**	**2009**	**Details**	**£**	**p**	
				10 Jul	Total S D B	156	00	

Dr	Sales Returns Account - footballs						Cr	
2009	**Details**	**£**	**p**	**2009**	**Details**	**£**	**p**	
10 Jul	Total S R D B	56	00					

Dr	Sales Returns Account - tennis balls						Cr	
2009	**Details**	**£**	**p**	**2009**	**Details**	**£**	**p**	
10 Jul	Total S R D B	48	00					

Dr	Value Added Tax Account						Cr	
2009	**Details**	**£**	**p**	**2009**	**Details**	**£**	**p**	
10 Jul	Total S R D B	18	20	10 Jul	Total S D B	71	05	

SALES DAY BOOKS TO LEDGER ACCOUNTS – A SUMMARY

debit or credit?

The problem when entering the figures from the day books into the ledger accounts is to decide whether the entry is a debit or a credit.

The diagram below shows the Zest Sports sales day book and sales returns day book which have been explained earlier in this chapter.

The notes in the boxes show:

- the ledger to which the day book figures should be posted
- the account to which the figures from the day books should be posted
- whether the entry made is a debit or a credit.

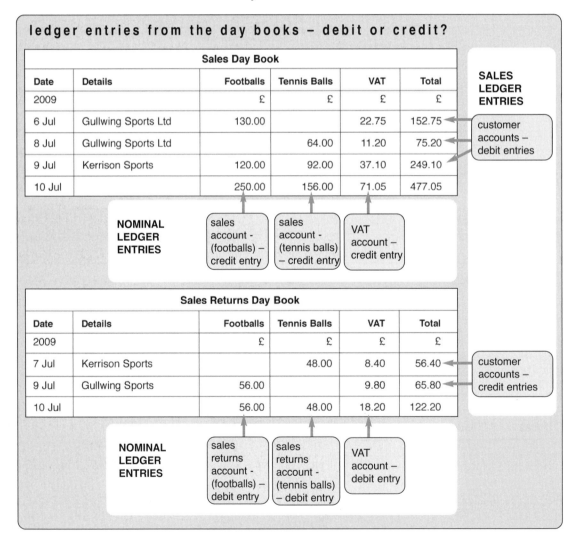

ledger entries from the day books – debit or credit?

Sales Day Book

Date	Details	Footballs	Tennis Balls	VAT	Total
2009		£	£	£	£
6 Jul	Gullwing Sports Ltd	130.00		22.75	152.75
8 Jul	Gullwing Sports Ltd		64.00	11.20	75.20
9 Jul	Kerrison Sports	120.00	92.00	37.10	249.10
10 Jul		250.00	156.00	71.05	477.05

SALES LEDGER ENTRIES

customer accounts – debit entries

NOMINAL LEDGER ENTRIES

sales account - (footballs) – credit entry

sales account - (tennis balls) – credit entry

VAT account – credit entry

Sales Returns Day Book

Date	Details	Footballs	Tennis Balls	VAT	Total
2009		£	£	£	£
7 Jul	Kerrison Sports		48.00	8.40	56.40
9 Jul	Gullwing Sports	56.00		9.80	65.80
10 Jul		56.00	48.00	18.20	122.20

customer accounts – credit entries

NOMINAL LEDGER ENTRIES

sales returns account - (footballs) – debit entry

sales returns account - (tennis balls) – debit entry

VAT account – debit entry

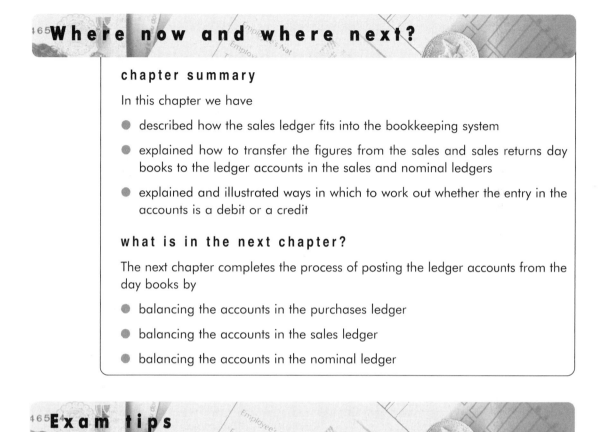

Where now and where next?

chapter summary

In this chapter we have

- described how the sales ledger fits into the bookkeeping system
- explained how to transfer the figures from the sales and sales returns day books to the ledger accounts in the sales and nominal ledgers
- explained and illustrated ways in which to work out whether the entry in the accounts is a debit or a credit

what is in the next chapter?

The next chapter completes the process of posting the ledger accounts from the day books by

- balancing the accounts in the purchases ledger
- balancing the accounts in the sales ledger
- balancing the accounts in the nominal ledger

Exam tips

- When setting up the customer accounts in the sales ledger, group them together.
- Check the names in the sales and sales returns day books against the names of the ledger accounts you have created to make sure you have not left any out.
- Work out a way of remembering whether the entries in the Sales Ledger and the Nominal Ledger are debits or credits, for example:
  - **S**ales ledger accounts: **S**ales are **D**ebits and **R**eturns are **C**redits

    Try the words '**S**aucy **S**ally **D**ances **R**eally **C**oolly'
  - **N**ominal ledger accounts: **S**ales are **C**redits and **R**eturns are **D**ebits

    Try the words '**N**aughty **S**usan **C**annot **R**eally **D**ance'

Exercises

3.1* It is August 14 2009 and you have just written up the sales day book and the sales returns day book for the week (see below) for Echo Design, a business which distributes kitchen and bathroom accessories which it buys from importers based in the UK. Its product lines are analysed according to the two categories, kitchens and bathrooms.

You are to set up ledger accounts in the sales and nominal ledgers, as listed below. Make sure that each ledger is headed up with the name of the ledger and all account names are set out clearly.

Sales Ledger:

Personal accounts for two customers: Modern Accessories and Stylish Living

Nominal Ledger

Sales - kitchens, Sales - bathrooms, Sales Returns - kitchens, Sales Returns - bathrooms, VAT

You are then to enter up the ledger accounts with the appropriate figures from the two day books.

Sales Day Book

Date	Details	Kitchens	Bathrooms	VAT	Total
2009		£	£	£	£
10 Aug	Modern Accessories	180.00	220.00	70.00	470.00
11 Aug	Stylish Living	144.00	172.00	55.30	371.30
12 Aug	Modern Accessories	56.00	130.00	32.55	218.55
14 Aug		380.00	522.00	157.85	1,059.85

Sales Returns Day Book

Date	Details	Kitchens	Bathrooms	VAT	Total
2009		£	£	£	£
11 Aug	Modern Accessories	72.00	120.00	33.60	225.60
12 Aug	Stylish Living		48.00	8.40	56.40
14 Aug		72.00	168.00	42.00	282.00

3.2   Best Feet Forward is a business which supplies two types of footwear for adults: trainers and shoes. The date is 26 June. The accounts manager has handed you the completed day books for the last two weeks. He asks you to enter them in the ledger accounts with entries for both Fridays, ie 19 June and 26 June. You will need to set up the accounts before posting the figures.

week 1   **Sales Day Book**

Date	Details	Trainers	Shoes	VAT	Total
2009		£	£	£	£
15 Jun	Fashion Footwear	256.00	192.00	78.40	526.40
16 Jun	Shoes4U		184.00	32.20	216.20
18 Jun	Fashion Footwear	108.00	160.00	46.90	314.90
19 Jun		364.00	536.00	157.50	1,057.50

Sales Returns Day Book

Date	Details	Trainers	Shoes	VAT	Total
2009		£	£	£	£
16 Jun	Fashion Footwear	112.00	154.00	46.55	312.55
18 Jun	Shoes4U		68.00	11.90	79.90
19 Jun		112.00	222.00	58.45	392.45

week 2   **Sales Day Book**

Date	Details	Trainers	Shoes	VAT	Total
2009		£	£	£	£
23 Jun	Fashion Footwear	728.00		127.40	855.40
24 Jun	Shoes4U		368.00	64.40	432.40
25 Jun	Fashion Footwear	120.00	84.00	35.70	239.70
26 Jun		848.00	452.00	227.50	1,527.50

Sales Returns Day Book

Date	Details	Trainers	Shoes	VAT	Total
2009		£	£	£	£
23 Jun	Fashion Footwear	56.00		9.80	65.80
24 Jun	Shoes4U		78.00	13.65	91.65
26 Jun		56.00	78.00	23.45	157.45

4 Balancing the ledger accounts

The last two chapters have dealt with the writing up of the double-entry accounts for purchase and sales transactions from the relevant day books into the three ledgers:

- purchase ledger
- sales ledger
- nominal ledger

This chapter describes how these ledger accounts are balanced, a process which you are likely to have covered in previous studies of bookkeeping.

This will be in preparation for the drawing up of the trial balance – a list of all the ledger account balances – which is covered in the next chapter. The trial balance is the last stage of your Unit 1 examination, which covers:

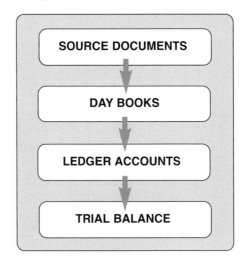

SOURCE DOCUMENTS

DAY BOOKS

LEDGER ACCOUNTS

TRIAL BALANCE

This chapter explains the processes of:

- balancing accounts in the purchase ledger
- balancing accounts in the sales ledger
- balancing accounts in the nominal ledger

BALANCING ACCOUNTS

You may well have learnt how to balance accounts in your previous studies. But in case you have not, or if by any chance you think you may need some revision, you should read the text that follows (pages 49 to 50).

At regular intervals, often at the end of each month, double-entry accounts are balanced in order to calculate the running total of the account to date. This provides the owner of the business with valuable information, such as:

- the amount owing to each supplier (creditor)
- the amount owing by each customer (debtor)
- the amount of sales and purchases made
- the amount of VAT due to, or from, HM Revenue & Customs

As you will have seen in the last three chapters, these accounts are set out in the purchase, sales and nominal ledgers:

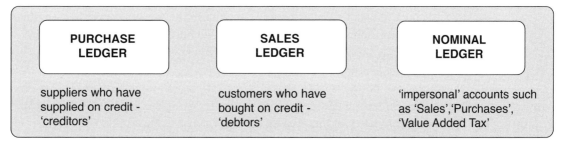

PURCHASE LEDGER	**SALES LEDGER**	**NOMINAL LEDGER**
suppliers who have supplied on credit - 'creditors'	customers who have bought on credit - 'debtors'	'impersonal' accounts such as 'Sales', 'Purchases', 'Value Added Tax'

BALANCING A PURCHASE LEDGER ACCOUNT

Set out below is an example of a supplier's account which has been written up in Zest Sport's purchase ledger during the month, but has not yet been balanced. Purchases made from the supplier during the month are entered on the credit (right-hand) side of the account and returns made to the supplier by Zest Sports are entered on the debit (left-hand) side of the account.

Dr				Olympic Supplies Account			Cr
2009	**Details**	**£**	**p**	**2009**	**Details**	**£**	**p**
14 Jul	Purchase returns	25	00	13 Jul	Purchases	320	00
22 Jul	Purchase returns	75	00	20 Jul	Purchases	80	00
				24 Jul	Purchases	200	00

Now study the way in which this account is balanced:

Dr				Olympic Supplies Account				Cr
2009	**Details**	**£**	**p**	**2009**	**Details**	**£**	**p**	
14 Jul	Purchase returns	25	00	13 Jul	Purchases	320	00	
22 Jul	Purchase returns	75	00	20 Jul	Purchases	80	00	
31 Jul	Balance c/d	**1** 500	00	24 Jul	Purchases	200	00	
		2 600	00		double-entry	**2** 600	00	
				1 Aug	Balance b/d	**3** 500	00	

The debit and the credit columns are separately added up and the totals noted down (eg on a piece of paper). The totals are £600 on the credit side (three purchase items) and £100 (two purchase returns items) on the debit side.

Nothing is entered in the account at this stage. You should then follow the following steps:

1 The difference between the totals of the two sides (ie £600 – £100 = £500) is the **balance** of the account ; this is entered in the account . . .

- in the money column on the side of the smaller total (here it is the debit side)
- on the next available line down on that side
- with the date of the balancing (here it is 31 July)
- with the words 'Balance c/d', which is an abbreviation of 'Balance carried down' in the details column

2 Both sides of the account are now added up and the totals (which should be identical, and the higher of the two totals calculated earlier) are entered in the money columns on both sides of the account; here the figure is £600.

A single line is drawn above the totals and a double line underneath the totals.

3 As we are dealing with double-entry bookkeeping, we need a second entry to go with the transaction of entering the balance (the debit for £500 in Step 1). This is done by entering a credit for £500 on the other side of the account, below the totals entered in Step 2. Note that the date here is not the month-end date (31 July) but the first day of the following month (1 August). The abbreviation 'Balance b/d' used here stands for 'Balance brought down'.

BALANCING A SALES LEDGER ACCOUNT

In the previous section we balanced a purchase ledger account. This showed how much a supplier, Olympic Supplies, is owed by Zest Sports at the end of the month. The balance of this account – £500 – is on the **credit** side of the account, representing an amount **owed by** a business, a liability.

It therefore follows that if you turn to the Sales Ledger which shows the opposite situation, ie amounts **owed to** Zest Sports by a customer, you will then find the balance of a customer account on the **debit** side of the ledger account, because an amount **owed to** a business is always a **debit**.

Study the example below of a balanced customer account – Trajan Sports – and read the notes that follow. You will see that sales are recorded on the left (debit side) and sales returns are on the right (credit side).

Dr			Trajan Sports Account				Cr	
2009	**Details**	**£**	**p**	**2009**	**Details**		**£**	**p**
6 Jul	Sales	200	00	Jul 9	Sales returns		20	00
8 Jul	Sales	50	00	Jul 16	Sales returns		30	00
22 Jul	Sales	150	00	Jul 31	Balance c/d	**1**	350	00
		2 400	00		*double-entry*	**2**	400	00
1 Aug	Balance b/d	**3** 350	00					

1 The balance of **£350** is the difference between the total of the debit entries (**£400**, ie £200 + £50 + £150) and the total of the debit entries (**£50**, ie £20 + £30). It is entered on the credit side, ie the side with the lower total.

2 Both sides are now added up to produce a total of £400. A single line is drawn above the totals and a double line underneath the totals.

3 As we are dealing with double-entry bookkeeping, the transaction of entering the £350 balance (Step 1, a credit) must be completed. This is done by entering the second entry on the debit side of the account, below the totals entered in Step 2. Again, the date here is not the month-end date (31 July) but the first day of the following month (1 August). The abbreviation 'Balance b/d' stands for 'Balance brought down'.

BALANCING NOMINAL LEDGER ACCOUNTS

balancing accounts: recap so far . . .

- balanced **purchase ledger** accounts (for suppliers) normally show an amount **owed by** a business – a **credit** balance
  - the balancing figure is entered on the debit side above the underlined total, described as 'balance c/d'
  - the balance is then brought down on the credit side after the totals have been entered; it is described as 'balance b/d'
- balanced **sales ledger** accounts (for customers) normally show an amount **owing to** a business – a **debit** balance
  - the balancing figure is entered on the credit side above the underlined total, described as 'balance c/d'
  - the balance is then brought down on the debit side after the totals have been entered; it is described as 'balance b/d'

In other words, you can normally rely on:

- purchase ledger account = balance brought down on the credit side
- sales ledger account = balance brought down on the debit side

nominal ledger balances

Nominal accounts, on the other hand, can show the final 'balance c/d' on either side of the account. One way of remembering the rules is:

- **debit balance** = **money going out** of the business: ie money spent on purchases, money refunded because of returns, expenses paid
- **credit balance** = **money going into** the business from sales, refunds and other items of income

We will now give examples of the nominal accounts you will need to balance in the examination.

nominal accounts with only one entry

The majority of nominal accounts you are likely to encounter in the examination will in fact have only one entry – the total you will have posted from the relevant day book.

The good news is that if there is only one entry to an account, you do not have to balance it – the entry is the balance!

The important thing is to work out whether the entry will be on the debit side or the credit side. One way of remembering this is was explained on the previous page:

money out (eg purchases) = debit balance

money in (eg sales) = credit balance

Here are two examples of balanced accounts in Zest Sports' Nominal Ledger relating to purchases and purchase returns:

Dr				Purchases Account - footballs			Cr
2009	**Details**	**£**	**p**	**2009**	**Details**	**£**	**p**
30 Apr	Total P D B	500	00				

On 30 April the total of the purchases column (footballs) in the Purchases Day Book (PDB) is transferred to the debit side of the Purchases Account (footballs) in the Nominal Ledger.

This becomes the balance of the account.

Dr				Purchase Returns Account - footballs			Cr
2009	**Details**	**£**	**p**	**2009**	**Details**	**£**	**p**
				30 Apr	Total P R D B	50	00

On 30 April the total of the purchase returns column (footballs) in the Purchase Returns Day Book (PRDB) is transferred to the credit side of the Purchase Returns Account (footballs) in the Nominal Ledger.

This becomes the balance of the account.

Here are two examples of balanced accounts in Zest Sports' Nominal Ledger which relate to sales:

Dr				Sales Account - footballs			Cr
2009	Details	£	p	2009	Details	£	p
				30 Apr	Total S D B	800	00

On 30 April the total of the sales column (footballs) in the Sales Day Book (SDB) is transferred to the credit side of the Sales Account (footballs) in the Nominal Ledger.

This becomes the balance of the account.

Dr				Sales Returns Account - footballs			Cr
2009	Details	£	p	2009	Details	£	p
30 Apr	Total S R D B	60	00				

On 30 April the total of the sales returns column (footballs) in the Sales Returns Day Book (SRDB) is transferred to the debit side of the Sales Returns Account (footballs) in the Nominal Ledger.

This becomes the balance of the account.

balancing Value Added Tax (VAT) Account

The only account that you are likely to have to balance in the Nominal Ledger by bringing down a calculated figure is Value Added Tax (VAT) Account.

The rules for which sides the totals from the day books are posted in the account are the same as those for the other accounts:

Debits = totals from Purchases Day Book, Sales Returns Day Book

Credits = totals from Purchase Returns Day Book, Sales Day Book

Study the account on the next page and read the notes that follow.

Dr	Value Added Tax Account						Cr	
2009	**Details**	**£**	**p**	**2009**	**Details**	**£**	**p**
30 Apr	Total P D B	250	00	30 Apr	Total P R D B	100	00
30 Apr	Total S R D B	50	00	30 Apr	Total S D B	800	00
30 Apr	Balance c/d	**1** 600	00				
		2 900	00		double-entry	**2** 900	00
				1 May	Balance b/d	**3** 600	00

1 The balance of **£600** is the difference between the total of the credit entries (**£900**, ie £100 + £800) and the total of the debit entries (**£300**, ie £250 + £50). It is entered on the debit side, ie the side with the lower total.

2 Both sides are now added up to produce a total of £900. A single line is drawn above the totals and a double line underneath the totals.

3 As we are dealing with double-entry bookkeeping, the transaction of entering the £600 balance (Step 1, a debit) must be completed. This is done by entering the second entry on the credit side of the account, below the totals entered in Step 2. Again, the date here is not the month-end date (30 April) but the first day of the following month (1 May). The abbreviation 'Balance b/d' stands for 'Balance brought down'.

a note on Value Added Tax (VAT)

VAT is a tax on spending. Most goods and services that you buy will have VAT added to them at standard rate. This can vary from time-to-time, and in this text an example rate of 17.5% is used. The tax is paid by the final purchaser of the goods and services and 'collected' by the business which sells the goods and services. The VAT is then paid periodically to the VAT authorities, the government agency HM Revenue & Customs.

The business which 'collects' the VAT is allowed to set off any VAT it has had to pay itself against the amount collected. This is where the VAT Account comes in: the credit side is a total of the VAT the business 'collects' from customers and the debit side is the total of the VAT it has had to pay out to suppliers. **The balance of the account (the credit side minus the debit side) is the amount owing to HM Revenue & Customs.**

Where now and where next?

chapter summary

In this chapter we have

● explained how to balance ledger accounts in:
  – the purchase ledger
  – the sales ledger
  – the nominal ledger

● explained the reason for maintaining a Value Added Tax (VAT) Account

what is in the next chapter?

The next chapter moves to the next stage in the accounting process:

● the transfer of the ledger account balances to the trial balance

● the totalling and the agreement of the debits and credits of the trial balance to check that the double-entry has been carried out correctly

Balancing ledger accounts - exam tips

● If there is only one entry on an account (eg in some Nominal Ledger accounts), it does not need to be balanced, as that entry will be the balance.

● When totalling the debits and credits in an account, always write the initial totals on a separate piece of paper, or somewhere other than in the account – but never in the account itself.

● Always enter the balancing figure in the column with the lower total, on the next line down.

● Always enter the underlined totals on the same line - never on different lines.

● The balancing figure should always have the description 'Balance carried down' or 'Balance c/d'. 'Balance' should never be abbreviated to 'Bal'.

● Always remember to complete the double-entry and enter 'Balance brought down' or 'Balance b/d' on the line below the underlined totals – and on the opposite side to the 'Balance c/d' figure.

● If you are not sure about 'c/d' and 'b/d' remember **c**/d = '**c**rown' and **b**/d = '**b**ottom' (one is normally on a higher level than the other)

● Always remember that the date of the 'Balance b/d' figure should be the next day after 'Balance c/d' entry.

4.1* You are working as a temporary bookkeeper for Zest Sports which acts a distributor for footballs and tennis balls. You have been handed the purchase ledger and asked to to deal with the accounts shown on the next two pages. The date is 31 March 2009. You are to:

(a) balance the five accounts

(b) explain what the balance of the accounts tells the owner of the business

It is recommended for this exercise that you rule up some blank accounts, or obtain them from your tutor, or download them from the Resources Section of www.osbornebooks.co.uk

Dr					Atletico Supplies Account			Cr
2009	**Details**	**£**	**p**	**2009**	**Details**	**£**	**p**
23 Mar	Purchase returns	80	00	24 Mar	Purchases	120	00
26 Mar	Purchase returns	70	00	27 Mar	Purchases	360	00
				30 Mar	Purchases	170	00

Dr					Alpha Supplies Account			Cr
2009	**Details**	**£**	**p**	**2009**	**Details**	**£**	**p**
24 Mar	Purchase returns	50	00	24 Mar	Purchases	280	00
25 Mar	Purchase returns	75	00	26 Mar	Purchases	144	00
				30 Mar	Purchases	320	00

Dr						Trax Supplies Account			Cr
2009	Details	£	p	**2009**	Details		£	p
26 Mar	Purchase returns	40	00	24 Mar	Purchases		195	00
30 Mar	Purchase returns	35	00	27 Mar	Purchases		236	00

Dr						Mercury Limited Account			Cr
2009	Details	£	p	**2009**	Details		£	p
24 Mar	Purchase returns	57	50	24 Mar	Purchases		161	60
25 Mar	Purchase returns	49	75	26 Mar	Purchases		352	79
				30 Mar	Purchases		642	10

Dr						Solo Supplies Account			Cr
2009	Details	£	p	**2009**	Details		£	p
				23 Mar	Purchases		248	00
				25 Mar	Purchases		78	75
				30 Mar	Purchases		180	00

4.2 You are working as a temporary bookkeeper for Zest Sports which acts a distributor for footballs and tennis balls. You have been handed the sales ledger and asked to to deal with the accounts shown on the next two pages. The date is 31 March 2009. You are to:

(a) balance the five accounts

(b) explain what the balance of the accounts tells the owner of the business

It is recommended for this exercise that you rule up some blank accounts, or obtain them from your tutor, or download them from the Resources Section of www.osbornebooks.co.uk

Dr					Trajan Sports Account			Cr
2009	Details	£	p	2009	Details	£	p
23 Mar	Sales	450	00	24 Mar	Sales returns	80	00
26 Mar	Sales	70	00	30 Mar	Sales returns	70	00
27 Mar	Sales	180	00				

Dr					Windermere Centre Account			Cr
2009	Details	£	p	2009	Details	£	p
24 Mar	Sales	195	00	23 Mar	Sales returns	67	00
25 Mar	Sales	271	00	24 Mar	Sales returns	123	00
30 Mar	Sales	64	00				

Dr				Hero Sports Account			Cr
2009	**Details**	**£**	**p**	**2009**	**Details**	**£**	**p**
24 Mar	Sales	191	00	25 Mar	Sales returns	45	00
25 Mar	Sales	378	00	27 Mar	Sales returns	87	50
30 Mar	Sales	580	00				

Dr				Baxter Sports Centre Account			Cr
2009	**Details**	**£**	**p**	**2009**	**Details**	**£**	**p**
26 Mar	Sales	486	00	23 Mar	Sales returns	38	00
30 Mar	Sales	396	00	24 Mar	Sales returns	64	00

Dr				Bentley Sports Account			Cr
2009	**Details**	**£**	**p**	**2009**	**Details**	**£**	**p**
23 Mar	Sales	486	50				
27 Mar	Sales	287	95				
30 Mar	Sales	94	20				

4.3 You are working as a trainee for a small local firm of accountants. You have been asked to deal with the three VAT accounts shown below. All the day book figures have already been transferred to the accounts. The date is 30 April 2009.

You are to:

(a) balance the three accounts

(b) explain what the balance of these accounts tells the owner of the business

Dr	Value Added Tax Account - Business A					Cr	
2009	**Details**	**£**	**p**	**2009**	**Details**	**£**	**p**
30 Apr	Total P D B	400	00	30 Apr	Total P R D B	80	00
30 Apr	Total S R D B	60	00	30 Apr	Total S D B	720	00

Dr	Value Added Tax Account - Business B					Cr	
2009	**Details**	**£**	**p**	**2009**	**Details**	**£**	**p**
30 Apr	Total P D B	550	00	30 Apr	Total P R D B	120	00
30 Apr	Total S R D B	75	00	30 Apr	Total S D B	840	00

Dr	Value Added Tax Account - Business C					Cr	
2009	**Details**	**£**	**p**	**2009**	**Details**	**£**	**p**
30 Apr	Total P D B	264	75	30 Apr	Total P R D B	49	21
30 Apr	Total S R D B	55	95	30 Apr	Total S D B	455	62

5 Balancing the trial balance

what this chapter covers . . .

In the last chapter we balanced a number of ledger accounts in:

- purchase ledger
- sales ledger
- nominal ledger

This chapter describes how the debit and credit balances of these ledger accounts are transferred and entered in a table known as a 'trial balance'. This contains two money columns:

- all the debit balances
- all the credit balances

These two columns are totalled and in theory the two totals should then agree.

This is because the balances are the result of double-entry bookkeeping in which the debit entry should always equal the credit entry.

It therefore follows that the total of the debit entries should equal the total of the credit entries.

This process is carried out regularly – often at the end of the month – to ensure the accuracy of the bookkeeping.

If the two totals do not agree this is because a mistake has been made somewhere in the bookkeeping or in entering the balances in the trial balance, or in adding up the trial balance columns.

This chapter explains how to trace these errors and correct the trial balance.

In the examination you will be penalised if your trial balance does not 'balance'.

This chapter, in short, explains the processes of:

- setting up the trial balance with the correct headings
- transferring the ledger account balances in an organised way
- totalling the debit and credit columns of the trial balance
- agreeing the totals of the debit and credit columns of the trial balance
- finding out the source of any mistakes if by any chance your trial balance does not balance

THE NEED FOR A TRIAL BALANCE

A trial balance is an important stage in the bookkeeping process. It sets out the debit balances and credit balances of the ledger accounts, totals them up, and shows, hopefully – if you have been accurate in your double-entry – two equal totals. It is therefore an important accuracy check. Also, if you take your studies further, you will see that the trial balance is the source of the figures for two important financial statements of a business:

- the profit statement – which shows how profitable a business is
- the balance sheet – which sets out the assets and liabilities of a business and shows the stake the owner has in the business (the 'capital')

At this stage, however, all you need to know is how to set up and complete a trial balance. This is explained in the next section.

FORMAT OF A TRIAL BALANCE - HEADINGS

Set out below is an example of the 'trial balance' table you may be given in the examination. It is likely to be blank, apart from the headings 'Trial Balance as at' and 'Name of business' after which you should enter the date and the appropriate name. You will have to enter up the other headings accurately and legibly. They are entered here, with explanatory notes. These are just the headings; explanation of the account entries are on the next page.

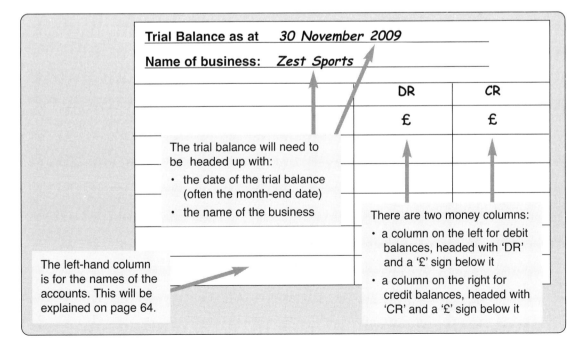

TRIAL BALANCE - ENTERING THE BALANCES

Set out on the next two pages are:

- summaries of the ledger accounts of Zest Sports for the month of January 2009, set out in the nominal, sales and purchase ledgers; the figures shown are the balance of each account at the end of the month
- the trial balance after those balances have been transferred and the columns have been added up and the totals agreed

You should study carefully

- the **columns** into which the account balances have been transferred:
    - **debit balances** to the **debit column** of the trial balance
    - **credit balances** to the **credit column** of the trial balance
- the **order** in which they have been transferred:
    - supplier accounts from the **purchase ledger** - credits
    - customer accounts from the **sales ledger** - debits
    - purchases accounts from the **nominal ledger** - debits
    - purchase returns accounts from the **nominal ledger** - credits
    - sales accounts from the **nominal ledger** - credits
    - sales returns accounts from the **nominal ledger** - debits
    - VAT account from the **nominal ledger** - a credit

NOMINAL LEDGER ACCOUNT BALANCES (SUMMARY)

	Dr (£)	Cr (£)
Purchases - footballs	2,014,40	
Purchases - tennis balls	4,438.82	
Purchase Returns - footballs		386.38
Purchase Returns - tennis balls		164.60
Sales - footballs		7,441.68
Sales - tennis balls		2,634.60
Sales Returns - footballs	569.72	
Sales Returns - tennis balls	175.40	
Value Added Tax		600.08

Trial Balance as at *31 January 2009*

Name of business: *Zest Sports*

	DR	CR
	£	£
Atletico Supplies		822.88
Alpha Supplies		3,502.06
Trax Supplies		2,610.18
Trajan Sports	4,597.02	
Windermere Centre	4,273.08	
Hero Sports	2,094.02	
Purchases - footballs	2,014,40	
Purchases - tennis balls	4,438.82	
Purchase Returns - footballs		386.38
Purchase Returns - tennis balls		164.60
Sales - footballs		7,441.68
Sales - tennis balls		2,634.60
Sales Returns - footballs	569.72	
Sales Returns - tennis balls	175.40	
Value Added Tax		600.08
	18,162.46	18,162.46

the account names entered in the left-hand column

the totals columns balance

SALES LEDGER ACCOUNT BALANCES (SUMMARY)

	Dr (£)	Cr (£)
Trajan Sports	4,597.02	
Windermere Centre	4,273.08	
Hero Sports	2,094.02	

PURCHASE LEDGER ACCOUNT BALANCES (SUMMARY)

	Dr (£)	Cr (£)
Atletico Supplies		822.88
Alpha Supplies		3,502.06
Trax Supplies		2,610.18

TRIAL BALANCE - A SUMMARY

Before we explain what to do if the debit and credit columns do not agree, make sure that you are completely familiar with:

- writing the headings in the trial balance
- entering up the account balances in the correct order
- adding up the debit and credit columns accurately
- agreeing the totals of the debit and credit columns

The entries you have to make are explained below in the grey boxes.

		DR	CR
Trial Balance as at	**31 January 2009**		
Name of business:	**Zest Sports**		
		£	**£**
enter the date / enter the business name / enter DR and CR / enter £ signs			
enter supplier balances from purchase ledger → Atletico Supplies			822.88
Alpha Supplies			3,502.06
Trax Supplies			2,610.18
enter customer balances from sales ledger → Trajan Sports		4,597.02	
Windermere Centre		4,273.08	
Hero Sports		2,094.02	
enter purchases and purchase returns balances from nominal ledger → Purchases - footballs		2,014.40	
Purchases - tennis balls		4,438.82	
Purchase Returns - footballs			386.38
Purchase Returns - tennis balls			164.60
enter sales and sales returns balances from nominal ledger → Sales - footballs			7,441.68
Sales - tennis balls			2,634.60
Sales Returns - footballs		569.72	
Sales Returns - tennis balls		175.40	
enter VAT balance from nominal ledger → Value Added Tax			600.08
		18,162.46	18,162.46

add up the two columns and then enter and agree the column totals

WHAT TO DO IF THE TRIAL BALANCE TOTALS DO NOT AGREE

the cause of the problem

It may happen that the total of the debits and the total of the credits in the trial balance are not the same figure – they do not agree. This will be because there is an error somewhere:

- in the double-entry bookkeeping, eg a debit entry for £200 and a credit entry for £220, or . . .

- in the preparation of the trial balance, eg a balance put in the debit column instead of in the credit column, or incorrect addition of the columns

procedure for identifying the difference

1   Add up the columns again to check your accuracy. If you find a mistake and the debit and credit totals this time are the same, cross out the incorrect total and neatly write in the correct amount. You need take no further action.

2   But if, on the other hand, the columns still do not agree when you check your arithmetic, find out the difference between the two totals by deducting the lower total from the higher total. Make a note of this difference.

   There are now a number of techniques for finding out where this error has been made:

3   Check carefully all the original ledger account balances to see if any of them is the same as the difference. You may have forgotten to transfer a ledger account balance to the trial balance. If this happens you should enter this figure in the correct trial balance column and amend the total.

4   Divide the difference by two and see if you can find a figure in the trial balance for this amount. If you can, it means that you have probably put this balance in the wrong trial balance column. If this happens you will then need to cross out the wrong entry neatly and enter it in the correct column and then re-do the column addition and correct the incorrect total (as in 3 above).

5   If you can divide the difference by nine and come up with a whole number, it is possible that you have transposed some figures when you were transferring them. For example if the difference is £45 (which is divisible by 9 to produce 5) you may have written £72 as £27 (£72 minus £27 = £45). If you can divide the difference by nine you should the check all the figures you have transferred and look for reversed figures.

what to do if there is still a difference

If you are working in a business it would be important to find this difference and this may mean looking back through your invoices, credit notes, daybook entries and calculations, ledger account entries and so on. In an examination situation you will not have so much time for this, but it is still worth checking through your work carefully if you have a difference and some time before you have to finish.

---

example trial balance - finding the difference

Add up the columns of this trial balance. What is the problem? What is the solution? The answer is printed at the bottom of this page, in case you need to check it.

Trial Balance as at   *30 June 2009*

Name of business: *Zest Sports*

	DR	CR
	£	£
Atletico Supplies		1262.54
Alpha Supplies		820.14
Trax Supplies		784.56
Trajan Sports	2,481.76	
Windermere Centre	1,728.66	
Hero Sports	1,762.92	
Purchases - footballs		1,534.50
Purchases - tennis balls	1,043.64	
Purchase Returns - footballs		68.00
Purchase Returns - tennis balls		69.92
Sales - footballs		3,295.60
Sales - tennis balls		1,911.06
Sales Returns - footballs	71.96	
Sales Returns - tennis balls	51.00	
Value Added Tax		462.62

Answer: the column totals are £7,139.94 and £10,208.94, the difference being £3069.00. This figure divided by 2 is £1,534.50, the balance of purchases (footballs) account, which should be on the debit side. When this figure is transferred to the debit side the columns then both total £8,674.44 and so the trial balance now balances.

Where now and where next?

chapter summary

In this chapter we have

- explained how to draw up a trial balance with correct headings

- shown how to transfer the balances of the ledger accounts to the trial balance debit and credit columns and then total those columns

- explained how to identify any difference between the two totals

what is in the next chapter?

The next chapter introduces Unit 2 of the Qualification 'process ledger transactions and prepare control accounts'. Control accounts are summary accounts which total up the account transactions of different areas of the business, suppliers or customers, for example. They are particularly useful for bigger businesses.

Documents to day books - exam tips

- Head up the trial balance carefully; it is especially important not to forget to enter the name of the business and the date.

- When entering the ledger account balances in the trial balance, do not abbreviate the account names.

- When entering the ledger account balances in the trial balance, remember that the balances go on the same side as in the ledger accounts – the trial balance is a summary and you are not doing double-entry.

- When entering the ledger account balances in the trial balance, be systematic and go though the ledgers in a set order, for example purchase ledger, sales ledger, nominal ledger.

- When entering personal ledger account balances in the trial balance, make sure that the names of customers and suppliers are spelt correctly.

- If you have to change a figure, rule neatly through the incorrect figure and write the amended figure next to the incorrect figure.

- If you do happen to have a difference, be organised in the way you look for it and memorise what you have to do, eg check arithmetic, check all entries, divide the difference by two, divide the difference by 9, and so on . . .

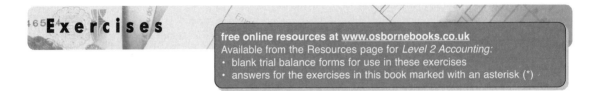

Situation

You work for a bookkeeping firm and are today processing the accounts for four customers. The ledger accounts have already been balanced and you have been asked to draw up the trial balance for each customer and date it 31 December 2009.

Each of the next four questions below relates to one of these customers.

5.1*   CUSTOMER 1 – PROFUMIA LIMITED

Profumia Limited is a small company which imports perfume from Italy.

The ledger account balances as at 31 December 2009 are shown below.

There is no subdivision in sales or purchases for types of product.

You are to draw up the trial balance for Profumia Limited as at 31 December 2009.

Purchase Ledger	£	
N Albanese	400.00	Cr
P Balmato	200.00	Cr
G Conti	550.00	Cr
Sales Ledger		
I F Sense Ltd	500.00	Dr
K Hallett & Co	600.00	Dr
Perfumes Unlimited	1,200.00	Dr
Nominal Ledger		
Purchases	1,100.00	Dr
Purchase Returns	55.00	Cr
Sales	2,300.00	Cr
Sales Returns	450.00	Dr
Value Added Tax	345.00	Cr

5.2* **CUSTOMER 2 – SCRIBE LIMITED**

Scribe Ltd is a small company which distributes high quality pens.

The ledger account balances as at 31 December 2009 are shown below.

There is no subdivision in sales or purchases for types of product.

You are to draw up the trial balance for Scribe Limited as at 31 December 2009.

Purchase Ledger	£	
Stationery Supplies Ltd	375.00	Cr
R S Hawes Ltd	212.00	Cr
R Mason & Co	964.70	Cr

Sales Ledger		
R S Stationery	610.50	Dr
James Lewis	635.00	Dr
Exclusivity Ltd	1,255.20	Dr

Nominal Ledger		
Purchases	1,420.00	Dr
Purchase Returns	103.70	Cr
Sales	2,050.65	Cr
Sales Returns	99.50	Dr
Value Added Tax	314.15	Cr

5.3 **CUSTOMER 3 – TEMPUS LIMITED**

Tempus Ltd is a company which buys and sells watches and clocks.

The ledger account balances as at 31 December 2009 are shown below.

The sales and purchases are subdivided into two categories in the accounts: watches and clocks.

You are to draw up the trial balance for Tempus Limited as at 31 December 2009.

Purchase Ledger	£	
TicToc Clock Supplies	1,500.00	Cr
Orologio Ltd	750.00	Cr
Secondo Watches Ltd	1,200.00	Cr

Sales Ledger

Wacky Watches	750.00	Dr
Sunhour Ltd	3,400.00	Dr
Waitamo Ltd	1,500.00	Dr

Nominal Ledger

Purchases – watches	1,250.00	Dr
Purchases – clocks	1,750.00	Dr
Purchase Returns – watches	56.00	Cr
Purchase Returns – clocks	45.00	Cr
Sales – watches	2,300.00	Cr
Sales – clocks	2,800.00	Cr
Sales Returns – watches	450.00	Dr
Sales Returns – clocks	120.00	Dr
Value Added Tax	569.00	Cr

5.4   CUSTOMER 3 – NEVESKI LIMITED

Neveski Ltd is a company which buys and sells skis and snowboards.

The ledger account balances as at 31 December 2009 are shown below.

The sales and purchases are subdivided into two categories in the accounts: skis and snowboards.

You are to draw up the trial balance for Neveski Limited as at 31 December 2009.

Purchase Ledger   £

Slalom Supplies Ltd	1,570.50	Cr
Skistuff Importers	810.50	Cr
Downhill Ltd	994.50	Cr

Sales Ledger

Snowsure Equipment	905.75	Dr
Speedsafe Ltd	3,456.00	Dr
Champion Ski	567.20	Dr

Nominal Ledger

Purchases – skis	1,067.00	Dr
Purchases – snowboards	1,725.60	Dr

Purchase Returns – skis	76.00	Cr
Purchase Returns – snowboards	64.00	Cr
Sales – skis	1,700.00	Cr
Sales – snowboards	2,235.90	Cr
Sales Returns – skis	198.95	Dr
Sales Returns – snowboards	120.50	Dr
Value Added Tax	589.60	Cr

5.5* **Note**: this question and questions 5.6 and 5.7 are not related to questions 5.1 to 5.4

An inexperienced colleague has passed you the trial balance shown below. She cannot get it to balance. She has followed the usual procedures, listing three purchase ledger accounts before three sales ledger accounts and then finishing with the nominal accounts. You have already checked the Value Added Tax Account and confirmed that it has a credit balance.

Identify all the errors that you can find, draw up a revised trial balance, and state what the debit column and credit column totals should be.

Trial Balance as at
Name of business

	DR	CR
	£	£
ABC Supplies	1,500.00	
J Costerman & Co	900.00	
Roman Supplies		750.00
D Martland	1,250.00	
Ranveer Singh		935.00
Jin Li Limited		840.00
Purchases		3,050.00
Purchase Returns		75.00
Sales	2,750.00	
Sales Returns	125.00	
Value Added Tax		225.00
	6,025.00	6,375.00

5.6 Hunter Electronics is a business which produces two sensors: the X104 and the X109. The bookkeeper has balanced the ledger accounts as at 30 June 2009 and has had them checked as correct. He has then attempted to draw up the trial balance at the same date but cannot get the debit and credit totals to agree. He asks you to help him out. The ledger balances and his attempt at a trial balance are shown below. You are to draw up a new and correct trial balance.

LEDGER BALANCES

Purchase Ledger	Onyx Supplies	758.00	Cr
	Laser Electronic Supplies	430.00	Cr
	Richard Thomas Limited	1,056.00	Cr
Sales Ledger	Delta Diagnostics	956.00	Dr
	Arco Engineering	490.00	Dr
	Electropulse Ltd	1,745.00	Dr
Nominal Ledger	Purchases - X104	742.00	Dr
	Purchases - X109	1,276.00	Dr
	Purchase Returns - X104	45.00	Cr
	Purchase Returns - X109	38.00	Cr
	Sales - X104	1,267.00	Cr
	Sales - X109	1,356.00	Cr
	Sales Returns - X104	56.00	Dr
	Sales Returns - X109	79.00	Dr
	Value Added Tax	394.00	Cr

Trial Balance as at 1 July 2009

Name of Company: Onyx Supplies

	Dr £	Cr £
Onyx Supplies		758.00
Laser Electronic Supplies		430.00
Richard Thomas Limited		1,056.00
Delta Diagnostics	956.00	
Arco Engineering	940.00	
Electropulse Ltd	1,745.00	
Purchases - X104	742.00	
Purchases - X109	1,276.00	
Purchase Returns - X104		45.00
Purchase Returns - X109		38.00
Sales - X104		1,267.00
Sales - X109		1,356.00
Sales Returns - X104	56.00	
Sales Returns - X109	79.00	
Value Added Tax		394.00
	5,794.00	5,344.00

5.7   Bevendo Limited is a specialist wholesaler dealing in products used for holding drinks: mugs and glasses. The bookkeeper has balanced the ledger accounts as at 30 June 2009 and has had them checked as correct. She has then drawn up the trial balance at the same date but is having problems in getting the trial balance to balance. She asks you for help. The ledger balances and her trial balance are shown below. You are to draw up a new and correct trial balance.

LEDGER BALANCES

Purchase Ledger	Vetro Glassware	1,510.00	Cr
	Padley Porcelain	1,260.00	Cr
	Houseware Supplies Ltd	2,228.60	Cr
Sales Ledger	Muggins Ltd	1,802.35	Dr
	Kitchen Specialities	956.75	Dr
	J W Smith & Co	2,985.00	Dr
Nominal Ledger	Purchases - mugs	1,945.00	Dr
	Purchases - glasses	2,860.50	Dr
	Purchase Returns - mugs	85.00	Cr
	Purchase Returns - glasses	78.45	Cr
	Sales - mugs	2,056.70	Cr
	Sales - glasses	3,185.89	Cr
	Sales Returns - mugs	102.56	Dr
	Sales Returns - glasses	348.50	Dr
	Value Added Tax	596.02	Cr

Trial Balance as at 30 June 2009		
Name of Company: Bevendo Limited		
	Dr	Cr
	£	£
Vetro Glassware		1,510.00
Padley Porcelain		1,260.00
Houseware Supplies Ltd		2,228.60
Muggins Ltd	1,820.65	
Kitchen Specialities	956.75	
J W Smith & Co	2,985.00	
Purchases - glasses	2,860.00	
Purchase Returns - mugs		58.00
Purchase Returns - glasses		78.45
Sales - mugs		2,056.70
Sales - glasses		3,185.89
Sales Returns - mugs	102.56	
Sales Returns - glasses	348.50	
Value Added Tax		596.02
	9,073.46	10,973.66

Introduction to the Unit 2 assignment

The Unit 2 title for the OCR Level 2 in Accounting is:

Process ledger transactions and prepare control accounts

You will have to sit an externally set assignment in examination conditions for your assessment. You will have two hours in which to complete the assignment plus ten minutes reading time. You should already be familiar with some of the formats and terminology used in this unit. If they are new to you, there will be notes in this text to explain them.

The processes you will have to carry out are:

● Set up double-entry accounts in the three ledgers: purchase ledger, sales ledger and nominal ledger.

● Enter opening balances in these accounts from a list of accounts provided.

● Enter transactions from the day books into the purchase ledger, sales ledger and nominal ledger.

● Enter transactions from the cash book into the purchase ledger, sales ledger and nominal ledger.

● Deal with non-routine transactions such as returned cheques and writing off bad debts by making the appropriate account entries in the ledgers.

● Balance all the accounts in the ledgers.

● Prepare control (total) accounts in the nominal ledger:
  - purchase ledger control account
  - sales ledger control account

● Balance the two control accounts: purchase ledger control account and sales ledger control account.

● Draw up separate lists of supplier account balances and customer account balances, total each list and agree the totals with the purchase ledger and sales ledger control account balances.

These processes are summarised in the diagram on the opposite page. Study this diagram and then work through the chapters that follow.

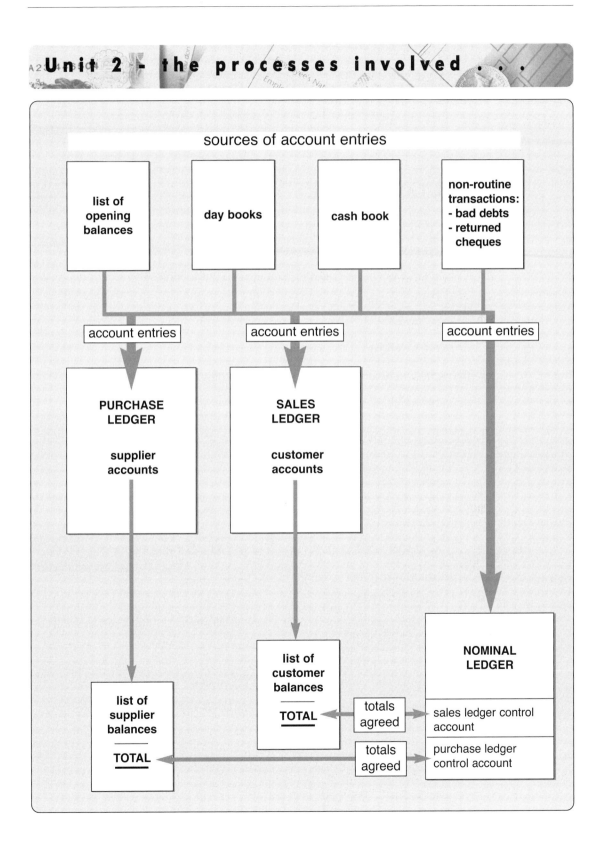

6 Setting up the ledgers

This chapter:

- shows how to set up the accounts in the following ledgers
  - purchase ledger
  - sales ledger
  - nominal ledger
- shows how to enter the opening balances in the ledger accounts
- explains the difference between personal and nominal accounts
- explains the rules for debits and credits in the double-entry bookkeeping system

Unit 2 Case Study – Supra Stationery

Supra Stationery

All the processes carried out in Unit 2 will be illustrated in this book by a Case Study of a business that supplies stationery, 'Supra Stationery'.

This business is run by Ranveer Singh, who supplies a number of local customers in the Midlands with stationery and office equipment.

Ranveer obtains his stock from a wide variety of UK and overseas manufacturers and sells his goods on credit.

His business 'Supra Stationery' operates a manual double-entry bookkeeping system incorporating purchase, sales and nominal ledgers.

SETTING UP LEDGER ACCOUNTS FROM A LIST OF BALANCES

Your starting point in the Unit 2 Assignment is a list of ledger account balances which you will have to enter into individual accounts. An example is shown below. Note that:

- the list is already organised by ledger and is dated
- the list shows whether the balance is a debit (Dr) or a credit (Cr)
- the balances are presented in a single column and are not added up as in the trial balance in Unit 1

SUPRA STATIONERY – LIST OF ACCOUNT BALANCES
(as at 1 April 2009)

Purchase Ledger	£	
Rapid Supply Ltd	840.20	Cr
AZ Supplies Ltd	725.60	Cr
T Khan Importers	963.90	Cr
Sales Ledger		
W Barnes Ltd	560.65	Dr
J Keetz	4,830.90	Dr
R S Thomas	1,340.10	Dr
W B Yates	1,074.70	Dr
Nominal Ledger		
Administration Expenses	32,350.10	Dr
Capital	65,600.00	Cr
Discount Allowed	510.65	Dr
Discount Received	690.00	Cr
Premises	50,000.00	Dr
Purchases	65,505.00	Dr
Purchase Returns	410.80	Cr
Sales	85,630.50	Cr
Sales Returns	240.50	Dr
Sundry Expenses	340.75	Dr
Value Added Tax	6,530.70	Cr

---

writing up the account balances

On the next four pages you will see how the accounts balances of Supra Stationery are entered in the Purchase Ledger, Sales Ledger and Nominal Ledger.

entering the balances in the purchase ledger

There are three supplier account balances which need to be entered in the purchase ledger. In the Assignment you will have to set up and head up the double-entry accounts. You also need to enter the words 'Purchase Ledger'.

Note that the supplier balances are all **credit balances** and are transferred to the **credit side** of the ledger account. The date used is the date of the balance list and the account description used is 'Balance b/d'.

LIST OF BALANCES as at 1 April 2009 (extract)

Purchase Ledger	£	
Rapid Supply Ltd	840.20	Cr
AZ Supplies Ltd	725.60	Cr
T Khan Importers	963.90	Cr

PURCHASE LEDGER

Dr					Rapid Supply Ltd Account			Cr
2009	**Details**	**£**	**p**	**2009**	**Details**		**£**	**p**
				1 Apr	Balance b/d		840	20

Dr					AZ Supplies Ltd Account			Cr
2009	**Details**	**£**	**p**	**2009**	**Details**		**£**	**p**
				1 Apr	Balance b/d		725	60

Dr					T Khan Importers Account			Cr
2009	**Details**	**£**	**p**	**2009**	**Details**		**£**	**p**
				1 Apr	Balance b/d		963	90

entering the balances in the sales ledger

There are four customer balances to be entered in the sales ledger. Note that this time the balances are **debit balances** and will have to be entered on the **debit side** of the accounts. Again the ledger and accounts will be headed up as appropriate and the details entered in each case as 'Balance b/d'.

LIST OF BALANCES as at 1 April 2009 (extract)

Sales Ledger

W Barnes Ltd	560.65	Dr
J Keetz	4,830.90	Dr
R S Thomas	1,340.10	Dr
W B Yates	1,074.70	Dr

SALES LEDGER

Dr					W Barnes Ltd Account			Cr
2009	**Details**	**£**	**p**	**2009**	**Details**		**£**	**p**
1 Apr	Balance b/d	560	65					

Dr					J Keetz Account			Cr
2009	**Details**	**£**	**p**	**2009**	**Details**		**£**	**p**
1 Apr	Balance b/d	4,830	90					

Dr					R S Thomas Account			Cr
2009	**Details**	**£**	**p**	**2009**	**Details**		**£**	**p**
1 Apr	Balance b/d	1,340	10					

Dr					W B Yates Account			Cr
2009	**Details**	**£**	**p**	**2009**	**Details**		**£**	**p**
1 Apr	Balance b/d	1,074	70					

entering the balances in the nominal ledger

Note that in the case of the nominal ledger there are both debit balances and credit balances. **Debit balances** go to the **debit side** and **credit balances** to the **credit side** of the appropriate account. As before, the ledger and accounts will need to be headed up, dated, and the details column entered in each case with the words 'Balance b/d'.

LIST OF ACCOUNT BALANCES (as at 1 April 2009)

Nominal Ledger

Administration Expenses	32,350.10	Dr
Capital	65,600.00	Cr
Discount Allowed	510.65	Dr
Discount Received	690.00	Cr
Premises	50,000.00	Dr
Purchases	65,505.00	Dr
Purchase Returns	410.80	Cr
Sales	85,630.50	Cr
Sales Returns	240.50	Dr
Sundry Expenses	340.75	Dr
VAT	6,530.70	Cr

NOMINAL LEDGER

Dr				Administration Expenses Account			Cr
2009	**Details**	**£**	**p**	**2009**	**Details**	**£**	**p**
1 Apr	Balance b/d	32,350	10				

Dr				Capital Account			Cr
2009	**Details**	**£**	**p**	**2009**	**Details**	**£**	**p**
				1 Apr	Balance b/d	65,600	00

Dr				Discount Allowed Account			Cr
2009	**Details**	**£**	**p**	**2009**	**Details**	**£**	**p**
1 Apr	Balance b/d	510	65				

Dr					Discount Received Account			Cr
2009	Details	£	p	2009	Details		£	p
				1 Apr	Balance b/d		690	00

Dr					Premises Account			Cr
2009	Details	£	p	2009	Details		£	p
1 Apr	Balance b/d	50,000	00					

Dr					Purchases Account			Cr
2009	Details	£	p	2009	Details		£	p
1 Apr	Balance b/d	65,505	00					

Dr					Purchase Returns Account			Cr
2009	Details	£	p	2009	Details		£	p
				1 Apr	Balance b/d		410	80

Dr					Sales Account			Cr
2009	Details	£	p	2009	Details		£	p
				1 Apr	Balance b/d		85,630	50

Dr					Sales Returns Account			Cr
2009	Details	£	p	2009	Details		£	p
1 Apr	Balance b/d	240	50					

Dr					Sundry Expenses Account			Cr
2009	Details	£	p	2009	Details		£	p
1 Apr	Balance b/d	340	75					

Dr					Value Added Tax Account			Cr
2009	Details	£	p	2009	Details		£	p
				1 Apr	Balance b/d		6,530	70

PERSONAL AND IMPERSONAL ACCOUNTS

The balances entered in the **purchase ledger** and **sales ledger** are named accounts for suppliers and customers, for example 'Rapid Supply Ltd Account' and 'J Keetz Account' These are known as **personal accounts**.

The other accounts in the account list are not connected with individual people but relate to items such as expenses and sales income, eg 'Purchases Account' and 'Sales Account'. These are known as **impersonal accounts** and are entered in the **nominal ledger**, as shown on the previous two pages.

BALANCES – DEBIT OR CREDIT?

The transfer of account balances to the ledger accounts explained on the last four pages is a useful illustration of the **rules of double-entry** at work. The entries to the various accounts in all three ledgers help to show you what balances are on the debit side and what are balances are on the credit side.

debits

Debit balances include:

- items owing to a business – eg customer accounts in the sales ledger
- items owned by a business (known as 'assets'), eg premises, equipment, money in the bank
- expenses – items such as administration and purchases

If you wish to increase the balance of assets and expenses accounts you will need to do so with a debit entry.

credit entries

Credit entries include:

- items owed by the business (known as 'liabilities'), eg:
    - supplier accounts in the purchase ledger
    - bank loans and overdrafts
- capital – this is money invested in the business by the owner and therefore owed to the owner by the business
- income – items such sales

If you wish to increase the balance of liability, capital or income accounts you will need to do so with a credit entry.

Where now and where next?

chapter summary

In this chapter we have

- described how to set up accounts and enter opening balances in the purchase ledger, sales ledger and nominal ledger
- explained the difference between personal accounts (in the purchase and sales ledger) and impersonal accounts (in the nominal ledger)
- explained the rules for debit and credit balances in ledger accounts

what is in the next chapter?

The next chapter describes the next stage in writing up the accounts – using figures from the purchase and sales day books.

Exam tips

- Allocate accounts for all three ledgers in your answer pages in the order shown in the list of balances. Tick off each balance in the list of balances as you carry out this process.
- Head up each ledger with the ledger title, eg 'Purchase Ledger' above the first account in that ledger.
- Write the name of each account above the appropriate account. Tick off each balance in the list of balances as you carry out this process. Check your spelling of the name.
- Identify from the balance list whether the balance is a debit (Dr) or credit (Cr).
- Enter the date shown on the list of balances in the account date column on the appropriate debit or credit side.
- Enter the description 'Balance b/d' in the details column. Never abbreviate this description to 'Bal b/d'.
- Enter the balance in the money column.
- Check the money amount carefully against the list of balances.
- Cross through each balance in the balance list when you have finished entering all the balance details, and then pass on to the next line.

6.1*   You work as an accounts assistant for R V Williams Ltd.

The date is 1 April 2009.

You have been handed a list of account balances and have been asked to

(a)   set up the accounts in the purchase, sales and nominal ledgers

(b)   enter the opening balances

R V WILLIAMS – LIST OF ACCOUNT BALANCES
(as at 1 April 2009)

Purchase Ledger	£	
Jaycee Bark Ltd	450.40	Cr
F J Hiden	766.70	Cr
Mendell & Son	756.23	Cr

Sales Ledger		
B Britten	340.67	Dr
J Rifkin	2,345.60	Dr
Joseph Green	1,280.00	Dr
M Tippit Ltd	1,670.50	Dr

Nominal Ledger		
Insurance	2,450.00	Dr
Capital	75,000.00	Cr
Discount Allowed	450.80	Dr
Discount Received	560.75	Cr
Equipment	45,000.00	Dr
Purchases	55,615.00	Dr
Purchase Returns	630.20	Cr
Sales	79,720.50	Cr
Sales Returns	320.50	Dr
General Expenses	1,630.25	Dr
Value Added Tax	5,940.20	Cr

6.2 You work as an accounts assistant for J Turner Ltd.

The date is 1 September 2009.

You have been handed a list of account balances and have been asked to set up the accounts in the purchase, sales and nominal ledgers and to enter the opening balances

---

J TURNER LTD – LIST OF ACCOUNT BALANCES
(as at 1 September 2009)

Purchase Ledger	£	
P Casso Ltd	510.20	Cr
J Constable	1,670.00	Cr
F Bacon Ltd	967.20	Cr
Sales Ledger		
Mike L Angelo	370.80	Dr
Donna Telloe	2,560.70	Dr
J Piper	1,560.55	Dr
J Miller	1,712.60	Dr
Nominal Ledger		
Advertising	2,450.00	Dr
Discount Allowed	340.10	Dr
Discount Received	485.00	Cr
Premises	200,000.00	Dr
Purchases	75,805.00	Dr
Purchase Returns	850.70	Cr
Sales	98,390.25	Cr
Sales Returns	410.50	Dr
Sundry Expenses	675.90	Dr
Capital	250,000.00	Cr
Value Added Tax	7,840.10	Cr

6.3 Identify any errors in the following chart which should show which account balances are normally on the debit side and which account balances are normally on the credit side. When you have identified the errors, redraw the chart to show the corrected version.

debit balances	**credit balances**
assets (items owned)	liabilities (items owed)
supplier balances	customer balances
income	expenses
capital	bank loan

7 Posting ledger entries from the day books

The last chapter dealt with the setting up of ledger accounts from a list of balances at a certain date.

This chapter continues the process of posting the ledgers (ie making entries in ledger accounts), but this time using the day books as source documents. The ledgers concerned are the purchase, sales and nominal ledgers.

As you work through the examples in the chapter – based on Supra Stationery – you will see how information builds up in the accounts relating to purchases, and sales transactions.

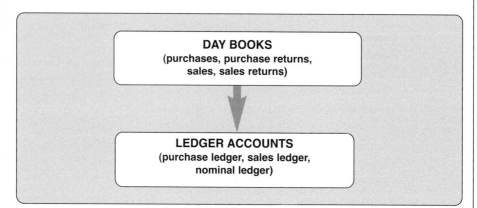

DAY BOOKS
(purchases, purchase returns, sales, sales returns)

LEDGER ACCOUNTS
(purchase ledger, sales ledger, nominal ledger)

This chapter, in short, explains the processes of

● posting entries in the ledger accounts from the day books:
  – purchases day book
  – purchase returns day book
  – sales day book
  – sales returns day book

POSTING FROM THE DAY BOOKS TO THE LEDGER ACCOUNTS

some terminology

You will note that there are various phrases used in this book for entering information into the ledger accounts, for example:'entering up the accounts', 'writing up the accounts' or 'posting entries in the accounts'. These all mean exactly the same thing, ie making a debit or credit entry in a double-entry account, writing in the date, details and the money amount.

information in the day books

The next stage in the process of entering figures in the accounts is to transfer details from the day books described earlier in this book. These are:

- **purchases day book**, which records purchases made on credit from suppliers using supplier invoices as the source of information

- **purchase returns day book**, which records returns made to suppliers using supplier credit notes as the source of information

- **sales day book**, which records sales made on credit to customers using customer invoices as the source of information

- **sales returns day book**, which records returns made by customers using customer credit notes as the source of information

The format of a purchases day book is shown below. Note that this day book has only one column for the goods supplied to the business rather than the two columns (for different products) used in your Unit 1 studies. The format here is simpler and will be used in your studies for the Unit 2 Assignment.

Purchases Day Book				
Date	**Details**	**Goods**	**VAT**	**Total**
2009		£ p	£ p	£ p
3 Mar	Rapid Supply	176.00	30.80	206.80
5 Mar	T Khan Importers	324.00	56.70	380.70

The date of each purchase invoice.

The name of each supplier.

The amount of the goods before VAT is added on.

VAT charged and added to the cost of goods.

Invoice total owing to each supplier.

PURCHASES DAY BOOK – WRITING UP THE ACCOUNTS

In your Assignment the day books will be presented already complete and totalled. All that you will be required to do is to transfer the necessary entries to the ledger accounts. In the case of the **Purchases Day Book** of Supra Stationery you should carry out the following steps methodically and accurately, checking and ticking off each entry as you go:

1   For each separate transaction, transfer the figure in the '**Total**' column to the individual supplier account in the purchase ledger as a **credit entry**. For example, the first entry is dated 6 April and represents an invoice received from Rapid Supply Ltd. The total amount of the invoice is £141.00 and this is the amount Supra Stationery will have to pay to Rapid Supply Ltd. The amount is shown (on the opposite page) as a credit to Rapid Supply Ltd Account in the Purchase Ledger. The amount has not yet been paid; it is shown as owing and is a **credit entry** because it is **an amount that the business owes**.

The next page shows all six supplier invoice entries in the day book posted as credit entries to the appropriate supplier accounts.

2   The total of the '**Goods**' column (not the individual entries) is transferred to Purchases Account in the Nominal Ledger as a **debit entry**. This is a debit because it represents an expense, the amount spent on purchases. Note that 'Purchases Day Book' is abbreviated to 'PDB'.

3   The total of the '**VAT**' column (not the individual entries) is transferred to Value Added Tax Account in the Nominal Ledger as a **debit entry**. This is a debit because it represents an expense, the VAT paid.

Purchases Day Book				
Date	Details	Goods	VAT	Total
2009		£ p	£ p	£ p
6 Apr	Rapid Supply	120.00	21.00	141.00
9 Apr	AZ Supplies	690.00	120.75	810.75
15 Apr	Rapid Supply	400.00	70.00	470.00
17 Apr	T Khan Importers	84.00	14.70	98.70
22 Apr	AZ Supplies	200.00	35.00	235.00
27 Apr	T Khan Importers	282.00	49.35	331.35
30 Apr		1,776.00	310.80	2,086.80

PURCHASE LEDGER

Dr	Rapid Supply Account					Cr	
2009	**Details**	**£**	**p**	**2009**	**Details**	**£**	**p**
15 Apr	Purchase returns	89	30	1 Apr	Balance b/d	840	20
				6 Apr	Purchases	141	00
				15 Apr	Purchases	470	00

Dr	AZ Supplies Account					Cr	
2009	**Details**	**£**	**p**	**2009**	**Details**	**£**	**p**
24 Apr	Purchase returns	37	60	1 Apr	Balance b/d	725	60
				9 Apr	Purchases	810	75
				22 Apr	Purchases	235	00

Dr	T Khan Importers Account					Cr	
2009	**Details**	**£**	**p**	**2009**	**Details**	**£**	**p**
17 Apr	Purchase returns	28	20	1 Apr	Balance b/d	963	90
				17 Apr	Purchases	98	70
				27 Apr	Purchases	331	35

NOMINAL LEDGER

Dr	Value Added Tax Account					Cr	
2009	**Details**	**£**	**p**	**2009**	**Details**	**£**	**p**
30 Apr	Total PDB	310	80	1 Apr	Balance b/d	6,530	70
				30 Apr	Total PRDB	23	10

Dr	Purchase Returns Account					Cr	
2009	**Details**	**£**	**p**	**2009**	**Details**	**£**	**p**
				1 Apr	Balance b/d	410	80
				30 Apr	Total PRDB	132	00

SALES DAY BOOK – WRITING UP THE ACCOUNTS

The **Sales Day Book** of Supra Stationery is compiled from invoices issued to customers, increasing the amount each customer owes to the business. As when posting transactions from the other day books, you should transfer the entries to the ledger accounts carefully, remembering to tick off each entry.

1   For each transaction, transfer the figure in the '**Total**' column to the individual customer account in the sales ledger as a **debit entry**.

For example, the first entry is dated 2 April and represents an invoice issued to W Barnes Ltd. The total amount of the invoice is £540.50 and this is the amount Supra Stationery is owed. The amount is shown (on the opposite page) as a debit to W Barnes Ltd Account in the Sales Ledger. The amount has not yet been paid and is a **debit entry** because it is **an amount that is owed to the business**.

The next page shows all six customer invoice entries in the day book posted as debit entries to the appropriate customer accounts.

2   The total of the '**Goods**' column (not the individual entries) is transferred to Sales Account in the Nominal Ledger as a **credit entry**. This is a credit because it represents an income item. Note that 'Sales Day Book' is abbreviated to 'SDB'.

3   The total of the '**VAT**' column (not the individual entries) is transferred to Value Added Tax Account in the Nominal Ledger as a **credit entry**. This is a credit because it represents VAT that is due to be paid to HM Revenue & Customs.

Sales Day Book				
Date	Details	Goods	VAT	Total
2009		£ p	£ p	£ p
2 Apr	W Barnes Ltd	460.00	80.50	540.50
7 Apr	J Keetz	640.00	112.00	752.00
15 Apr	R S Thomas	386.00	67.55	453.55
20 Apr	W B Yates	828.00	144.90	972.90
23 Apr	W Barnes Ltd	466.00	81.55	547.55
28 Apr	J Keetz	120.00	21.00	141.00
30 Apr		2,900.00	507.50	3,407.50

SALES LEDGER

Dr	W Barnes Ltd Account						Cr
2009	Details	£	p	2009	Details	£	p
1 Apr	Balance b/d	560	65				
2 Apr	Sales	540	50				
23 Apr	Sales	547	55				

Dr	J Keetz Account						Cr
2009	Details	£	p	2009	Details	£	p
1 Apr	Balance b/d	4,830	90				
7 Apr	Sales	752	00				
28 Apr	Sales	141	00				

Dr	R S Thomas Account						Cr
2009	Details	£	p	2009	Details	£	p
1 Apr	Balance b/d	1,340	10				
15 Apr	Sales	453	55				

Dr	W B Yates Account						Cr
2009	Details	£	p	2009	Details	£	p
1 Apr	Balance b/d	1,074	70				
20 Apr	Sales	972	90				

NOMINAL LEDGER

Dr	Value Added Tax Account						Cr
2009	Details	£	p	2009	Details	£	p
30 Apr	Total PDB	310	80	1 Apr	Balance b/d	6,530	70
				30 Apr	Total PRDB	23	10
				30 Apr	Total SDB	507	50

Dr	Sales Account						Cr
2009	Details	£	p	2009	Details	£	p
				1 Apr	Balance b/d	85,630	50
				30 Apr	Total SDB	2,900	00

SALES RETURNS DAY BOOK – WRITING UP THE ACCOUNTS

The **Sales Returns Day Book** of Supra Stationery is compiled from credit notes issued to customers, reducing in each case the amount owed to Supra Stationery. You should, as with the sales day book, transfer the entries methodically and accurately, checking and ticking off each entry.

1   For each transaction, transfer the figure in the '**Total**' column to the individual customer account in the Sales Ledger as a **credit entry**. For example, the first entry is dated 6 April and represents a credit note issued to W Barnes Ltd. The total amount of the credit note is £37.60 and this is the amount Supra Stationery is deducting from what it is owed. The amount is shown (on the opposite page) as a **credit** to W Barnes Ltd Account in the Sales Ledger.

   The next page shows all three supplier credit note entries in the day book posted as credit entries to the appropriate customer accounts.

2   The total of the '**Goods**' column (not the individual entries), ie £162.00, is transferred to Sales Returns Account in the Nominal Ledger as a **debit entry**. 'Sales Returns Day Book' is abbreviated to 'SRDB'.

3   The total of the '**VAT**' column (not the individual entries), ie £28.35, is transferred to Value Added Tax Account in the Nominal Ledger as a **debit entry**. 'Sales Returns Day Book' is abbreviated to 'SRDB'.

Sales Returns Day Book				
Date	**Details**	**Goods**	**VAT**	**Total**
2009		£ p	£ p	£ p
6 Apr	W Barnes Ltd	32.00	5.60	37.60
14 Apr	R S Thomas	88.00	15.40	103.40
17 Apr	J Keetz	42.00	7.35	49.35
30 Apr		162.00	28.35	190.35

SALES LEDGER

Dr	W Barnes Ltd Account							Cr
2009	Details	£	p	**2009**	Details	£	p	
1 Apr	Balance b/d	560	65	6 Apr	Sales returns	37	60	
2 Apr	Sales	540	50					
23 Apr	Sales	547	55					

Dr	J Keetz Account							Cr
2009	Details	£	p	**2009**	Details	£	p	
1 Apr	Balance b/d	4,830	90	17 Apr	Sales returns	49	35	
7 Apr	Sales	752	00					
28 Apr	Sales	141	00					

Dr	R S Thomas Account							Cr
2009	Details	£	p	**2009**	Details	£	p	
1 Apr	Balance b/d	1,340	10	14 Apr	Sales returns	103	40	
15 Apr	Sales	453	55					

Dr	W B Yates Account							Cr
2009	Details	£	p	**2009**	Details	£	p	
1 Apr	Balance b/d	1,074	70					
20 Apr	Sales	972	90					

NOMINAL LEDGER

Dr	Value Added Tax Account							Cr
2009	Details	£	p	**2009**	Details	£	p	
30 Apr	Total PDB	310	80	1 Apr	Balance b/d	6,530	70	
30 Apr	Total SRDB	28	35	30 Apr	Total PRDB	23	10	
				30 Apr	Total SDB	507	50	

Dr	Sales Returns Account							Cr
2009	Details	£	p	**2009**	Details	£	p	
1 Apr	Balance b/d	240	50					
30 Apr	Total SRDB	162	00					

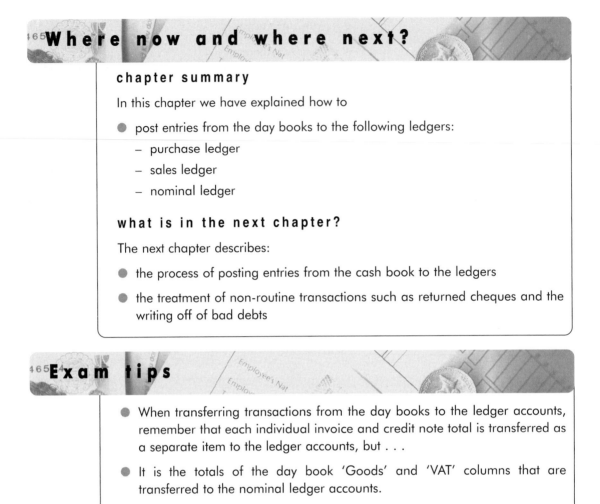

Where now and where next?

chapter summary

In this chapter we have explained how to

● post entries from the day books to the following ledgers:
  - purchase ledger
  - sales ledger
  - nominal ledger

what is in the next chapter?

The next chapter describes:

● the process of posting entries from the cash book to the ledgers

● the treatment of non-routine transactions such as returned cheques and the writing off of bad debts

Exam tips

● When transferring transactions from the day books to the ledger accounts, remember that each individual invoice and credit note total is transferred as a separate item to the ledger accounts, but . . .

● It is the totals of the day book 'Goods' and 'VAT' columns that are transferred to the nominal ledger accounts.

● The total of the 'Total' column (the bottom right-hand figure in the day book) is not transferred anywhere at all at this stage.

● Always tick off each entry as you work through the transactions.

● When dealing with the Purchases Day Book, remember that the total amount owing to the supplier is entered in the supplier account as a **credit** as it is an **amount owed by the business** to the supplier.

● When dealing with the Purchase Returns Day Book, remember that the credit note amount is entered on the other side of the supplier account as a **debit.**

● When dealing with the Sales Day Book, remember that the total amount owing to the business is entered in the customer account as a **debit** as it is an **amount owed to the business** by the customer.

● When dealing with the Sales Returns Day Book, remember that the credit note amount is entered in the customer account as a **credit.**

The Purchases and Sales Day Books shown on this page have been produced by the bookkeeper of Victor Design in the first week of September. Answer the questions set out below each Day Book.

7.1*

Purchases Day Book					
Date	Details		Goods	VAT	Total
2009			£ p	£ p	£ p
1 Sep	Jethro Furniture		240.00	42.00	282.00
3 Sep	Lumos Lighting Company		1,320.00	231.00	1,551.00
6 Sep	Roger Grant		840.00	147.00	987.00
7 Sep			2,400.00	420.00	2,820.00

(a)   From what source documents has this Purchases Day Book been prepared?

(b)   To what accounts will each of the figures in the 'Total' column be transferred? Will they be debit or credit entries?

(c)   To which accounts will the totals of the Goods column and the VAT column be transferred? Will they be debit or credit entries?

7.2*

Sales Day Book					
Date	Details		Goods	VAT	Total
2009			£ p	£ p	£ p
1 Sep	R Khan		200.00	35.00	235.00
3 Sep	L Jones Ltd		256.00	44.80	300.80
6 Sep	Gina Riccardo		520.00	91.00	611.00
7 Sep			976.00	170.80	1,146.80

(a)   From what source documents has this Sales Day Book been prepared?

(b)   To what accounts will each of the figures in the 'Total' column be transferred? Will they be debit or credit entries?

(c)   To which accounts will the totals of the Goods column and the VAT column be transferred? Will they be debit or credit entries?

7.3 You work as an accounts assistant for B Johnson Ltd. You have been handed the four day books shown on these two pages. It is the end of the month of August.

You have also been provided with a list of relevant opening balances for the following ledger accounts as at 1 August:

Purchase Ledger	£	
T H Ackeray	345.00	Cr
C Dickens Supplies	562.50	Cr
K Khan	136.90	Cr
Sterne Importers	298.40	Cr
Sales Ledger		
S Hollow Ltd	645.00	Dr
Redshade Ltd	795.00	Dr
H Pinta	410.00	Dr
Nominal Ledger		
Purchases	45,100.00	Dr
Purchase Returns	4,300.00	Cr
Sales	76,120.00	Cr
Sales Returns	5,690.00	Dr
Value Added Tax	3,285.25	Cr

You are to:

(a) Set up the ledger accounts for the accounts listed above and enter the opening balances as at 1 August.

(b) Enter the transactions from the four day books into the purchase, sales and nominal ledgers of B Johnson Ltd.

Purchases Day Book				
Date	**Details**	**Goods**	**VAT**	**Total**
2009		£ p	£ p	£ p
4 Aug	T H Ackeray Ltd	840.00	147.00	987.00
6 Aug	C Dickens Supplies	144.00	25.20	169.20
12 Aug	Sterne Importers	282.00	49.35	331.35
15 Aug	K Khan	196.00	34.30	230.30
19 Aug	T H Ackeray Ltd	416.00	72.80	488.80
26 Aug	C Dickens Supplies	132.00	23.10	155.10
31 Aug		2,010.00	351.75	2,361.75

Purchase Returns Day Book				
Date	**Details**	**Goods**	**VAT**	**Total**
2009		£ p	£ p	£ p
10 Aug	T H Ackeray Ltd	96.00	16.80	112.80
15 Aug	C Dickens Supplies	144.00	25.20	169.20
20 Aug	Sterne Importers	84.00	14.70	98.70
31 Aug		324.00	56.70	380.70

Sales Day Book				
Date	**Details**	**Goods**	**VAT**	**Total**
2009		£ p	£ p	£ p
3 Aug	S Hollow Ltd	910.00	159.25	1,069.25
7 Aug	Redshade Ltd	540.00	94.50	634.50
13 Aug	H Pinta	316.00	55.30	371.30
18 Aug	Redshade Ltd	726.00	127.05	853.05
20 Aug	S Hollow Ltd	432.00	75.60	507.60
26 Aug	H Pinta	392.00	68.60	460.60
31 Aug		3,316.00	580.30	3,896.30

Sales Returns Day Book				
Date	**Details**	**Goods**	**VAT**	**Total**
2009		£ p	£ p	£ p
6 Aug	S Hollow Ltd	88.00	15.40	103.40
18 Aug	H Pinta	140.00	24.50	164.50
24 Aug	Redshade Ltd	122.00	21.35	143.35
31 Aug		350.00	61.25	411.25

8 Posting ledger entries from the cash book

The last chapter dealt with the posting of ledger accounts from four day books: purchases day book, purchase returns day book, sales day book and sales returns day book.

This chapter continues the process of posting the ledgers by using the cash book as the source document (see diagram below).

This chapter also deals with the problems caused to a business by bad payers; it describes the treatment in the accounts of returned cheques and debts that have to be written off (bad debts).

By the end of the chapter the ledger accounts will be ready for balancing, a process that will be carried out in the next chapter.

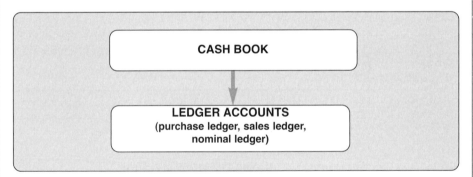

This chapter, in short, explains the processes of

● posting entries in the ledger accounts from the cash book:

- payments in cash and by cheque

- receipts in cash and by cheque

- discounts received from suppliers

- discounts allowed to customers

● posting non-routine items to the ledgers, for example:

- making the required account entry for a returned cheque

- setting up an account for writing off bad debts

CASH BOOK TO LEDGER ACCOUNTS

The next stage in the transfer of data to the ledger accounts is from the cash book of the business. This is a bookkeeping record which you will have probably already encountered in your studies.

The most common format of cash book is illustrated below. The left-hand (debit) side is the **Receipts** side in which all receipts are entered, and the right-hand (credit) side is the **Payments** side where all the payments are recorded. 'Money in' is on the left, 'Money out' is on the right.

There are three money columns on the left-hand **debit side (money in)**:

- **discount allowed** – discount allowed to customers for early settlement of sales invoices
- **cash** – cash paid into the business (not cash paid into the bank)
- **bank** – all the money paid into the bank, eg cheques, cash, bank giro credits, standing orders, direct debits received

There are three money columns on the right-hand **credit side (money out)**:

- **discount received** – discount received by the business for early settlement of supplier invoices
- **cash** – cash paid out of the business, eg cash wages, small purchases
- **bank** – all the money paid out of the bank, eg cheques issued by the business, cash withdrawals, standing orders paid, direct debits paid

FROM CASH BOOK TO LEDGER ACCOUNTS

Set out below is a cash book with the type of transactions you should expect to see in your Assessment. Many of these transactions will need to be entered in the ledger accounts.

Not all the entries in the cash book, however, are transferred to the accounts. The **exceptions** include 'Balances c/d' and 'Balances b/d' in the cash and bank columns and figures relating to 'Contra' transactions (where there is a 'C' in the narrow column). A 'contra' in this context means that both the debit and the credit entries are in the cash book and so will not need to be entered anywhere else.

The transactions that **will be** transferred to the ledger accounts are indicated in the cash book below by grey tinted boxes. Study this cash book and read the explanatory notes that follow.

cash book: receipts side (debits)					cash book: payments side (credits)					

Dr					Cash Book					Cr
Date	Details		Discount allowed	Cash	Bank	Date	Details		Discount received	Cash	Bank
2009			£ p	£ p	£ p	2009			£ p	£ p	£ p
3 Mar	Balances b/d			300.00	550.00	5 Mar	T Hardy		125.00		1,175.00
4 Mar	Cash sales			100.00		6 Mar	R Wilde (R/D)				200.00
4 Mar	VAT			17.50		6 Mar	Cash purchases			235.00	
5 Mar	R Wilson		175.00		3,325.00	6 Mar	Insurance				275.00
6 Mar	Cash	C			150.00	6 Mar	Bank	C		150.00	
						7 Mar	Balances c/d				32.50 2,375.00
			175.00	417.50	4,025.00				125.00	417.50	4,025.00
9 Mar	Balances b/d			32.50	2,375.00						

	= transactions to be posted to the ledgers	**money in**			**money out**

debit side

- **Cash sales** and **VAT**: here a total of £117.50 cash has been received, which is split into sales and VAT amounts, recorded in the cash column:

   The entries to be made in the ledgers are as follows (the account details for each entry is in brackets):

   − Credit Sales Account £100 (Cash)

   − Credit Value Added Tax Account £17.50 (Cash).

- **R Wilson**: this is a cheque received from a customer (R Wilson) settling an account and deducting discount for early settlement. There are two entries made in the customer's account:
  - Credit R Wilson Account £3,325 (Bank)
  - Credit R Wilson Account £175 (Discount Allowed)
- **Discount Allowed column total**: this is the total of all the early settlement discount amounts which have been allowed to customers (here there is only one amount). The ledger entry here is:
  - Debit Discount Allowed Account £175 (Cash Book)

Note that there is a 'C' in the narrow 'contra' column. On 6 March £150 cash is paid into the bank account from the cash held by the business. A contra column is included on the credit side of the cash book, also with a 'C' against the relevant transaction. These items are **not** posted to the ledger accounts.

credit side

- **T Hardy**: this is a cheque paid to a supplier in settlement of an account and deducting discount of £125 for early settlement. The entries are:
  - Debit T Hardy Account £1,175 (Bank)
  - Debit T Hardy Account £125 (Discount Received)
- **R Wilde (R/D)**: this is a 'returned cheque', ie a cheque which has been received from a R Wilde, a customer, and paid into the bank, but then returned **R/D** (which stands for 'Refer to Drawer') by R Wilde's bank because the customer does not have the money in the account. This is bad news for the business because it means that the cheque is then deducted from its bank account, making the balance of the account go down. This is 'money out' of the bank account and so the cheque is entered on the credit side of the cash book with the customer's name and the letters 'R/D'. The entry in the Sales Ledger is therefore:
  - Debit R Wilde Account £200 (Bank R/D)
- **Cash purchases**: this relates to purchases paid for in cash. The entry is:
  - Debit Purchases Account £235.00 (Cash)

There is no VAT charged to the business in this case, probably because the supplier is not VAT-registered. If these purchases had included VAT, there would have been two entries: a £200 debit to Purchases Account and a £35 debit to Value Added Tax Account.

- **Insurance**: this is payment of an expense and involves a single entry:
  - Debit Insurance Account £275.00 (Bank)
- **Discount Received column total**: this is the total of all the cash discount amounts which have been received from suppliers (here there is only one amount). The ledger entry here is:
  - Credit Discount Received Account £125 (Cash Book)

CASH BOOK (DEBIT SIDE) TO LEDGER ACCOUNTS

We will now describe in a worked example how the **debit side** of the cash book of Supra Stationery is posted to accounts in the Sales Ledger and Nominal Ledger. The whole cash book is shown below. The transactions are shown here with reference numbers and are highlighted with a grey background. They are also explained in the text below the cash book.

Dr							Supra Stationery: Cash Book				Cr
Date	Details	Discount allowed	Cash	Bank	Date	Details	Discount received	Cash	Bank
2009		£ p	£ p	£ p	2009		£ p	£ p	£ p
1 Apr	Balances b/d		993.70	3,644.65	14 Apr	AZ Supplies	40.54		770.21
6 Apr	Cash sales		**1** 200.00		15 Apr	Rapid Supply			840.20
6 Apr	VAT		**2** 35.00		21 Apr	Administration			290.00
14 Apr	J Keetz	**4** 37.60		**3** 714.40	24 Apr	Cash purchases		320.00	
22 Apr	W Barnes Ltd			**5** 560.65	24 Apr	VAT		56.00	
28 Apr	J Keetz			**6** 240.00	27 Apr	W Barnes R/D			560.65
					30 Apr	Balances c/d		852.70	2,698.64
		7 37.60	1,228.70	5,159.70			40.54	1,228.70	5,159.70
1 May	Balances b/d		852.70	2,698.64					

postings from the debit side of the cash book:

ref. no.	Dr or Cr	ledger	account	description	amount (£)
1	Credit	Nominal	Sales	Cash	200.00
2	Credit	Nominal	Value Added Tax	Cash	35.00
	Note: items 1 and 2 relate to £235 cash received for goods sold, £35 of which is VAT.				
3	Credit	Sales	J Keetz	Bank	714.40
4	Credit	Sales	J Keetz	Discount Allowed	37.60
	Note: items 3 and 4 relate to a payment from which cash discount has been deducted; the amounts are entered in the account J Keetz and add up to £752.00 (see debit entry, 7 April).				
5	Credit	Sales	W Barnes Ltd	Bank	560.65
	Note: W Barnes Ltd pays by cheque the balance owing from last month.				
6	Credit	Sales	J Keetz	Bank	240.00
	Note: J Keetz pays a further amount owing by cheque. No discount is taken this time.				
7	Debit	Nominal	Discount Allowed	Cash Book	37.60
	Note: this entry is a debit entry which relates to an expense of the business, ie the total discount allowed by the business for the month. The date is the month-end date, 30 April.				

SALES LEDGER

Dr						W Barnes Ltd Account		Cr
2009	**Details**	**£**	**p**	**2009**	**Details**		**£**	**p**
1 Apr	Balance b/d	560	65	6 Apr	Sales returns		37	60
2 Apr	Sales	540	50	22 Apr	Bank	**5**	560	65
23 Apr	Sales	547	55					

Dr						J Keetz Account		Cr
2009	**Details**	**£**	**p**	**2009**	**Details**		**£**	**p**
1 Apr	Balance b/d	4,830	90	17 Apr	Sales returns		49	35
7 Apr	Sales	752	00	14 Apr	Bank	**3**	714	40
28 Apr	Sales	141	00	14 Apr	Discount Allowed	**4**	37	60
				28 Apr	Bank	**6**	240	00

NOMINAL LEDGER

Dr					Discount Allowed Account		Cr
2009	**Details**	**£**	**p**	**2009**	**Details**	**£**	**p**
1 Apr	Balance b/d	510	65				
30 Apr	Cash book **7**	37	60				

Dr					Sales Account		Cr
2009	**Details**	**£**	**p**	**2009**	**Details**	**£**	**p**
				1 Apr	Balance b/d	85,630	50
				30 Apr	Total SDB	2,900	00
				6 Apr	Cash **1**	200	00

Dr					Value Added Tax Account		Cr
2009	**Details**	**£**	**p**	**2009**	**Details**	**£**	**p**
30 Apr	Total PDB	310	80	1 Apr	Balance b/d	6,530	70
30 Apr	Total SRDB	28	35	30 Apr	Total PRDB	23	10
				30 Apr	Total SDB	507	50
				6 Apr	Cash **2**	35	00

CASH BOOK (CREDIT SIDE) TO LEDGER ACCOUNTS

We will now continue the worked example to show how the **credit side** of the cash book of Supra Stationery is posted to accounts in the Purchase Ledger and Nominal Ledger (see the opposite page). The transactions are shown with reference numbers and are highlighted with a grey background.

Dr					Supra Stationery: Cash Book						Cr
Date	Details	Discount allowed	Cash	Bank	Date	Details		Discount received	Cash	Bank	
2009		£ p	£ p	£ p	2009			£ p	£ p	£ p	
1 Apr	Balances b/d		993.70	3,644.65	14 Apr	AZ Supplies	**2**	40.54		**1** 770.21	
6 Apr	Cash sales		200.00		15 Apr	Rapid Supply				**3** 840.20	
6 Apr	VAT		35.00		21 Apr	Administration				**4** 290.00	
14 Apr	J Keetz	37.60		714.40	24 Apr	Cash purchases			**5** 320.00		
22 Apr	W Barnes Ltd			560.65	24 Apr	VAT			**6** 56.00		
28 Apr	J Keetz			240.00	27 Apr	W Barnes R/D				**7** 560.65	
					30 Apr	Balances c/d			852.70	2,698.64	
		37.60	1,228.70	5,159.70			**8**	40.54	1,228.70	5,159.70	
1 May	Balances b/d		852.70	2,698.64							

ref. no.	Dr or Cr	ledger	account	description	amount (£)
1	Debit	Purchase	AZ Supplies	Bank	770.21
2	Debit	Purchase	AZ Supplies	Discount Received	40.54
	Note: items 1 and 2 relate to a payment from which cash discount has been deducted; the amounts are entered in the account AZ Supplies and add up to £810.75 (see entry, 9 April).				
3	Debit	Purchase	Rapid Supply	Bank	840.20
	Note: item 3 is a payment by cheque to a supplier, Rapid Supply.				
4	Debit	Nominal	Administration	Bank	290.00
	Note: item 4 is a cheque payment for Administration expenses (expenses are debit entries)				
5	Debit	Nominal	Purchases	Cash	320.00
6	Debit	Nominal	Value Added Tax	Cash	56.00
	Note: items 5 and 6 relate to £376 for cash paid for goods purchased, £56 of which is VAT.				
7	Debit	Sales	W Barnes Ltd	Bank R/D	560.65
	Note: item 7 is a returned cheque which was paid into the bank account on 22 April.				
8	Credit	Nominal	Discount Received	Cash Book	40.54
	Note: this entry is a credit entry which relates to income for the business, ie the total discount received by the business for the month. The date is the month-end date, 30 April.				

PURCHASE LEDGER

Dr				AZ Supplies Account					Cr
2009	Details		£	p	2009	Details		£	p
24 Apr	Purchase returns		37	60	1 Apr	Balance b/d		725	60
14 Apr	Bank	**1**	770	21	9 Apr	Purchases		810	75
14 Apr	Discount Received	**2**	40	54	22 Apr	Purchases		235	00

Dr				Rapid Supply Account					Cr
2009	Details		£	p	2009	Details		£	p
15 Apr	Purchase returns		89	30	1 Apr	Balance b/d		840	20
15 Apr	Bank	**3**	840	20	6 Apr	Purchases		141	00
					15 Apr	Purchases		470	00

NOMINAL LEDGER

Dr				Administration Expenses Account					Cr
2009	Details		£	p	2009	Details		£	p
1 Apr	Balance b/d		32,350	10					
21 Apr	Bank	**4**	290	00					

Dr				Purchases Account					Cr
2009	Details		£	p	2009	Details		£	p
1 Apr	Balance b/d		65,505	00					
30 Apr	Total PDB		1,776	00					
24 Apr	Cash	**5**	320	00					

Dr				Value Added Tax Account					Cr
2009	Details		£	p	2009	Details		£	p
30 Apr	Total PDB		310	80	1 Apr	Balance b/d		6,530	70
30 Apr	Total SRDB		28	35	30 Apr	Total PRDB		23	10
24 Apr	Cash purchases	**6**	56	00	30 Apr	Total SDB		507	50
					6 Apr	Cash sales		35	00

NOMINAL LEDGER (continued)

Dr	Discount Received Account						Cr
2009	Details	£	p	2009	Details	£	p
				1 Apr	Balance b/d	690	00
				30 Apr	Cash Book [8]	40	54

SALES LEDGER

Dr	W Barnes Ltd Account						Cr
2009	Details	£	p	2009	Details	£	p
1 Apr	Balance b/d	560	65	6 Apr	Sales returns	37	60
2 Apr	Sales	540	50	22 Apr	Bank	560	65
23 Apr	Sales	547	55				
27 Apr	Bank R/D [7]	560	65				

WRITING OFF BAD DEBTS

A **bad debt** is a debt that a customer owes which a business decides to 'write off' because the business cannot realistically get that money back from the customer. This will happen, for example, if the customer goes 'bust'.

Let us take the case of W Barnes Ltd, the customer of Supra Stationery who has already issued a cheque to Supra Stationery for £560.65 which was returned 'R/D' (Refer to Drawer) and so has been unpaid. This debt is therefore still outstanding on the ledger account of W Barnes Ltd following the adjustment debit entry from the cash book made on 27 April. The account is shown above.

Suppose that Supra Stationery is then informed on the next day, 28 April, that W Barnes Ltd has gone into administration, in other words it has 'gone bust'. Supra Stationery now stands little, if any, chance of getting its money back. This debt has therefore become 'bad' and will have to be written off as an expense to the business.

In your Assessment you may have a task which tells you that a customer owing money has been declared bankrupt. The task might say something like:

> 'On 28 April 2009, you receive notification that W Barnes Ltd has gone into administration. The balance on this account should be written off as a bad debt.'

The actions you should take are as follows:

1   Set up a Bad Debts Account in the Nominal Ledger, if it does not already exist.

2   Work out the amount of the bad debt from the account of the customer in the Sales Ledger. This will be the balance of the account (ie total debits minus total credits). In the case of W Barnes Ltd this is:

Total debits £560.65 + £540.50 + £547.55 + £560.65	£2,209.35
minus	
Total credits £560.65 + £37.60 =	£598.25
equals	
Balance (ie the 'bad debt')	£1,611.10

The double-entry account postings will therefore be:

Debit	Bad Debts Account in the Nominal Ledger	£1,611.10
Credit	W Barnes Account in the Sales Ledger	£1,611.10

NOMINAL LEDGER

Dr				Bad Debts Account			Cr
2009	**Details**	**£**	**p**	**2009**	**Details**	**£**	**p**
28 Apr	W Barnes Ltd	1,611	10				

SALES LEDGER

Dr				W Barnes Ltd			Cr
2009	**Details**	**£**	**p**	**2009**	**Details**	**£**	**p**
1 Apr	Balance b/d	560	65	6 Apr	Sales returns	37	60
2 Apr	Sales	540	50	22 Apr	Bank	560	65
23 Apr	Sales	547	55	28 Apr	Bad debts	1,611	10
27 Apr	Bank R/D	560	65				
		2,209	35			2,209	35

Note:

•   The account balance of W Barnes Ltd is Nil (it has been written off) and so there is no balancing figure to enter; the final total is entered on both sides and underlined.

•   There is no transfer from any source financial document such as a day book or cash book; instead the bad debt write-off will be requested within the business by a memo, email, or (see Chapter 14) it may be carried out by a journal entry (a form of internal account adjustment).

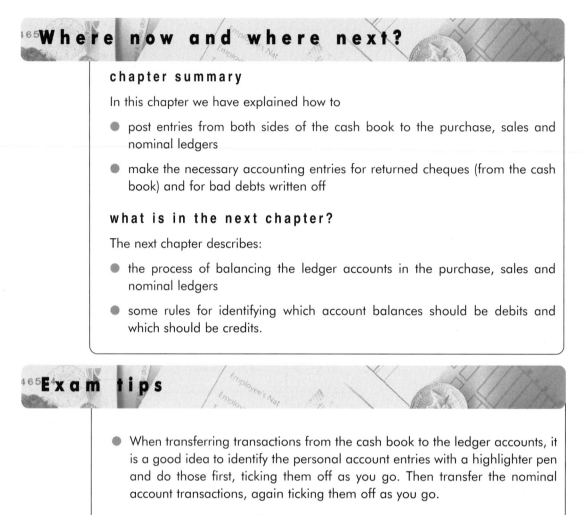

Where now and where next?

chapter summary

In this chapter we have explained how to

- post entries from both sides of the cash book to the purchase, sales and nominal ledgers

- make the necessary accounting entries for returned cheques (from the cash book) and for bad debts written off

what is in the next chapter?

The next chapter describes:

- the process of balancing the ledger accounts in the purchase, sales and nominal ledgers

- some rules for identifying which account balances should be debits and which should be credits.

Exam tips

- When transferring transactions from the cash book to the ledger accounts, it is a good idea to identify the personal account entries with a highlighter pen and do those first, ticking them off as you go. Then transfer the nominal account transactions, again ticking them off as you go.

- Remember that you will effectively enter the discount column entries twice: firstly the individual amounts to the personal accounts and secondly the column total to the appropriate discount account in the nominal ledger.

- Look out for any returned cheques ('R/D' entries) on the cash book credit side. This will require a debit entry in the appropriate customer account.

- If you are told to write off a customer account as a bad debt you will have to set up a Bad Debts Account in the Nominal Ledger (if it does not already exist) and post a debit to that account and then a credit to the customer account in the Sales Ledger.

- Remember that when you are writing off a bad debt through Bad Debts Account you are not transferring the figures from the day books or the cash book, but acting on an internal message such as a memo, email or (see Chapter 14) a journal entry.

8.1* Study the cash book of R Dorrell shown below.

Dr						R Dorrell: Cash Book					Cr
Date	Details		Discount allowed	Cash	Bank	Date	Details		Discount received	Cash	Bank
2009			£ p	£ p	£ p	2009			£ p	£ p	£ p
1 Sep	Balances b/d			250.60	1,657.25	2 Sep	R McElwee		20.00		380.00
7 Sep	Cash sales			200.00		3 Sep	Impex Ltd (R/D)				401.00
7 Sep	VAT			35.00		15 Sep	Rent				456.83
15 Sep	C Beatty		28.00		532.00	24 Sep	Cash purchases			160.00	
22 Sep	D Patel		12.00		228.00	24 Sep	VAT			28.00	
28 Sep	N Romavic		25.00		475.00	29 Sep	Cash	C		180.00	
29 Sep	Bank	C			180.00	30 Sep	Balances c/d			117.60	1,834.42
			65.00	485.60	3,072.25				20.00	485.60	3,072.25
1 Oct	Balances b/d			117.60	1,834.42						

You are to draw up a table headed '**Account Postings from the Cash Book**' using the format shown below. Complete the columns to describe how the items should be posted. (Use a spreadsheet if you wish).

Date 2009	Details	Amount £	Ledger	Account name	Details entered	credit or debit?
2 Sep	R McElwee	20.00				
2 Sep	R McElwee	380.00				
3 Sep	Impex Ltd	401.00				
7 Sep	Cash sales	200.00				
7 Sep	VAT	35.00				
15 Sep	C Beatty	28.00				
15 Sep	C Beatty	532.00				
15 Sep	Rent	456.83				
24 Sep	Cash purchases	160.00				
24 Sep	VAT	28.00				
29 Sep	Contra (x2)	180.00				
none	Discount allowed	65.00				
none	Discount received	20.00				

8.2   You work as an accounts assistant for K Livingstone Ltd.

You have been handed the company's cash book for the month of August (see next page) and also a list of account balances as at 1 August (see below).

You are to:

(a)   Set up accounts in the purchase, sales and nominal ledger, based on the list of balances and enter the balances as at 1 August in the accounts.

Blank ledger accounts are available for download from www.osbornebooks.co.uk

(b)   Enter the appropriate transactions from the cash book in the purchase, sales and nominal ledgers of K Livingstone Ltd.

(c)   Deal with an email from your line manager who has some bad news:

> *On 26 August 2009, we received formal notification that Ladro Ltd has gone into administration.*
>
> *The balance on this account should now be written off as a bad debt.*

You are to make the necessary account entries to write off the bad debt (the date of the write off is 28 August).

K Livingstone Ltd: Balances as at 1 August 2009

Purchase Ledger

XPO Supplies	1,256.70	Cr

Sales Ledger £

C Darwin	550.00	Dr
Itza Breeze Ltd	520.00	Dr
Ladro Ltd	760.50	Dr
R Preston Ltd	451.10	Dr

Nominal

Bad Debts	679.50	Dr
Discount Allowed	451.00	Dr
Discount Received	720.95	Cr
Insurance	693.50	Dr
Purchases	24,507.90	Dr
Sales	32,720.00	Cr
Value Added Tax	5,970.00	Cr

Dr						K Livingstone Ltd: Cash Book					Cr
Date	Details		Discount allowed	Cash	Bank	Date	Details		Discount received	Cash	Bank
2009			£ p	£ p	£ p	2009			£ p	£ p	£ p
1 Aug	Balances b/d			250.50	4,456.78	3 Aug	XPO Supplies		32.00		608.00
6 Aug	Cash sales			100.00		4 Aug	Ladro Ltd (R/D)				120.00
6 Aug	VAT			17.50		15 Aug	Insurance				283.00
15 Aug	C Darwin		42.00		798.00	26 Aug	Cash purchases			144.00	
22 Aug	R Preston Ltd				195.25	26 Aug	VAT			25.20	
28 Aug	Itza Breeze Ltd		12.00		228.00	29 Aug	Cash	C		100.00	
29 Aug	Bank	C			100.00	31 Aug	Balances c/d			98.80	4,767.03
			54.00	368.00	5,778.03				32.00	368.00	5,778.03
1 Sep	Balances b/d			98.80	4,767.03						

what this chapter covers . . .

In the last three chapters we have:

- set up the double-entry accounts in the purchase, sales and nominal ledgers from a list of opening balances
- posted transactions from the purchases and sales day books – and also the purchase and sales returns day books – into the ledger accounts
- posted transactions from the cash book into the ledger accounts
- dealt with returned cheques and written off bad debts

The three ledgers are now fully written up and all that remains to be done at this stage is to balance all the ledger accounts.

The diagram below summarises the stage reached in your Unit 2 studies.

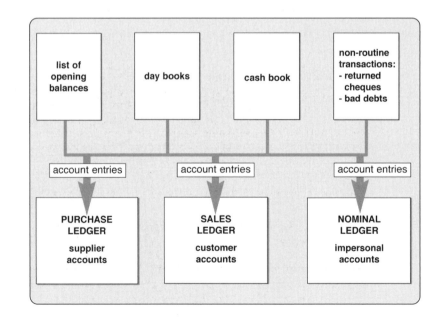

This chapter, in short, explains the processes of

- balancing the purchase, sales and nominal ledgers in preparation for the drawing up of control accounts

BALANCING THE PURCHASE LEDGER ACCOUNTS

A business using a manual accounting system will regularly balance all its ledger accounts and extract a trial balance, partly to check the accuracy of the system and also to enable the owners and managers to monitor the figures. This routine is commonly carried out at the end of each month.

In your assessment you will normally be required to balance **all** the ledger accounts – purchase, sales and nominal – after you have posted the ledgers from the day books and cash book (see last chapter). Balancing of accounts has already been explained in Chapter 4 (pages 48 - 55). If you are unsure of the procedure you should read these pages again.

This chapter starts with the supplier accounts in the Purchase Ledger. Set out below are the three supplier accounts which form the Purchase Ledger of Supra Stationery.

These accounts have now been balanced (see entries in bold type). You should note that most businesses are likely to have more than three supplier accounts. The number has been limited in this text for the sake of simplicity.

SUPRA STATIONERY: PURCHASE LEDGER

Dr	AZ Supplies Account						Cr	
2009	Details	£	p	2009	Details	£	p
24 Apr	Purchase returns	37	60	1 Apr	Balance b/d	725	60
14 Apr	Bank	770	21	9 Apr	Purchases	810	75
14 Apr	Discount Received	40	54	22 Apr	Purchases	235	00
30 Apr	**Balance c/d**	**923**	**00**				
		1,771	35			1,771	35
				1 May	Balance b/d	923	00

Dr	Rapid Supply Account						Cr	
2009	Details	£	p	2009	Details	£	p
15 Apr	Purchase returns	89	30	1 Apr	Balance b/d	840	20
15 Apr	Bank	840	20	6 Apr	Purchases	141	00
30 Apr	**Balance c/d**	**521**	**70**	15 Apr	Purchases	470	00
		1,451	20			1,451	20
				1 May	Balance b/d	521	70

continued on next page

Dr				T Khan Importers Account			Cr
2009	Details	£	p	2009	Details	£	p
17 Apr	Purchase returns	28	20	1 Apr	Balance b/d	963	90
30 Apr	**Balance c/d**	**1,365**	**75**	17 Apr	Purchases	98	70
				27 Apr	Purchases	331	35
		1,393	95			1,393	95
				1 May	**Balance b/d**	**1,365**	**75**

technical notes

- the 'balance c/d' in each case is the difference between the totals of the credit and debit sides
- the date of the 'Balance c/d' in each case is the last day of the current month (here it is 30 April)
- the date of the 'Balance b/d' in each case is the first day of the next month (1 May)
- the 'Balance c/d' is inserted on the next available line on the side with the lower total; note that 'balance' is never abbreviated to 'bal'
- the total figure of both columns is always double or bold underlined and is always on the same level, even it means leaving a gap (as on the debit side of the T Khan Importers Account shown above)

You should note that the supplier accounts all have a **credit balance**. This is because these balances are amounts **owed by** the business and are **liabilities**.

We will see in the next chapter how the balances of the accounts in the Purchase Ledger are brought together in a checking and control device known as a 'control account'. The same control account process will be carried out with the Sales Ledger accounts (see below and in Chapter 11).

BALANCING THE SALES LEDGER ACCOUNTS

Set out on the next page are the four customer accounts which form the Sales Ledger of Supra Stationery. These accounts have been balanced (see entries in bold type). You should note that most businesses are likely to have many more than four customer accounts.

As with the Purchase Ledger this text is illustrating the principles of ledger accounting as simply as possible with a limited number of customer accounts. These accounts include W Barnes Ltd Account, which was written off as a bad debt in the last chapter (see pages 110-111).

SUPRA STATIONERY: SALES LEDGER

Dr				W Barnes Ltd				Cr
2009	Details	£	p	**2009**	Details	£	p
1 Apr	Balance b/d	560	65	6 Apr	Sales returns	37	60
2 Apr	Sales	540	50	22 Apr	Bank	560	65
23 Apr	Sales	547	55	28 Apr	Bad debts	1,611	10
27 Apr	Bank R/D	560	65				
		2,209	35			2,209	35

Dr				J Keetz Account				Cr
2009	Details	£	p	**2009**	Details	£	p
1 Apr	Balance b/d	4,830	90	17 Apr	Sales returns	49	35
7 Apr	Sales	752	00	14 Apr	Bank	714	40
28 Apr	Sales	141	00	14 Apr	Discount Allowed	37	60
				28 Apr	Bank	240	00
				30 Apr	**Balance c/d**	**4,682**	**55**
		5,723	90			5,723	90
1 May	Balance b/d	4,682	55				

Dr				R S Thomas Account				Cr
2009	Details	£	p	**2009**	Details	£	p
1 Apr	Balance b/d	1,340	10	14 Apr	Sales returns	103	40
15 Apr	Sales	453	55	**30 Apr**	**Balance c/d**	**1,690**	**25**
		1,793	65			1,793	65
1 May	Balance b/d	1,690	25				

Dr				W B Yates Account				Cr
2009	Details	£	p	**2009**	Details	£	p
1 Apr	Balance b/d	1,074	70	**30 Apr**	**Balance c/d**	**2,047**	**60**
20 Apr	Sales	972	90				
		2,047	60			2,047	60
1 May	Balance b/d	2,047	60				

technical notes

- the W Barnes Ltd account has been written off as a bad debt and therefore has a nil balance, which is why there is no 'Balance c/d'.
- the remaining accounts all have **debit** balances; this is because they are amounts **owed to** Supra Stationery.

BALANCING THE NOMINAL LEDGER

Your Assessment will also require you to balance all the other accounts in the Nominal Ledger.

The Supra Stationery nominal accounts are shown below with individual explanatory notes.

The balancing figures are shown in bold type.

Control accounts for purchases and sales are normally included at the end of the Nominal Ledger and will be dealt with in the next two chapters.

NOMINAL LEDGER

Dr		Administration Expenses Account						Cr	
2009	**Details**	**£**	**p**	**2009**	**Details**		**£**	**p**
1 Apr	Balance b/d	32,350	10	**30 Apr**	**Balance c/d**		**32,640**	**10**
21 Apr	Bank	290	00					
		32,640	10				32,640	10
1 May	**Balance b/d**	**32,640**	**10**					

*The balance of Administration Expenses Account is brought down on the **debit** side; it is an **expense** of the business.*

Dr		Capital Account					Cr	
2009	**Details**	**£**	**p**	**2009**	**Details**	**£**	**p**
				1 Apr	Balance b/d	65,600	00

*Capital Account does not need balancing as there are no entries for the month and the balance shown is still correct. It is a **credit** entry because it is capital introduced and is **owed to** the owner.*

Dr		Discount Allowed Account					Cr	
2009	**Details**	**£**	**p**	**2009**	**Details**	**£**	**p**
1 Apr	Balance b/d	510	65	**30 Apr**	**Balance c/d**	**548**	**25**
30 Apr	Cash book	37	60				
		548	25			548	25
1 May	**Balance b/d**	**548**	**25**				

*The balance of Discount Allowed Account is brought down on the **debit** side; it is an **expense** of the business.*

Dr					Discount Received Account			Cr
2009	Details	£	p	2009	Details		£	p
30 Apr	Balance c/d	730	54	1 Apr	Balance b/d		690	00
				30 Apr	Cash Book		40	54
		730	54				730	54
				1 May	Balance b/d		730	54

The balance of Discount Received Account is brought down on the **credit** side; it is an **income item** received by the business.

Dr					Premises Account			Cr
2009	Details	£	p	2009	Details		£	p
1 Apr	Balance b/d	50,000	00					

Premises Account does not need balancing as there are no entries for the month and the balance shown is still correct. It is a **debit** entry because it is an asset, an **item owned** by the business.

Dr					Purchases Account			Cr
2009	Details	£	p	2009	Details		£	p
1 Apr	Balance b/d	65,505	00	30 Apr	Balance c/d		67,601	00
30 Apr	Total PDB	1,776	00					
24 Apr	Cash	320	00					
		67,601	00				67,601	00
1 May	Balance b/d	67,601	00					

The balance of Purchases Account is brought down on the **debit** side; it is an **expense** of the business.

Dr					Purchase Returns Account			Cr
2009	Details	£	p	2009	Details		£	p
30 Apr	Balance c/d	542	80	1 Apr	Balance b/d		410	80
				30 Apr	Total PRDB		132	00
		542	80				542	80
				1 May	Balance b/d		542	80

The balance of Purchase Returns Account is brought down on the **credit** side; it is a **reduction in the amount owed** by the company.

Dr		Sales Account						Cr
2009	Details	£	p	2009	Details	£	p
30 Apr	Balance c/d	88,730	50	1 Apr	Balance b/d	85,630	50
				30 Apr	Total SDB	2,900	00
				6 Apr	Cash	200	00
		88,730	50			88,730	50
				1 May	Balance b/d	88,730	50

The balance of Sales Account is brought down on the **credit** side; it is **income** received by the business.

Dr		Sales Returns Account						Cr
2009	Details	£	p	2009	Details	£	p
1 Apr	Balance b/d	240	50	30 Apr	Balance c/d	402	50
30 Apr	Total SRDB	162	00				
		402	50			402	50
1 May	Balance b/d	402	50				

The balance of Sales Returns Account is brought down on the **debit** side; it is a **reduction** in the amount owed to the business.

Dr		Sundry Expenses						Cr
2009	Details	£	p	2009	Details	£	p
1 Apr	Balance b/d	340	75				

Sundry Expenses Account does not need balancing as there are no entries for the month and the balance shown is still correct. It is a **debit** entry because it is an **expense** of the business.

Dr		Value Added Tax Account						Cr
2009	Details	£	p	2009	Details	£	p
30 Apr	Total PDB	310	80	1 Apr	Balance b/d	6,530	70
30 Apr	Total SRDB	28	35	30 Apr	Total PRDB	23	10
24 Apr	Cash purchases	56	00	30 Apr	Total SDB	507	50
30 Apr	Balance c/d	6,701	15	6 Apr	Cash sales	35	00
		7,096	30			7,096	30
				1 May	Balance b/d	6,701	15

The balance of Value Added Tax Account is brought down on the **credit** side; it is an **amount owed** by the business to HM Revenue & Customs.

Dr				Bad Debts Account			Cr
2009	**Details**	**£**	**p**	**2009**	**Details**	**£**	**p**
28 Apr	W Barnes Ltd	1,611	10				

*Bad Debts Account does not need balancing as there is only one entry and this is the balance. It is a **debit** entry because it is effectively an **expense** of the business and will reduce profit.*

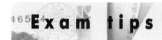

Where now and where next?

chapter summary

In this chapter we have explained how to

● balance accounts in the purchase, sales and nominal ledgers

what is in the next chapter?

The next chapter explains how to set up control accounts for purchases using account balances in the purchase and nominal ledger and information from the day books and cash book.

Exam tips

● When totalling the debits and credits in an account, always enter the balancing figure in the column with the lower total, on the next line down.

● Always enter the underlined totals on the same line - never on different lines.

● The balancing figure should always have the description 'Balance carried down' or 'Balance c/d'. 'Balance' should never be abbreviated to 'Bal'.

● Remember that supplier accounts in the Purchase Ledger normally have credit balances because they are items owed by the business, ie they are liabilities.

● Remember that customer accounts in the Sales Ledger normally have debit balances because they are items owed to the business.

● Account balances in the Nominal Ledger are a mix of debit balances and credit balances. Debit balances include expenses and assets (items owned). Credit balances include liabilities (items owed), capital (the owner's investment) and income items such as sales.

9.1* You are to draw up and then balance the following accounts in the Purchase Ledger of a business

Dr				J Carlisle Account			Cr
2009	**Details**	**£**	**p**	**2009**	**Details**	**£**	**p**
14 Apr	Purchase returns	45	20	1 Apr	Balance b/d	945	20
24 Apr	Bank	760	00	20 Apr	Purchases	800	00
24 Apr	Discount Received	40	00	29 Apr	Purchases	146	80

Dr				M Benjamin Account			Cr
2009	**Details**	**£**	**p**	**2009**	**Details**	**£**	**p**
15 Apr	Purchase returns	56	95	1 Apr	Balance b/d	875	10
23 Apr	Bank	875	10	6 Apr	Purchases	329	50
				28 Apr	Purchases	619	72

Dr				T Wood Account			Cr
2009	**Details**	**£**	**p**	**2009**	**Details**	**£**	**p**
17 Apr	Purchase returns	66	50	1 Apr	Balance b/d	720	20
15 Apr	Bank	532	00	9 Apr	Purchases	560	00
15 Apr	Discount Received	28	00	27 Apr	Purchases	470	00

9.2* You are to draw up and then balance the following accounts in the Sales Ledger of a business.

Dr				H Randeep Ltd			Cr
2009	**Details**	**£**	**p**	**2009**	**Details**	**£**	**p**
1 Apr	Balance b/d	3,810	50	17 Apr	Sales returns	30	30
17 Apr	Sales	852	75	14 Apr	Bank	160	40
28 Apr	Sales	145	10	14 Apr	Sales returns	137	60
				28 Apr	Bank	3,642	60

Dr	V Handley Ltd Account					Cr	
2009	Details	£	p	2009	Details	£	p
1 Apr	Balance b/d	2,760	21	17 Apr	Sales returns	66	15
7 Apr	Sales	860	00	14 Apr	Bank	817	00
28 Apr	Sales	1,346	90	14 Apr	Discount Allowed	43	00
				28 Apr	Bank	2,760	21

Dr	H Parry Ltd					Cr	
2009	Details	£	p	2009	Details	£	p
1 Apr	Balance b/d	420	25	9 Apr	Sales returns	89	75
14 Apr	Sales	190	30	20 Apr	Bank	420	25
23 Apr	Sales	620	15	30 Apr	Bad debts	1,140	95
24 Apr	Bank R/D	420	25				

9.3 You are to draw up and then balance the following accounts in the Nominal Ledger of a business.

Dr	Insurance Account					Cr	
2009	Details	£	p	2009	Details	£	p
1 Mar	Balance b/d	725	75				

Dr	Discount Allowed Account					Cr	
2009	Details	£	p	2009	Details	£	p
1 Apr	Balance b/d	340	55				
30 Apr	Cash book	42	90				

Dr	Value Added Tax Account					Cr	
2009	Details	£	p	2009	Details	£	p
30 Apr	Total PDB	630	70	1 Apr	Balance b/d	4,920	30
30 Apr	Total SRDB	56	40	30 Apr	Total PRDB	46	20
14 Apr	Cash purchases	125	00	30 Apr	Total SDB	1,230	85
				6 Apr	Cash sales	82	90

10 Purchase ledger control account

The last chapter described how to balance the accounts in the purchase, sales and nominal ledgers.

In this chapter we will explain the workings of 'control' accounts which summarise the account entries in the individual ledgers over a period of time (eg a month) and provide a check on the accuracy of the posting to the accounts.

We will use as a working example the Purchase Ledger Control Account which is a summary and 'total' account of all the supplier (creditor) accounts which make up the purchase ledger.

As a check of the accuracy of our account workings we will agree the total of a list of the balances of the supplier (creditor) accounts against the final balance of the Purchase Ledger Control Account.

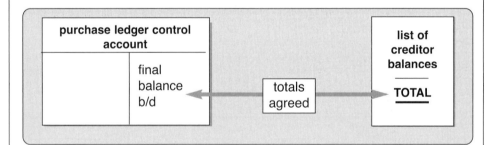

This chapter, in short, explains the processes of

- drawing up a Purchase Ledger Control Account, which summarises
  - the total of the opening balances of the supplier accounts
  - totals of transactions on the supplier accounts, eg purchases made, purchases returns made, payment for purchases, discounts received
  - the total of the final balances of the supplier accounts
- totalling up a separate list of the final balances of the supplier accounts and agreeing the total with the final balance brought down of the Purchase Ledger Control Account

BALANCING THE PURCHASE LEDGER ACCOUNTS

As seen in the last chapter, a business using a manual accounting system will regularly balance all its accounts, including its Purchase Ledger accounts. This routine is often carried out at the end of each month. The balanced Purchase Ledger accounts of Supra Stationery are shown below.

SUPRA STATIONERY: PURCHASE LEDGER

Dr						AZ Supplies Account			Cr
2009	**Details**	**£**	**p**	**2009**	**Details**		**£**	**p**	
24 Apr	Purchase returns	37	60	1 Apr	Balance b/d		725	60	
14 Apr	Bank	770	21	9 Apr	Purchases		810	75	
14 Apr	Discount Received	40	54	22 Apr	Purchases		235	00	
30 Apr	Balance c/d	923	00						
		1,771	35				1,771	35	
				1 May	Balance b/d		923	00	

Dr						Rapid Supply Account			Cr
2009	**Details**	**£**	**p**	**2009**	**Details**		**£**	**p**	
15 Apr	Purchase returns	89	30	1 Apr	Balance b/d		840	20	
15 Apr	Bank	840	20	6 Apr	Purchases		141	00	
30 Apr	Balance c/d	521	70	15 Apr	Purchases		470	00	
		1,451	20				1,451	20	
				1 May	Balance b/d		521	70	

Dr						T Khan Importers Account			Cr
2009	**Details**	**£**	**p**	**2009**	**Details**		**£**	**p**	
17 Apr	Purchase returns	28	20	1 Apr	Balance b/d		963	90	
30 Apr	Balance c/d	1,365	75	17 Apr	Purchases		98	70	
				27 Apr	Purchases		331	35	
		1,393	95				1,393	95	
				1 May	Balance b/d		1,365	75	

PURCHASE LEDGER CONTROL ACCOUNT

The next stage after all the ledger accounts have been balanced is to prepare **control accounts** which are **summaries** of groups of ledger accounts and also **checking devices** which should pick up any errors in the double-entry bookkeeping. The most common control accounts are also the control accounts which feature in your Unit 2 Assessment:

- **Purchase Ledger Control Account** which summarises the supplier accounts in the Purchase Ledger (as shown on the previous page)
- **Sales Ledger Control Account** which summarises the customer accounts in the Sales Ledger (this will be dealt with in the next chapter)

Control accounts are 'total' accounts which bring together the totals of the transactions which are recorded in the individual ledger accounts. The Purchase Ledger Control Account, for example, is a 'total' account for the individual Purchase Ledger supplier accounts.

The following details will enable you to work out the combined total balance of all the Purchase Ledger customer accounts. The calculation is as follows:

- The total opening balances of all the supplier accounts; these are normally credit balances, **plus . . .**

- **credits**: the additions to the supplier balances, eg further credit purchases made and recorded in the Purchases Day Book (PDB) **minus . . .**

- **debits**: the deductions from the supplier balances, eg purchase returns recorded in the Purchase Returns Day Book (PRDB), cheques sent to suppliers, early settlement discounts received from suppliers, **equals . . .**

- the total of the combined Purchase Ledger account balances 'carried down' at the end of the period.

The Purchase Ledger Control Account for Supra Stationery is shown below.

Dr				Purchase Ledger Control Account			Cr
2009	**Details**	**£**	**p**	**2009**	**Details**	**£**	**p**
30 Apr	PRDB	155	10	1 Apr	Balance b/d	2,529	70
30 Apr	Bank	1,610	41	30 Apr	PDB	2,086	80
30 Apr	Discount Received	40	54				
30 Apr	Balance c/d	2,810	45				
		4,616	50			4,616	50
				1 May	Balance b/d	2,810	45

The three supplier accounts of Supra Stationery and the completed control account are shown below. Note that the control account entries – eg 'Bank' and 'Discount Received' – are **always on the same side of the account** as the entries in the customer accounts in the Purchase Ledger.

The way in which the information for the Purchase Ledger Control Account is collected together is explained on the next two pages.

Dr	AZ Supplies Account						Cr	
2009	**Details**	**£**	**p**	**2009**	**Details**	**£**	**p**	
24 Apr	Purchase returns	37	60	1 Apr	Balance b/d	725	60	
14 Apr	Bank	770	21	9 Apr	Purchases	810	75	
14 Apr	Discount Received	40	54	22 Apr	Purchases	235	00	
30 Apr	Balance c/d	923	00					
		1,771	35			1,771	35	
				1 May	Balance b/d	923	00	

Dr	Rapid Supply Account						Cr	
2009	**Details**	**£**	**p**	**2009**	**Details**	**£**	**p**	
15 Apr	Purchase returns	89	30	1 Apr	Balance b/d	840	20	
15 Apr	Bank	840	20	6 Apr	Purchases	141	00	
30 Apr	Balance c/d	521	70	15 Apr	Purchases	470	00	
		1,451	20			1,451	20	
				1 May	Balance b/d	521	70	

Dr	T Khan Importers Account						Cr	
2009	**Details**	**£**	**p**	**2009**	**Details**	**£**	**p**	
17 Apr	Purchase returns	28	20	1 Apr	Balance b/d	963	90	
30 Apr	Balance c/d	1,365	75	17 Apr	Purchases	98	70	
				27 Apr	Purchases	331	35	
		1,393	95			1,393	95	
				1 May	Balance b/d	1,365	75	

Dr	Purchase Ledger Control Account						Cr	
2009	**Details**	**£**	**p**	**2009**	**Details**	**£**	**p**	
30 Apr	PRDB	155	10	1 Apr	Balance b/d	2,529	70	
30 Apr	Bank	1,610	41	30 Apr	PDB	2,086	80	
30 Apr	Discount Received	40	54					
30 Apr	Balance c/d	2,810	45					
		4,616	50			4,616	50	
				1 May	Balance b/d	2,810	45	

Purchase Ledger Control Account – how it works

The Purchase Ledger Control Account for Supra Stationery for the month of April is shown in the diagram on the next page, together with numbered arrows which show where each piece of information comes from in the accounting system.

Set out below are explanations of the numbers in the diagram which refer to individual arrows. Read the explanations carefully and study the diagram on the next page.

You will see that in practice a variety of sources of information is used: the Purchase Ledger accounts, the Purchases Day Book, the Purchase Returns Day Book and the credit side of the Cash Book.

1 'Balance b/d' is the total of the opening balances of all the supplier accounts in the Purchase Ledger.

2 'PDB' is the total of the 'Total' column of the Purchases Day Book - it is the total of all the credit purchases made by Supra Stationery in April.

3 'PRDB' is the total of the 'Total' column of the Purchase Returns Day Book - it is the total of all the purchase returns made by Supra Stationery in April.

4 'Bank' is taken from entries in the Cash Book (bank column, credit side) – it is the total of all the cheque payments made by Supra Stationery in April to settle supplier invoices. The total of any cash payments to suppliers would be calculated from entries in the credit 'Cash' column in the Cash Book and the total would be recorded as 'Cash' in the control account (debit side).

5 'Discount Received' is taken from the total of the Discount Received column in the Cash Book (credit side) – it is the amount of cash discount given to Supra Stationery by its suppliers in April.

6 The 'Balance' of the control account is worked out by deducting the total of the debit side from the total of the credit side – this balance is the total amount owed by Supra Stationery to its suppliers at the end of April, according to the control account.

This control account balance will then have to be agreed ('reconciled') with a listing of the individual supplier account totals (see page 132).

If there is any difference between the balance of the control account and the listing of supplier balances, there is a error in the accounts which will have to be investigated.

Supra Stationery: writing up the Purchase Ledger Control Account

Purchase Returns Day Book (PRDB)

Purchase Returns Day Book				
Date	Details	Goods	VAT	Total
2009		£ p	£ p	£ p
15 Apr	Rapid Supply Ltd	76.00	13.30	89.30
17 Apr	T Khan Importers	24.00	4.20	28.20
24 Apr	AZ Supplies Ltd	32.00	5.60	37.60
30 Apr		132.00	23.10	155.10

Purchases Day Book (PDB)

Purchases Day Book				
Date	Details	Goods	VAT	Total
2009		£ p	£ p	£ p
6 Apr	Rapid Supply Ltd	120.00	21 00	141.00
9 Apr	AZ Supplies Ltd	690.00	120.75	810.75
15 Apr	Rapid Supply Ltd	400.00	70.00	470.00
17 Apr	T Khan Importers	84.00	14.70	98.70
22 Apr	AZ Supplies Ltd	200.00	35.00	235.00
27 Apr	T Khan Importers	282.00	49.35	331.35
30 Apr		1,776.00	310.80	2,086.80

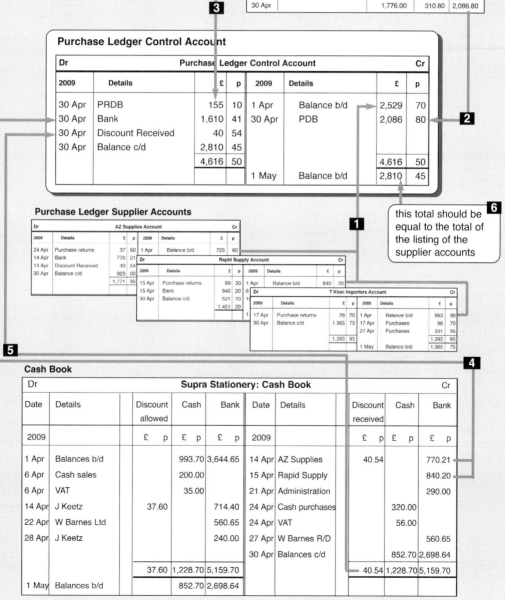

Purchase Ledger Control Account

Dr	Purchase Ledger Control Account						Cr
2009	Details	£	p	2009	Details	£	p
30 Apr	PRDB	155	10	1 Apr	Balance b/d	2,529	70
30 Apr	Bank	1,610	41	30 Apr	PDB	2,086	80
30 Apr	Discount Received	40	54				
30 Apr	Balance c/d	2,810	45				
		4,616	50			4,616	50
				1 May	Balance b/d	2,810	45

Purchase Ledger Supplier Accounts

Dr	AZ Supplies Account					Cr
2009	Details	£	p	2009	Details	£	p
24 Apr	Purchase returns	37	60	1 Apr	Balance b/d	725	60
14 Apr	Bank	770	21				
14 Apr	Discount Received	40	54				
30 Apr	Balance c/d	923	00				
		1,771	35				

Dr	Rapid Supply Account					Cr
2009	Details	£	p	2009	Details	£	p
15 Apr	Purchase returns	89	30	1 Apr	Balance b/d	840	20
15 Apr	Bank	840	20				
30 Apr	Balance c/d	521	70				
		1,451	20				

Dr	T Khan Importers Account					Cr
2009	Details	£	p	2009	Details	£	p
17 Apr	Purchase returns	28	20	1 Apr	Balance b/d	963	90
30 Apr	Balance c/d	1,365	75	17 Apr	Purchases	98	70
				27 Apr	Purchases	331	35
		1,393	95			1,393	95
				1 May	Balance b/d	1,365	75

this total should be equal to the total of the listing of the supplier accounts

Cash Book

Dr	Supra Stationery: Cash Book								Cr
Date	Details	Discount allowed	Cash	Bank	Date	Details	Discount received	Cash	Bank
2009		£ p	£ p	£ p	2009		£ p	£ p	£ p
1 Apr	Balances b/d			993.70	3,644.65	14 Apr	AZ Supplies	40.54		770.21
6 Apr	Cash sales		200.00		15 Apr	Rapid Supply			840.20
6 Apr	VAT		35.00		21 Apr	Administration			290.00
14 Apr	J Keetz	37.60		714.40	24 Apr	Cash purchases		320.00	
22 Apr	W Barnes Ltd			560.65	24 Apr	VAT		56.00	
28 Apr	J Keetz			240.00	27 Apr	W Barnes R/D			560.65
					30 Apr	Balances c/d		852.70	2,698.64
		37.60	1,228.70	5,159.70			40.54	1,228.70	5,159.70
1 May	Balances b/d		852.70	2,698.64					

reconciling the Purchase Ledger Control Account

You will see from the previous two pages that the only figure in the Purchase Ledger Control Account which is not taken from the accounts, day books or cash book is the final balance carried down, which is calculated within the control account.

One of the main reasons for constructing the control account is to check the workings in the accounts. If the total of the supplier account balances in the Purchase Ledger is not the same as the balance calculated in the control account there will be an error somewhere. This will either be in the control account itself (which should be checked first) or in the accounts.

These two total figures – the total of the supplier account balances and the control account balance carried down – are checked in a formal way known as a **'reconciliation'**.

Each time the control account is updated (often every month) a list of the supplier account balances – the **Creditors' List** – is drawn up. In the case of Supra Stationery there are only three creditors; most businesses may have a far greater number of balances to list.

The reconciliation will appear as follows:

Supra Stationery: Creditors' List as at 30 April 2009

	£	
AZ Supplies	923.00	
Rapid Supply	521.70	
T Khan Importers	1,365.75	
	2,810.45	= balance on Purchase Ledger Control Account

You will see from the previous page that this Creditors' List total agrees with the Purchase Ledger Control Account balance as at 30 April 2009.

The accounts are in order.

If this control account balance does not agree with the total of the list of supplier balances, this indicates an error in the accounts which must be investigated and corrected.

Where now and where next?

chapter summary

In this chapter we have explained how to:

- draw up a Purchase Ledger Control Account from entries in the day books, cash book and ledger accounts

- balance the Purchase Ledger Control Account and agree the balance with the total of the Creditors' List which sets out the supplier account balances

what is in the next chapter?

The next chapter describes:

- the preparation and balancing of the Sales Ledger Control Account

- the reconciliation of the Sales Ledger Control Account balance with the total of the Debtors' List which sets out the customer account balances

Exam tips

- When transferring figures from Purchase Ledger accounts to the Purchase Ledger Control Account, the figures ALWAYS go on the same side.

- Remember which items are debits and which are credits:

debit	Purchase Ledger Control Account	credit
items which <u>decrease</u> the amount owing to suppliers:		items which <u>increase</u> the amount owing to suppliers:
• Purchase Returns Day Book total - ie credit notes issued by suppliers		• Supplier account balances brought down
• Bank: cheques sent to suppliers paying off the amounts owing to them		• Purchases Day Book total – ie invoices issued by suppliers increasing the amount owing to them
• Discount received from suppliers, reducing the amount owing to them		

10.1* You work for A Mason & Co, a firm of accountants and have been given the following data for three businesses for the month of May:

	Business A	Business B	Business C
	£	£	£
Opening supplier balances	23,500	16,700	46,820
Credit purchases for the month	30,800	21,000	58,300
Purchase returns for the month	3,600	455	864

You are to calculate the closing supplier balances as at the end of May for all three businesses.

10.2 You work for C Campbell & Co, a firm of accountants and have been given the following data for three businesses for the month of June:

	Business D	Business E	Business F
	£	£	£
Opening supplier balances	65,300	86,200	32,920
Credit purchases for the month	46,100	64,300	41,920
Purchase returns for the month	975	1,560	2,783
Cheque payments to suppliers	59,500	82,900	29,500
Discount received from suppliers	450	620	406

You are to calculate the closing supplier balances as at the end of June for all three businesses.

10.3* You work for T Cirillo, a local book-keeper, and have been given the following data for three businesses for the month of July.

	Business J	Business K	Business L
	£	£	£
Opening supplier balances	34,500	56,300	6,970
Credit purchases for the month (PDB)	29,405	45,100	5,160
Purchase returns for the month (PRDB)	1,240	620	340
Cheque payments to suppliers during July	28,640	52,500	6,970
Discount received from suppliers during July	105	215	56

You are to draw up and balance a Purchase Ledger Control Account for each of the three businesses for the month of July.

10.4 You work as an accounts assistant for Addey Tupp & Co, a firm of accountants.

A client, Leo Petrov Limited, has a problem because the company accountant has been off sick since the weekend. You have been handed the books of the business and find that the end-of-the-month balancing in the Purchase Ledger has not been carried out, and the Purchase Ledger Control Account has gone missing. The day books and cash book have been completed. The date is 1 October 2009.

You are to:

(a) Balance the three Purchase Ledger accounts shown below and on the next page (all relevant transactions have been entered).

(b) Draw up and balance a Purchase Ledger Control Account from the data in the documents provided on this and the next two pages.

(c) Draw up a Creditors' List as at 30 September and reconcile the total with the balance carried down on the Purchase Ledger Control Account as at 30 September.

A specimen format is shown on page 137.

Question 10.4:
Purchase Ledger accounts

Dr				Axis Supplies Account				Cr
2009	**Details**	**£**	**p**	**2009**	**Details**	**£**	**p**
2 Sep	Purchase returns	56	90	1 Sep	Balance b/d	567	90
4 Sep	Bank	332	50	7 Sep	Purchases	728	50
4 Sep	Discount Received	17	50	15 Sep	Purchases	493	50

Dr				Pronto Importers Account				Cr
2009	**Details**	**£**	**p**	**2009**	**Details**	**£**	**p**
3 Sep	Purchase returns	128	55	1 Sep	Balance b/d	215	50
9 Sep	Bank	199	50	10 Sep	Purchases	145	70
9 Sep	Discount Received	10	50	21 Sep	Purchases	131	60

Dr	RTI Supplies Account						Cr
2009	**Details**	**£**	**p**	**2009**	**Details**	**£**	**p**
4 Sep	Purchase returns	288	50	1 Sep	Balance b/d	591	20
18 Sep	Bank	522	50	8 Sep	Purchases	223	25
18 Sep	Discount Received	27	50	24 Sep	Purchases	658	00

Question 10.4:
Completed day books.

Purchases Day Book				
Date	**Details**	**Goods**	**VAT**	**Total**
2009		£ p	£ p	£ p
7 Sep	Axis Supplies	620.00	108.50	728.50
8 Sep	RTI Supplies	190.00	33.25	223.25
10 Sep	Pronto Importers	124.00	21.70	145.70
15 Sep	Axis Supplies	420.00	73.50	493.50
21 Sep	Pronto Importers	112.00	19.60	131.60
24 Sep	RTI Supplies	560.00	98.00	658.00
30 Sep		2,026.00	354.55	2,380.55

Purchase Returns Day Book				
Date	**Details**	**Goods**	**VAT**	**Total**
2009		£ p	£ p	£ p
15 Sep	Axis Supplies	48.43	8.47	56.90
17 Sep	Pronto Importers	109.40	19.15	128.55
24 Sep	RTI Supplies	245.53	42.97	288.50
30 Sep		403.36	70.59	473.95

Question10.4:
Completed cash book extract – credit side.

Cash Book					Cr
Date	Details	Discount rec'd		Cash	Bank
2009		£ p		£ p	£ p
4 Sep	Axis Supplies	17.50			332.50
9 Sep	Pronto Importers	10.50			199.50
18 Sep	RTI Supplies	27.50			522.50
24 Sep	Insurance				760.00
25 Sep	Electricity				570.50
30 Sep	Balances c/d			100.50	1,690.30
		55.50		100.50	4,075.30

Question 10.4:
Format for creditors' list.

Creditors' List as at 30 September 2009

£

Axis Supplies

Pronto Importers

RTI Supplies

_____

========   = balance on Purchase Ledger
Control Account

11 Sales ledger control account

The last chapter dealt with the balancing of the Purchase Ledger accounts and the drawing up of the Purchase Ledger Control Account which summarises the account entries in the Purchase Ledger over the period of a month. It also showed how the total of the Purchase Ledger account balances should be reconciled with the balance of the control account.

In this chapter we will carry out the same processes by drawing up a Sales Ledger Control Account which acts as a summary account for the customer (debtor) accounts in the Sales Ledger.

We will also check the total of a list of the final balances of the customer (debtor) accounts against the final balance of the Sales Ledger Control Account.

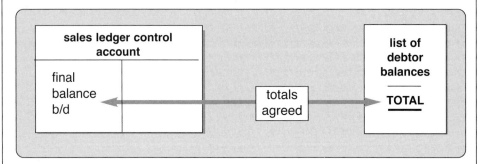

This chapter, in short, explains the processes of

- drawing up a Sales Ledger Control Account, which summarises
  - the total of the opening balances of the customer accounts
  - totals of transactions on the customer accounts, eg credit sales made, sales returns, payment received from customers, discounts allowed, returned cheques and bad debts
  - the total of the final balances of the customer (debtor) accounts
- totalling a separate list of the final balances of the customer accounts and agreeing the total with the final balance brought down of the sales ledger control account

BALANCING THE SALES LEDGER ACCOUNTS

As seen in Chapter 9, a business using a manual accounting system will regularly balance its Sales Ledger accounts. This routine is often carried out at the end of each month. The balanced Sales Ledger accounts of Supra Stationery (including the W Barnes Ltd bad debt) are shown below.

Dr		W Barnes Ltd					Cr	
2009	Details	£	p	2009	Details	£	p
1 Apr	Balance b/d	560	65	6 Apr	Sales returns	37	60
2 Apr	Sales	540	50	22 Apr	Bank	560	65
23 Apr	Sales	547	55	28 Apr	Bad debts	1,611	10
27 Apr	Bank R/D	560	65				
		2,209	35			2,209	35

Dr		J Keetz Account					Cr	
2009	Details	£	p	2009	Details	£	p
1 Apr	Balance b/d	4,830	90	17 Apr	Sales returns	49	35
7 Apr	Sales	752	00	14 Apr	Bank	714	40
28 Apr	Sales	141	00	14 Apr	Discount Allowed	37	60
				28 Apr	Bank	240	00
				30 Apr	Balance c/d	4,682	55
		5,723	90			5,723	90
1 May	Balance b/d	4,682	55				

Dr		R S Thomas Account					Cr	
2009	Details	£	p	2009	Details	£	p
1 Apr	Balance b/d	1,340	10	14 Apr	Sales returns	103	40
15 Apr	Sales	453	55	30 Apr	Balance c/d	1,690	25
		1,793	65			1,793	65
1 May	Balance b/d	1,690	25				

Dr		W B Yates Account					Cr	
2009	Details	£	p	2009	Details	£	p
1 Apr	Balance b/d	1,074	70	30 Apr	Balance c/d	2,047	60
20 Apr	Sales	972	90				
		2,047	60			2,047	60
1 May	Balance b/d	2,047	60				

SALES LEDGER CONTROL ACCOUNT

We have seen that **control accounts** are 'total' accounts which bring together the totals of the transactions which are recorded in the individual ledger accounts. The **Sales Ledger Control Account** is a 'total' account for the individual Sales Ledger customer accounts. The following details will enable you to work out the combined total balance of all the Sales Ledger customer accounts. The calculation is as follows:

- The total opening balances of all the customer (debtor) accounts; these are normally debit balances

plus . . .

- **debits**: the additions to the customer balances, eg:
  - credit sales made to customers, recorded in the Sales Day Book (SDB)
  - cheques returned to the bank 'R/D' (which will increase the amount owing to Supra Stationery)

minus . . .

- **credits**: the deductions from the customer balances, eg:
  - sales returns, recorded in the Sales Returns Day Book (SRDB)
  - cheques and cash received from customers and paid into the bank
  - early settlement discounts given (allowed) to customers
  - bad debts incurred and written off in the Sales Ledger account

equals . . .

- the total of the combined Sales Ledger balances 'carried down' at the end of the period.

The Sales Ledger Control Account for Supra Stationery is shown below. Note that all the entries, apart from the balance b/d, are dated 30 April, the date on which the account is drawn up.

Dr				Sales Ledger Control Account			Cr
2009	Details	£	p	2009	Details	£	p
1 Apr	Balance b/d	7,806	35	30 Apr	SRDB	190	35
30 Apr	Bank R/D	560	65	30 Apr	Bank	1,515	05
30 Apr	SDB	3,407	50	30 Apr	Discount Allowed	37	60
				30 Apr	Bad debts	1,611	10
				30 Apr	Balance c/d	8,420	40
		11,774	50			11,774	50
1 May	Balance b/d	8,420	40				

The four customer accounts of Supra Stationery and the completed control account are shown below. Note that the control account entries – eg 'Bank' 'Discount Allowed' and 'Bad Debts' – are **always on the same side of the account** as the entries in the customer accounts in the Sales Ledger.

The way in which the information for this control account is collected together is explained on the next two pages.

Dr	W Barnes Ltd						Cr	
2009	Details	£	p	2009	Details		£	p
1 Apr	Balance b/d	560	65	6 Apr	Sales returns		37	60
2 Apr	Sales	540	50	22 Apr	Bank		560	65
23 Apr	Sales	547	55	28 Apr	Bad debts		1,611	10
27 Apr	Bank R/D	560	65					
		2,209	35				2,209	35

Dr	J Keetz Account						Cr	
2009	Details	£	p	2009	Details		£	p
1 Apr	Balance b/d	4,830	90	17 Apr	Sales returns		49	35
7 Apr	Sales	752	00	14 Apr	Bank		714	40
28 Apr	Sales	141	00	14 Apr	Discount Allowed		37	60
				28 Apr	Bank		240	00
				30 Apr	Balance c/d		4,682	55
		5,723	90				5,723	90
1 May	Balance b/d	4,682	55					

Dr	R S Thomas Account						Cr	
2009	Details	£	p	2009	Details		£	p
1 Apr	Balance b/d	1,340	10	14 Apr	Sales returns		103	40
15 Apr	Sales	453	55	30 Apr	Balance c/d		1,690	25
		1,793	65				1,793	65
1 May	Balance b/d	1,690	25					

Dr	W B Yates Account						Cr	
2009	Details	£	p	2009	Details		£	p
1 Apr	Balance b/d	1,074	70	30 Apr	Balance c/d		2,047	60
20 Apr	Sales	972	90					
		2,047	60				2,047	60
1 May	Balance b/d	2,047	60					

Dr	Sales Ledger Control Account						Cr	
2009	Details	£	p	2009	Details		£	p
1 Apr	Balance b/d	7,806	35	30 Apr	SRDB		190	35
30 Apr	Bank R/D	560	65	30 Apr	Bank		1,515	05
30 Apr	SDB	3,407	50	30 Apr	Discount Allowed		37	60
				30 Apr	Bad debts		1,611	10
				30 Apr	Balance c/d		8,420	40
		11,774	50				11,774	50
1 May	Balance b/d	8,420	40					

Sales Ledger Control Account – how it works

The Sales Ledger Control Account for Supra Stationery for the month of April is shown in the diagram on the next page, together with numbered arrows which show where each piece of information comes from in the accounting system.

Set out below are explanations of the numbers in the diagram which refer to individual arrows. Read the explanations carefully and study the diagram on the next page. You will see that in practice a variety of sources of information is used: the Sales Ledger accounts, the related day books and the debit side of the cash book.

1 Balance b/d' is the total of the opening debit balances of the customer accounts in the Sales Ledger. (In practice, if the control account is already open this figure will be there as the 'Balance b/d' from the previous month.)

2 'Bank R/D' is taken from the W Barnes Ltd account (debit side) in the Sales Ledger – it is the returned cheque which was added back to the W Barnes Ltd account as a debit.

3 'SDB' is the total of the 'Total' column of the Sales Day Book - it is the total of all the credit sales made by Supra Stationery to customers in April.

4 'SRDB' is the total of the 'Total' column of the Sales Returns Day Book - it is the total of all the sales returns made to Supra Stationery in April.

5 'Bank' is taken from entries in the Cash Book (Bank column, debit side) – it is the total of all the cheque payments made by customers to Supra Stationery in April. The total of any cash payments made by customers to settle credit accounts would be taken from the 'Cash' column on the debit side of the Cash Book and added to the 'Bank' figure and recorded as 'Bank and Cash' in the control account (credit side).

6 'Discount Allowed' is taken from the total of the Discount Allowed column in the Cash Book (debit side) – it is the amount of early settlement discount given to customers by Supra Stationery in April.

7 'Bad debts' is the balance of the W Barnes Ltd account written off to Bad Debts account on 28 April.

8 The 'Balance c/d' of the control account is worked out by deducting the total of the credit side from the total of the debit side – this balance is the total amount owed to Supra Stationery by its customers at the end of April. This figure is then agreed ('reconciled') with a listing of the individual customer (debtor) account totals (see page 144). In this case the total is £8,420.40, which agrees with the customer balance total.

Supra Stationery: writing up the Sales Ledger Control Account

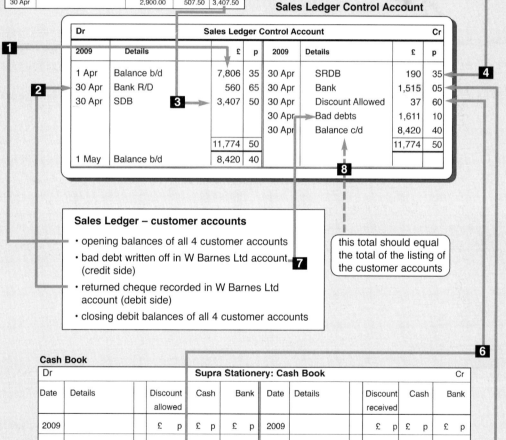

Sales Day Book (SDB)

	Sales Day Book			
Date	Details	Goods	VAT	Total
2009		£ p	£ p	£ p
2 Apr	W Barnes Ltd	460.00	80.50	540.50
7 Apr	J Keetz	640.00	112.00	752.00
15 Apr	R S Thomas	386.00	67.55	453.55
20 Apr	W B Yates	828.00	144.90	972.90
23 Apr	W Barnes Ltd	466.00	81.55	547.55
28 Apr	J Keetz	120.00	21.00	141.00
30 Apr		2,900.00	507.50	3,407.50

Sales Returns Day Book (SRDB)

	Sales Returns Day Book			
Date	Details	Goods	VAT	Total
2009		£ p	£ p	£ p
6 Jul	W Barnes Ltd	32.00	5.60	37.60
7 Jul	R S Thomas	88.00	15.40	103.40
9 Jul	J Keetz	42.00	7.35	49.35
10 Jul		162.00	28.35	190.35

Sales Ledger Control Account

1
2
3
4
8

Dr	Sales Ledger Control Account					Cr	
2009	Details	£	p	2009	Details	£	p
1 Apr	Balance b/d	7,806	35	30 Apr	SRDB	190	35
30 Apr	Bank R/D	560	65	30 Apr	Bank	1,515	05
30 Apr	SDB	3,407	50	30 Apr	Discount Allowed	37	60
				30 Apr	Bad debts	1,611	10
				30 Apr	Balance c/d	8,420	40
		11,774	50			11,774	50
1 May	Balance b/d	8,420	40				

Sales Ledger – customer accounts

- opening balances of all 4 customer accounts
- bad debt written off in W Barnes Ltd account (credit side) **7**
- returned cheque recorded in W Barnes Ltd account (debit side)
- closing debit balances of all 4 customer accounts

this total should equal the total of the listing of the customer accounts

6

Cash Book

Dr					Supra Stationery: Cash Book				Cr	
Date	Details	Discount allowed	Cash	Bank	Date	Details	Discount received	Cash	Bank	
2009		£ p	£ p	£ p	2009		£ p	£ p	£ p	
1 Apr	Balances b/d		993.70	3,644.65	14 Apr	AZ Supplies	40.54		770.21	
6 Apr	Cash sales		200.00		15 Apr	Rapid Supply			840.20	
6 Apr	VAT		35.00		21 Apr	Administration			290.00	
14 Apr	J Keetz	37.60		714.40	24 Apr	Cash purchases		320.00		
22 Apr	W Barnes Ltd			560.65	24 Apr	VAT		56.00		
28 Apr	J Keetz			240.00	27 Apr	W Barnes R/D			560.65	
					30 Apr	Balances c/d		852.70	2,698.64	
		37.60	1,228.70	5,159.70			40.54	1,228.70	5,159.70	
1 May	Balances b/d		852.70	2,698.64						

5

reconciling the Sales Ledger Control Account

You will see from the previous two pages that the only figure in the Sales Ledger Control Account which is not taken from the accounts, day books or cash book is the final balance carried down, which is calculated within the control account.

One of the main reasons for constructing the control account is to check the workings in the accounts. If the total of the customer account balances in the Sales Ledger is not the same as the balance calculated in the control account there will be an error somewhere. This will either be in the control account itself (which should be checked first) or in the accounts.

These two total figures – the total of the customer account balances and the control account balance carried down – are checked in a formal way known as a '**reconciliation**'.

Each time the control account is updated (often every month) a list of the customer account balances – the **Debtors' List** – is drawn up. In the case of Supra Stationery there are only three customers with account balances (W Barnes Ltd was written off as a bad debt). Most businesses selling on credit will have a higher number of customer accounts in the Sales Ledger.

The reconciliation will appear as follows:

Supra Stationery: Debtors' List as at 30 April 2009

	£	
J Keetz	4,682.55	
R S Thomas	1,690.25	
W B Yates	2,047.60	
	8,420.40	= balance on Sales Ledger Control Account

You will see from the previous page that this Debtors' List total agrees with the Sales Ledger Control Account balance as at 30 April 2009.

If there had been a difference in these totals, the control account and the accounts in the ledgers would need to be checked carefully to identify the error (or errors).

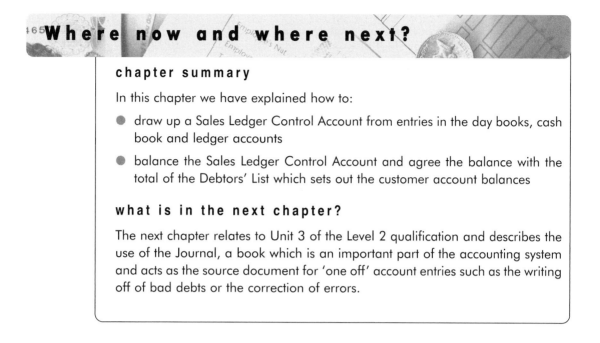

Where now and where next?

chapter summary

In this chapter we have explained how to:

- draw up a Sales Ledger Control Account from entries in the day books, cash book and ledger accounts

- balance the Sales Ledger Control Account and agree the balance with the total of the Debtors' List which sets out the customer account balances

what is in the next chapter?

The next chapter relates to Unit 3 of the Level 2 qualification and describes the use of the Journal, a book which is an important part of the accounting system and acts as the source document for 'one off' account entries such as the writing off of bad debts or the correction of errors.

Exam tips

- When transferring figures from Sales Ledger accounts to the Sales Ledger Control Account, the figures ALWAYS go on the same side.

- Remember which items are debits and which are credits:

debit	Sales Ledger Control Account	credit
items which <u>increase</u> the amount owed by customers who have bought on credit:		**items which <u>decrease</u> the amount owing by customers:**
• Customer account balances brought down, ie amounts owed by customers		• Sales Returns Day Book total - ie credit notes issued to customers
• Sales Day Book total – ie invoices issued by the business to customers, increasing the amount owed to the business		• Bank: cheques received from customers paying off the amounts owed by them
• Returned (R/D) cheques which have been issued by customers but returned by the bank unpaid		• Discount allowed to customers, reducing the amount owed by them
		• Bad debts written off to Bad Debts Account, reducing the customer account balance to nil

11.1* You work for Puccini & Co, a firm of accountants and have been given the following data for three businesses for the month of June:

	Business L	Business M	Business N
	£	£	£
Opening customer balances	56,600	36,930	94,782
Credit sales for the month	34,820	21,750	32,804
Sales returns for the month	1,348	856	743

You are to calculate the closing customer balances as at the end of June for all three businesses.

11.2 You work for Azhar Saleem Associates, a firm of accountants and have been given the following data for three businesses for the month of July:

	Business P	Business Q	Business R
	£	£	£
Opening customer balances	74,120	92,700	63,945
Credit sales for the month	23,206	46,920	27,630
Sales returns for the month	420	1,295	982
Cheque payments from customers	23,600	38,507	26,815
Discount allowed to customers	230	420	125

You are to calculate the closing customer balances as at the end of July for all three businesses.

11.3 You work for Zemenides & Co, a firm of accountants, and have been given the following data for three businesses for the month of September:

	Business S	Business T	Business U
	£	£	£
Opening customer balances	47,950	54,650	45,027
Credit sales for the month (SDB)	10,750	26,840	25,385
Sales returns for the month (SRDB)	850	1,560	1,420
Cheque payments from customers	12,856	29,742	28,673
Returned (R/D) cheques	458	-	-
Discount allowed to customers	62	122	72
Bad debts written off	-	978	-

You are to draw up and balance a Sales Ledger Control Account for each of the three businesses for the month of September on the last day of the month.

11.4 You work as an accounts assistant for O'Shea Associates, a firm of accountants. You have been called in at the end of August to help a client, Zenith Limited, to complete their end-of-month routines. You have been provided with the following documents:

1. Three sales ledger accounts which have been written up, but not balanced at the end of the month (see page 148).

2. A Sales Day Book recording total credit sales for the month amounting to £2,099.05.

3. A Sales Returns Day Book recording total Sales Returns for the month amounting to £322.90.

4. A balanced cash book (see extract on page 149) showing the debit side.

The date is 31 August 2009.

You are to:

(a) Balance the three Sales Ledger accounts shown on the next page (all relevant transactions have been entered).

(b) Draw up and balance a Sales Ledger Control Account, using the data in the documents provided on the next two pages.

(c) Draw up a Debtors' List as at 31 August and reconcile the total with the balance carried down on the Sales Ledger Control Account as at 31 August.

A specimen format is shown on page 149.

(d) Explain what difference it would make to the control account if R M Walker's account had been written off as a bad debt on 31 August.

SALES LEDGER

Dr	R M Walker Account						Cr
2009	Details	£	p	2009	Details	£	p
1 Aug	Balance b/d	6,740	20	18 Aug	Sales returns	96	00
12 Aug	Sales	460	00	14 Aug	Bank	6,437	00
18 Aug	Bank R/D	6,437	00	14 Aug	Discount Allowed	23	20

Dr	I Tabrizi Account						Cr
2009	Details	£	p	2009	Details	£	p
1 Aug	Balance b/d	4,939	50	12 Aug	Sales returns	171	90
18 Aug	Sales	295	55	25 Aug	Bank	4,597	36
20 Aug	Sales	628	80	25 Aug	Discount Allowed	31	44

Dr	W Murray Account						Cr
2009	Details	£	p	2009	Details	£	p
1 Aug	Balance b/d	929	20	18 Aug	Sales returns	55	00
12 Aug	Sales	160	70	27 Aug	Bank	1,055	55
24 Aug	Sales	269	00	27 Aug	Discount Allowed	13	45

CASH BOOK

Cash Book (Extract)		Discount allowed	Cash	Dr Bank
Date	Details			
2009		£ p	£ p	£ p
1 Aug	Balances b/d		120.00	567.00
14 Aug	R M Walker	23.20		6,437.00
25 Aug	I Tabrizi	31.44		4,597.36
26 Aug	Cash sales		100.00	
26 Aug	VAT		17.50	
27 Aug	W Murray	13.45		1,055.55
		68.09	237.50	12,656.91

Question 11.4:
Format for debtors' list.

Debtors' List as at 31 August 2009

                              £

R M Walker

I Tabrizi

W Murray

                    _____

                    _____   = balance on Sales Ledger
                                    Control Account

Introduction to the Unit 3 Assignment

The Unit 3 title for the OCR Level 2 in Accounting is:

Make journal entries and adjustments and produce a revised trial balance

You will have to sit an externally set assignment in examination conditions for your assessment. You will have two hours in which to complete the assignment plus ten minutes reading time.

● In the assignment you will be given an initial trial balance together with various documents from which you will have to make entries in a book known as 'the journal'.

● These documents include invoices, credit notes, memorandums and cheques. They relate to 'one-off' financial transactions which have not yet been entered in the ledger accounts and will need to be entered in the books.

● You will have to identify the relevant ledger accounts and the debit and credit entries for each journal entry and write down the 'T' accounts on working papers before making the entries in the journal. The entries require the date, the title of each account affected, amounts entered in the appropriate debit or credit column and a suitable narrative describing the entry.

● Each of the journal entries will affect an account and the account's balance in the trial balance.

● You will then be asked to prepare a 'Revised Trial Balance'. Using the journal entries prepared earlier you will be required to make the adjustments in the accounts in the 'Revised Trial Balance' . In some instances it may be necessary to add a new account to the trial balance

● Finally you will be required to total the trial balance which should balance if all the journal entries, adjustments and calculations have been carried out correctly.

These processes are summarised in the diagram on the opposite page. Study this diagram and then work through the chapters that follow.

Unit 3 – the processes involved . . .

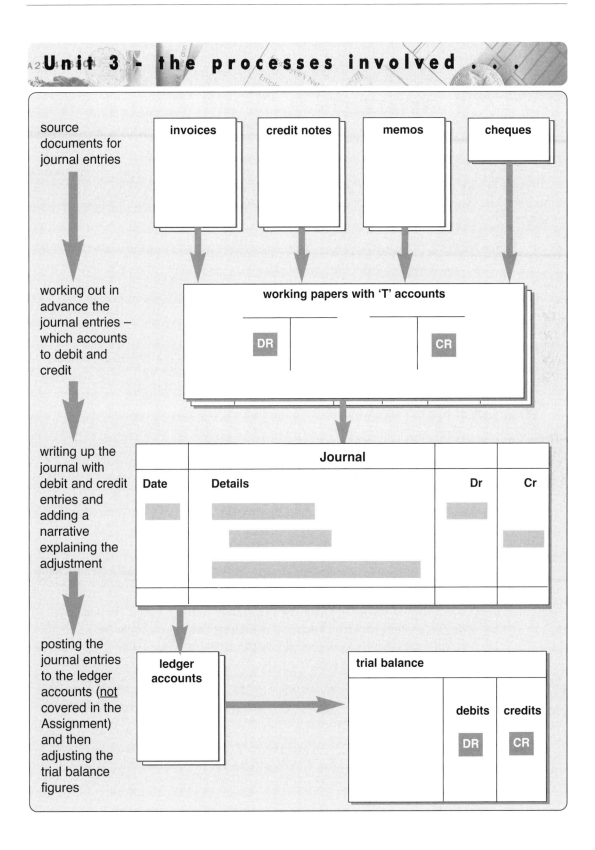

source documents for journal entries				

invoices **credit notes** **memos** **cheques**

working out in advance the journal entries – which accounts to debit and credit

working papers with 'T' accounts

DR CR

writing up the journal with debit and credit entries and adding a narrative explaining the adjustment

Journal			
Date	Details	Dr	Cr

posting the journal entries to the ledger accounts (not covered in the Assignment) and then adjusting the trial balance figures

ledger accounts

trial balance

	debits	credits
	DR	CR

12 Introduction to the journal

what this chapter covers . . .

This chapter:

- introduces the journal as an original book of entry

- shows the sequence of entries into the journal

- identifies the various uses of the journal

- illustrates simple journal entries using double-entry accounting procedures

- shows how the journal entry is posted to the ledger accounts

- considers the advantages of journal entries

Unit 3 Case Study – Cucina Zone

Cucina Zone

All the entries carried out in Unit 3 will be illustrated in this book by a Case Study of a wholesaler, Cucina Zone, which supplies kitchen equipment and utensils.

The business is owned and run by sole trader, Maria Fornara, who supplies a wide range of goods to the trade and retailers throughout the UK. Maria obtains her stock from various sources within the UK and specialises in high quality goods.

Maria purchases and sells goods on credit on a daily basis which involves a number of invoices and credit notes being issued to customers and received from suppliers.

In addition Maria may find it relevant to write a memo or an email if there is any particular financial issue that requires attention from her book-keeper.

THE JOURNAL

The **journal** is known as an original book of entry, which simply means that it is a place where a financial transaction is first entered. Other books of original entry that you may already have come across in your studies are the day books in Unit 1.

The journal is often referred to as a kind of diary in which the book-keeper enters transactions of a different nature, for example, 'writing off a debt as bad' or perhaps correcting an error that has occurred in one of the ledgers.

format of a journal

The journal is set out in a series of columns to enable details of the various transactions to be recorded from the source documents, for example an invoice or credit note or perhaps a memo.

The journal of Cucina Zone is shown below with a sample entry correcting an error in the accounts. The columns are as follows (from left to right):

	Journal		
Date	**Details**	**Dr**	**Cr**
2009		£	£
1 July	Sales	500.00	
	Office equipment		500.00
	Correction of an error in account posting.		

Date   - the year date is shown on the first line

    - the month and date of the invoice/credit note/memo is entered on the lines underneath

    - you should never enter a ditto mark (") in the date column

Details - the name of the account to be **debited** is always entered first

    - the name of the account to be **credited** is then entered underneath; this entry may be slightly indented to distinguish it from the debit entry

    - lastly, a brief narrative describing the situation is included, making reference to the source document whenever possible

Dr   - the total amount to be debited is entered in the debit column under the £ sign

Cr   - the total amount to be credited is entered in the credit column under the £ sign

Note: Each journal entry should be ruled off when completed.

sequence of entries into the journal

Entries into the journal are initially generated from a source document such as an invoice, credit note, memo or cheque. An entry to record the particular transaction is made in the journal and is then posted to a ledger account. Finally, the adjusted balance on the particular ledger account is entered onto the trial balance. The diagram below shows this sequence of entries involving the journal as the second stage.

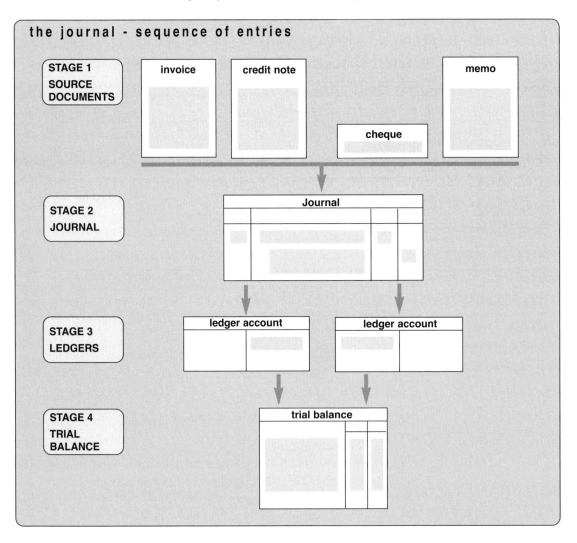

USES OF THE JOURNAL

All business transactions must be recorded in a book of original entry before being posted to the sales, purchase or nominal ledger. The journal is entered with details of transactions that are out of the ordinary or adjustments that are not recorded in any other book of original entry.

The types of transaction that fall into this category are as follows:

- recording errors of omission
- writing off bad debts
- dealing with partial bad debts
- bad debts recovered
- dealing with dishonoured cheques
- purchase and sale of fixed assets
- correction of errors
- other adjustments such as transfers between accounts

Sometimes a journal entry is necessary because of an **internal** error or adjustment that has occurred in the business, such as omitting to enter an invoice or credit note or perhaps dealing with an item such as the owner of the business taking goods for his or her own use.

Occasionally the error may be due to **external** factors such as a customer becoming bankrupt or perhaps disallowing a cash discount that had been taken. In this and the next chapter we will look at the various types of journal entries, starting with simple **internal** errors.

dealing with journal entries

Students often find journal entries difficult, therefore, to make this topic easier to understand you may find it helpful to use the following sequence of steps when you are undertaking an assessment:

1   Assume you are the book-keeper for the business.

2   Identify the name of the business you work for, in this case it will be Cucina Zone. Highlight the business name on your assignment paper.

3   Think double-entry, ie which account needs to be debited and which account is to be credited.

   Remember! - a debit entry is always an asset or an expense

                   - a credit entry is a liability, capital or income

4   Most students find it easier to draw up the 'T' accounts entering the name(s) of the accounts to be debited and credited before preparing the

journal entry. You could do this on an actual document provided with the assignment, ie an invoice or credit note; or you could use your answer book, in which case you must clearly identify your workings.

5   Enter the transaction in the 'T' accounts, perhaps using an 'x' for the amount since this is only a working document to decide where to make the debit and credit entries.

6   Record the journal entry:

  •   date (the date of the invoice/credit note/memo)

  •   details of the account to be debited

  •   enter the amount in the 'Dr' column

  •   details of the account to be credited (slightly indented to distinguish it from the debit entry)

  •   enter the amount in the 'Cr' column

  •   add a brief narrative

  •   finally rule the entry off

7   If you are using your assignment answer book to write down your workings, mark up the relevant page 'workings' and make sure you complete the journal entries after you have carried out your workings.

errors of omission

It is important for businesses to ensure that all documentation relating to financial data is recorded in the books of account. Occasionally, however, a document may be overlooked and is not entered in the books of account. When this occurs, the mistake is known as an **error of omission**. Examples of documents that may have missed being entered are as follows:

• invoices

• credit notes

• payments made by the bank but not entered in the cash book, ie direct debits and standing orders

• memos containing internal transactions, ie the owner/proprietor withdrawing cash or goods from the business for his/her personal use, or perhaps introducing additional cash or assets as capital into the business

We will now explain how the various transactions listed above are carried out.

documents not entered in the accounts – invoice

The sales invoice shown on the next page has been prepared by Cucina Zone in respect of purchases made by one of its customers, J Peters & Co.

<table>
<tr><td colspan="3" align="center">

INVOICE
Cucina Zone
Dovedale Way, Derby, DE3 7EP
Tel 01335 401278

VAT Reg 470 6352 81

</td></tr>
</table>

J Peters & Co 26 Hammond Place Derby DE2 6JK	**invoice number** 3754 **date** 6 October 2009

quantity	description	unit price £	£
6	Casserole dishes (Ref 1792C)	30.00	180.00
10	Frying pans (Ref 1521F)	40.00	400.00
			580.00
		VAT at 17.5%	101.50
			681.50

terms:
30 days

The top copy of this invoice had been sent to J Peters & Co, but unfortunately the office copy had not been entered in the books of account.

You are required to prepare a journal entry recording the sale of goods to J Peters. Remember the following steps:

- Assume the role of the book-keeper for Cucina Zone. Identify who our customer is, in this instance, J Peters & Co, they are our debtor, ie they owe us money.

- Prepare 'T' accounts on your working paper or document (invoice). If using the assignment answer book remember to mark your paper 'workings'. The date is the date of the invoice.

- Enter the invoice figures, thinking all the time '**double-entry**'.
- The goods are being received by J Peters & Co, so the total of the invoice is **debited** to their account, ie £681.50. Remember a debit is an asset and debtors are assets to the business because they owe us money.
- **Credit** - Sales Account with the net price of the goods £580.00
- **Credit** - Value Added Tax Account with £101.50 (this is money owed to HM Revenue & Customs, the VAT authorities)

Your workings will look like this:

WORKINGS					
Dr	**J Peters & Co Account**				Cr
2009					
6 Oct	Sales	681.50			
Dr	**Sales Account**				Cr
		2009			
		6 Oct	J Peters & Co		580.00
Dr	**Value Added Tax Account**				Cr
		2009			
		6 Oct	J Peters & Co		101.50

When you have decided which account needs to be debited and which accounts need to be credited, you prepare the journal entry as follows, using the date of the invoice.

	Journal			
Date	**Details**		**Dr**	**Cr**
2009			£	£
6 Oct	J Peters & Co		681.50	
	Sales			580.00
	Value Added Tax			101.50
	Correction of error of omission, invoice not entered			

After the transaction has been entered in the journal it is normal practice to post the entry to the ledger accounts, ie

(i)   Debit – J Peters & Co Account   £681.50

(ii)   Credit – Sales Account   £580.00

        Credit – Value Added Tax Account   £101.50

The diagram below illustrates this procedure.

posting a journal entry

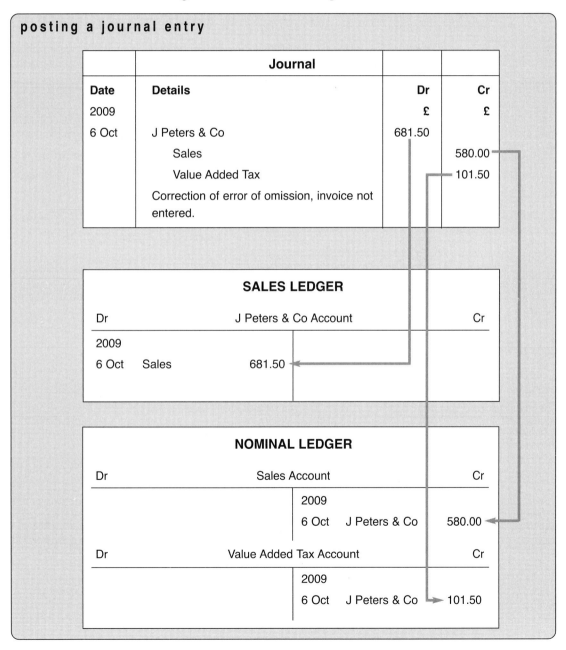

a note on the double-entry

In your assignment you are **not required** to complete the double-entry. You are only required to show the journal entry and the adjustment to the balances in the trial balance (the latter will be dealt with in Chapter 15). The ledger accounts shown in your 'workings' (see pages 155-156) are a suggested method to help you with the journal entry. In normal practice, postings to the ledger accounts are done **after** the journal entry has been completed.

credit note not entered in the accounts

Cucina Zone recently returned goods damaged in transit to the supplier, Fosters Ltd. A credit note in respect of the damaged goods was received by Cucina Zone but had not been entered in the accounts. The credit note from Fosters Ltd is shown below.

CREDIT NOTE			
		Fosters Limited	
		78 Union Street, Chesterfield CH4 8NX	
		Tel 01246 435237	
		VAT Reg 375 6471 03	

Cucina Zone Dovedale Way Derby DE3 7EP	**credit note number** C/N 739 **date** 12 October 2009

quantity	description	unit price £	£
10	Roasting tins	13.00	130.00
			130.00
	VAT at 17.5%		22.75
			152.75

reason for credit: Goods damaged in transit

You are required to prepare the journal entry.

- Assume the role of the book-keeper for Cucina Zone. Our supplier is Fosters Ltd, they are our creditor, ie we owe them money.

- Prepare 'T' accounts on your working paper or document (credit note). If you are using the assignment answer book remember to mark your paper 'workings'. The date is the date of the credit note.

- Enter the credit note, thinking all the time '**double-entry**'.

- The goods are being sent back to Fosters Ltd so the total amount on the credit note is **debited** to Fosters Ltd account ie £152.75, so reducing our liability to the company.

- **Credit** – Purchase Returns Account with the net price of the goods returned £130.00

- **Credit** – Value Added Tax Account with £22.75

Your workings will look like this:

WORKINGS				
Dr	**Fosters Limited Account**			Cr
2009				
12 Oct	Purchase returns	152.75		
Dr	**Purchase Returns Account**			Cr
		2009		
		12 Oct	Fosters Limited	130.00
Dr	**Value Added Tax Account**			Cr
		2009		
		12 Oct	Fosters Limited	22.75

The journal entry appears as shown below. Please note that you will **not** have to post the ledger accounts in your assignment.

	Journal		
Date	**Details**	**Dr**	**Cr**
2009		£	£
12 Oct	Fosters Limited	152.75	
	Purchase returns		130.00
	Value Added Tax		22.75
	Correction of error of omission, credit note not entered.		

JOURNAL ENTRIES FROM A MEMORANDUM

Occasionally financial issues arise that are different from normal trading activities, for example, the proprietor may decide to take cash or goods from the business for his or her personal use. Another instance maybe that the proprietor decides that the business could do with some extra funds and decides to contribute additional capital or a fixed asset, such as a car or equipment, into the business.

Another situation that could arise is if some transactions listed on the bank statement for which no documents have been generated - eg direct debit or standing order payments - are overlooked by the book-keeper.

All these transactions will, of course, require entry into the books of account. To ensure that the financial details are accurately recorded in the books the Accountant (or equivalent) may send a memo or email to the book-keeper setting out the details for the entries that need to be made into the ledger accounts. These situations commonly occur in your assignment for Unit 3.

the owner draws out cash for personal use

We will now look at some examples illustrating the situations described above. Firstly the proprietor, Maria Fornara, takes cash out of the business for her own use. The Accountant sends the following memo to the book-keeper.

MEMORANDUM

to   Book-keeper

from Accountant   **Date** 23 October 2009

On 23 October 2009, Maria Fornara took £100.00 cash from the business for her own use.

No entries have been made in the books. You are required to prepare the journal entry.

- Assume the role of the book-keeper for Cucina Zone.
- Prepare 'T' accounts on your working paper or document (the memo). If you use the assignment answer book remember to mark your paper 'workings'. The date is the date of the memo.

- Record the details set out in the memo, thinking all the time '**double-entry**'.
- Maria has taken £100.00 cash from the business, therefore a credit entry is required in the cash account in the cash book (payment made) and a corresponding debit in drawings account:
  - **Debit** Drawings Account with the £100.00 that Maria has received for her own personal use.
  - **Credit** Cash Account with £100.00 taken out as cash.

Your workings will look like this:

WORKINGS			
Dr	**Drawings Account**		Cr
2009			
23 Oct Cash	100.00		
Dr	**Cash Account**		Cr
		2009	
		23 Oct Drawings	100.00

Now prepare the journal entry as follows, using the date of the memo. Remember - start with the debit:

		Journal		
Date	**Details**		**Dr**	**Cr**
2009			£	£
23 Oct	Drawings		100.00	
	Bank			100.00
	Cash taken by the owner for own use.			

the owner draws out goods for personal use

In this example, Maria takes a set of pans for use at home. These pans are in the stock room of the business and have been recorded as part of the purchases of the business. This has been cleared with the Accountant who sends a memo to the book-keeper. Withdrawal of goods in this way is known as 'drawings' in the same way as the withdrawal of cash is known as 'drawings'.

MEMORANDUM

to   Book-keeper

from   Accountant   **Date** 11 November 2009

On 11 November 2009, Maria Fornara took a set of pans, valued at £82.00, from the business for her own use.

No entries have been made in the books. You are required to prepare the journal entry.

- Assume the role of the book-keeper for Cucina Zone.

- Prepare 'T' accounts on your working paper or document (the memo). If you are using the assignment answer book, remember to mark your paper 'workings'. Use the date of the memo.

- Record the details in the memo thinking all the time '**double-entry**'.

- Maria had taken goods valued £82.00 from the business for personal use. The double entry required is:

    (i)   **Debit** - Drawings Account with the £82.00 goods for own use. The goods have gone into Maria's Drawings Account.

    (ii) **Credit** – Purchases Account £82.00 - so reducing the amount of goods available for sale to customers.

Your workings will look like this:

WORKINGS

Dr   **Drawings Account**   Cr

2009		
11 Nov Purchases	82.00	

Dr   **Purchases Account**   Cr

	2009	
	11 Nov Drawings	82.00

Now prepare the journal entry as follows:

	Journal		
Date	**Details**	**Dr**	**Cr**
2009		£	£
11 Nov	Drawings	82.00	
	Purchases		82.00
	Goods taken by the owner for own use.		

the owner introduces capital into the business

'Capital' is the money invested by the owner in a business. This obviously happens when a business is first started, but an owner may from time to time 'top up' the capital of the business as and when more money is needed, eg for expansion. The capital of a business is recorded in a Capital Account. This type of payment will need a journal entry.

In this example Maria is paying in her personal cheque for £5,000 as additional capital. The Accountant prepares a suitable memo for the book-keeper:

MEMORANDUM

to   Book-keeper

from Accountant   **Date** 1 December 2009

The owner of the business, Maria Fornara, introduced a further £5,000.00 into the business by cheque.

No entries have been made in the books. You are required to prepare the journal entry.

- Assume the role of the book-keeper for Cucina Zone.
- Prepare 'T' accounts on your working paper or document (the memo). If you are using the assignment answer book remember to mark your paper 'workings'.
- Record the details in the memo thinking all the time '**double-entry**'.

- Maria had introduced a further £5,000.00 into the business by cheque. The double-entry required is:

  (i) **Debit** - Bank Account with the £5,000.00 cheque which was paid into the bank (payments into the bank are debits)

  (ii) **Credit** - Capital Account £5,000.00 - the amount invested increases the owner's capital account.

The workings will appear as follows:

WORKINGS				
Dr		**Bank Account**		Cr
2009				
1 Dec	Capital	5,000.00		
Dr		**Capital Account**		Cr
		2009		
		1 Dec	Bank	5,000.00

The journal entry will then be prepared as follows:

		Journal		
Date	**Details**		**Dr**	**Cr**
2009			£	£
1 Dec	Bank		5,000.00	
	Capital			5,000.00
	Capital of £5,000 introduced by the owner.			

You may also encounter a business owner contributing an asset, eg a computer, as capital. In this case the entries will be: Debit Computer Equipment Account; Credit Capital Account.

a note on double-entry

The above examples – cash and goods withdrawn and assets (money and computers) introduced – have involved drawings account and capital account. As with the other examples of journals in this chapter, you should note that normally after the book-keeper has written up the journal, he/she will post the entries to the ledger accounts, as shown in the workings. For the purpose of your assignment, postings to the ledger accounts is not required.

the journal – direct debits/standing orders

The final example in this chapter of the use of the journal to regularise the double-entry bookkeeping relates to direct debits and standing orders.

Most businesses make regular payments by direct debit or standing order through BACS, the automatic electronic transfer system operated by the banks. Examples of this type of payment include insurance premiums, local authority rates, and transfers for the repayment of bank loans.

Normally these payments are recorded in the cash book of the business when the bank statement arrives or by reference to an internal schedule of these payments. There may be occasions, however, when the book-keeper for some reason or other fails to enter a payment in the accounts. One way of regularising the situation is for the payment to be recorded in the journal before being entered in the accounts. If this occurs in your assignment you are likely to be instructed to do this by a memo, as in the example shown below.

Let us assume that Cucina Zone receives a bank statement which records the following payment made from the current account:

Direct debit   Payment of £315.00 for rates

This item was overlooked when the cash book was written up. The book-keeper has received the following memo from the Accountant and the payment now requires entering in the books of account following a journal entry.

MEMORANDUM

to   Book-keeper
from   Accountant   **Date** 30 October 2009

The following payment has not been entered in the books:
A direct debit payment of £315.00 for rates.

In your assignment you should:

- Assume the role of the book-keeper for Cucina Zone.

- Prepare 'T' accounts on your working paper or document (ie the memo). If using the assignment answer book remember to mark your paper 'workings'. Use the date of the memo.

- Enter the payment made on behalf of the business by the bank, thinking all the time '**double-entry**'.

- The payment made by the bank was for rates and was paid out of the bank account of the business, therefore:

  Debit Rates Account – £315.00

  Credit Bank Account – £315.00

Your workings will look like this:

WORKINGS			
Dr	**Rates Account**		Cr
2009			
30 Oct Bank	315.00		
Dr	**Bank Account**		Cr
		2009	
		30 Oct D/D Rates	315.00

The journal entry is prepared as follows:

		Journal		
Date	**Details**		**Dr**	**Cr**
2009			£	£
30 Oct	Rates		315.00	
	Bank			315.00
	Direct debit payment for rates made by the bank, not previously entered.			

After the journal entry has been prepared the transaction is posted to the bank account in the cash book and the rates account in the nominal ledger, as shown in your workings.

Note that for the purpose of this assignment, posting to the ledger accounts is not required.

ADVANTAGES OF USING THE JOURNAL

Lastly we list the main advantages of using a journal:

- it provides a book of original entry for transactions of an irregular nature

- it acts as a form of diary providing a permanent record of the transaction with reference to the documentation

- it saves relying on members of staff to remember transaction details

- it helps to avoid the risk of errors being made by ensuring that the transaction is recorded in the books of account correctly

- it reduces the risk of fraudulent transactions taking place by preventing unauthorised entries being made into the accounting system

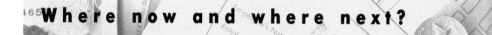

Where now and where next?

chapter summary

In this chapter we have

- introduced the journal into the accounting system and identified its uses and advantages

- shown how simple errors of omission are entered into the journal by working out the entries required

- explained the process of posting the journal entries into the ledger accounts

what is in the next chapter?

The next chapter covers further journal entries which are required for students undertaking Unit 3 – 'Make journal entries and adjustments and produce a revised trial balance' assessment.

As mentioned earlier in this chapter, errors that may occur within the business are often described as '**internal**' errors. In the next chapter we will be looking at more of these which involve:

- wrong postings

- dealing with transfers between nominal accounts

- other adjustments/correction of errors

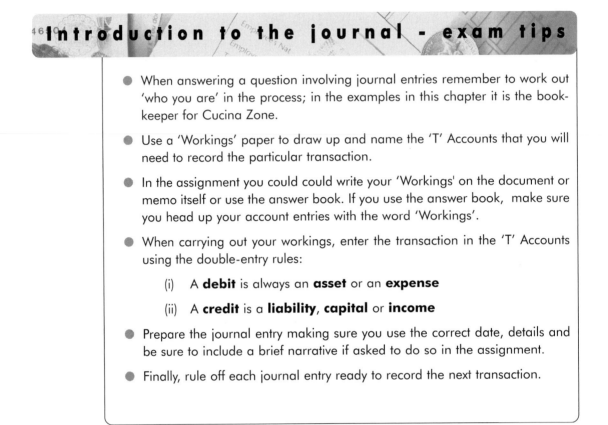

Introduction to the journal – exam tips

- When answering a question involving journal entries remember to work out 'who you are' in the process; in the examples in this chapter it is the book-keeper for Cucina Zone.

- Use a 'Workings' paper to draw up and name the 'T' Accounts that you will need to record the particular transaction.

- In the assignment you could could write your 'Workings' on the document or memo itself or use the answer book. If you use the answer book, make sure you head up your account entries with the word 'Workings'.

- When carrying out your workings, enter the transaction in the 'T' Accounts using the double-entry rules:

  (i)   A **debit** is always an **asset** or an **expense**

  (ii) A **credit** is a **liability**, **capital** or **income**

- Prepare the journal entry making sure you use the correct date, details and be sure to include a brief narrative if asked to do so in the assignment.

- Finally, rule off each journal entry ready to record the next transaction.

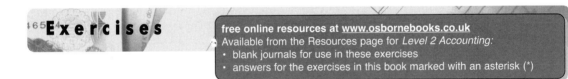

Exercises

free online resources at www.osbornebooks.co.uk
Available from the Resources page for *Level 2 Accounting:*
- blank journals for use in these exercises
- answers for the exercises in this book marked with an asterisk (*)

12.1* You are the book-keeper for a small printing business, Lewin Printers. When you are tidying your desk at the end of the week you discover that the following two purchase invoices have not been entered into the books of account.

You are required to prepare journal entries with suitable narratives for each of the two invoices shown on the next page.

You should show your workings on a separate piece of paper headed up 'Workings'.

INVOICE
MANNINGS LTD

West Street, Bury, Lancs, BL20 3TQ

VAT Reg 152 4793 260

| Lewin Printers |
| Church Street |
| Bury |
| Lance |
| BE10 17P |

invoice number   K 2071

date   3 September 2009

quantity	description	unit price £	£
10	Deluxe printing paper A4 (ream)	20.00	200.00
			200.00
	VAT at 17.5%		35.00
			235.00

terms:
30 days

INVOICE
CHANG & LAU

Office Equipment Suppliers
Market Street, Manchester M60 2KN

VAT Reg 372 8142 351

| Lewin Printers |
| Church Street |
| Bury |
| Lance |
| BE10 17P |

invoice number   3578

date   8 September 2009

quantity	description	unit price £	£
1	Computer Desk (oak)	100.00	100.00
1	Computer Chair (black)	40.00	40.00
			140.00
	VAT at 17.5%		24.50
			164.50

terms:
30 days

12.2* Yates Stationers employ you as their accounts clerk. One of your tasks is to enter all the sales invoices each month. After entering all the sales invoices into the sales day book your colleague produces another sales invoice that had been omitted from the rest of the month's invoices.

You are required to prepare a journal entry with suitable narrative for the invoice shown below..

You should show your workings on a separate piece of paper headed up 'Workings'.

INVOICE

YATES STATIONERS

Market Place, Leek, Staffs
ST23 5TG

VAT Reg 712 7068 349

Frasers Church Street Congleton Cheshire CW2 7SG	**invoice number** 09/273 **date** 28 July 2009

quantity	description	unit price £	£
2	Envelopes 110 x 220 self-seal (boxes)	7.00	14.00
36	Ballpoint pens (black)	0.45	16.20
			30.20
	VAT at 17.5%		5.28
			35.48

terms:
30 days

12.3 Yates Stationers employ you as their accounts clerk (see previous question). Another of your tasks is to enter in the accounts all the purchase credit notes received each month. After entering all the purchase credit notes into the day book and posting the accounts your colleague then produces another credit note that had been incorrectly filed and not posted to the accounts.

You are required to prepare a journal entry with suitable narrative for the credit note shown below.

You should show your workings on a separate piece of paper headed up 'Workings'.

CREDIT NOTE
Stationery Supplies Limited
67 Station Road, Newcastle
NE19 8VC

VAT Reg 342 1268 069

| Yates Stationers
Market Place
Leek
Staffs ST23 5TG | **credit note number** 105

date 27 July 2009 |

quantity	description	unit price £	£
5	Box files (black)	4.00	20.00
			20.00
	VAT at 17.5%		3.50
			23.50

reason for credit:
damaged goods

12.4* You work as a book-keeper for a computer supplies business run by Steven Moran. The company Accountant sends you the following memo:

MEMORANDUM

to   Book-keeper

from Accountant   **Date** 12 October 2009

On 12 October 2009, Steven Moran took £100.00 cash from the business for his own use.

You are required to prepare a journal entry with suitable narrative for the memo shown above.

You should show your workings on a separate piece of paper headed up 'Workings'.

12.5 You work as a book-keeper for a hair care products company run by Nikki Capelli. The company Accountant sends you the following memo:

MEMORANDUM

to   Book-keeper

from Accountant   **Date** 22 May 2009

On 22 May 2009, Nikki Capelli introduced a further £7,500.00 of capital into the business by cheque.

You are required to prepare a journal entry with suitable narrative for the memo shown above.

You should show your workings on a separate piece of paper headed up 'Workings'.

12.6* Martin works in the accounts department for a company which provides equipment for exhibitions. The accountant informed Martin by memo that the proprietor of the business, Georgio Napper, on 30 April 2009 took goods valued £63.00 out of the business for his own use.

MEMORANDUM

to   Book-keeper

from Accountant   **Date** 30 April 2009

The owner, Georgio Napper, on 30 April 2009 took goods valued £63.00 out of the business for his own use.

You are required to prepare a journal entry, with suitable narrative, to record the above transaction.

You should show your workings on a separate piece of paper headed up 'Workings'.

12.7* James works as a book-keeper for Snowdon Sports Ltd. It comes to his attention from a memo sent by the Accountant that a direct debit on the company bank statement dated 31 July 2009 has not been entered in the company's cash book.

MEMORANDUM

to   Book-keeper

from   Accountant   **Date**   31 July 2009

The following payment has not been entered in the books:
A direct debit payment of £93.00 for insurance.

You are required to prepare a journal entry, with suitable narrative, to record the above transaction.

You should show your workings on a separate piece of paper headed up 'Workings'.

12.8 Rashid works as a book-keeper for Importers Ltd. It comes to his attention from a memo sent by the Accountant that a standing order for a bank loan repayment on the company bank statement dated 30 June 2009 has not been entered in the company's cash book.

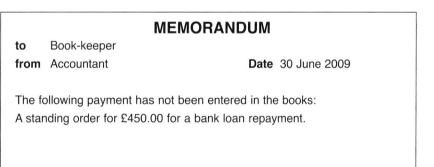

MEMORANDUM

to   Book-keeper

from   Accountant   **Date**   30 June 2009

The following payment has not been entered in the books:
A standing order for £450.00 for a bank loan repayment.

You are required to prepare a journal entry, with suitable narrative, to record the above transaction.

You should show your workings on a separate piece of paper headed up 'Workings'.

13 Journal entries – internal errors and adjustments

what this chapter covers . . .

The last chapter introduced the journal as a book of original entry in which non-regular entries are recorded.

These entries include situations such as invoices and credit notes omitted from the books, the proprietor investing further capital into the business or withdrawing cash or goods for his or her own use.

This chapter will describe further journal entries which are needed to correct errors such as duplication of entries, postings to the wrong accounts and also for making other internal adjustments such as the creation of new accounts.

The sequence of entering a transaction into the journal and the books of account is as follows. This chapter deals with the first two steps shown in the diagram:

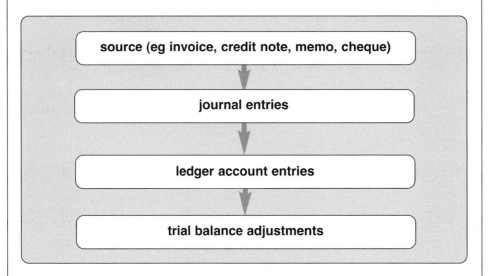

This chapter, in short, explains the processes of creating journal entries for:

● invoices and credit notes entered twice in error

● wrong postings between personal accounts, nominal accounts and cash book entries

● adjusting for incorrect transfers between personal and nominal accounts

● for the creation of new accounts

DEALING WITH JOURNAL ENTRIES

It is important to remember the procedures when dealing with journal entries. Here is a quick reminder for when you are doing exercises or an assignment:

1   Assume the role of book-keeper.

2   Highlight the name of the business.

3   Identify the double-entry adjustments needed, remembering:
    - a **debit entry** is always as **asset** or an **expense**
    - a **credit entry** is a **liability**, **capital** or **income**

4   In your 'Workings' use 'T' Accounts to decide which accounts to use and which account needs debiting and which account you will need to credit.

5   Record the journal entry making sure you use the correct date; show the debit entry first followed by the credit entry and add a brief narrative.

6   When the journal entry has been carried out it is normal practice to post the entry to the ledger accounts; however, for the purpose of your assessment you are not required to carry out these postings.

Now read the remainder of the chapter which comprises a series of short case studies based around the Cucina Zone kitchen supplies business.

JOURNALS FOR DOCUMENTS ENTERED TWICE IN ERROR

purchase invoice – entered twice in error

The invoice shown on the next page has been received by Cucina Zone from a supplier, Austin Kitchenware. The book-keeper for Cucina Zone has entered the invoice in the accounting records twice by mistake. You are required to prepare a journal entry to correct the error.

Using the rules shown at the top of this page, and all the time thinking 'double-entry', you need to decide:

- which accounts you will need to use to correct the error
- which account(s) to debit and which account(s) to credit

The goods were purchased from Austin Kitchenware for £352.50 including VAT, therefore the document is a **purchase invoice**. The following three 'T' accounts will be needed in your 'Workings' to put right this error:

- Austin Kitchenware Account
- Purchases Account
- Value Added Tax Account

INVOICE
Austin Kitchenware
Tickhill Road, Rotherham, S96 9RQ
Tel 01335 401278

VAT Reg 608 7219 73

Cucina Zone
Dovedale Way
Derby
DE3 7EP

invoice number   06113

date   3 November 2009

quantity	description	unit price £	£
6	Mechanical Scales	10.00	60.00
6	Slimline Digital Scales	25.00	150.00
6 sets	Measuring jugs	15.00	90.00
			300.00
		VAT at 17.5%	52.50
			352.50

This invoice has been entered in the books twice

terms:
30 days

The purchase invoice that was entered twice in error – see the note on the invoice.

your 'workings'

The first step is to draw up the three 'T' accounts on a separate piece of paper and write in the entries already made by the book-keeper, showing that the invoice has been entered twice in error. These accounts are set out at the top of the next page. The set of accounts at the bottom of the next page shows the adjusting account entries. The journal is shown on page 180.

Dr			**Purchases Account**			Cr
2009			2009			
3 Nov	Austin Kitchenware	300.00				
3 Nov	Austin Kitchenware	300.00				

Dr			**Value Added Tax Account**			Cr
2009			2009			
3 Nov	Austin Kitchenware	52.50				
3 Nov	Austin Kitchenware	52.50				

Dr		**Austin Kitchenware Account**			Cr
2009		2009			
		3 Nov	Purchases	352.50	
		3 Nov	Purchases	352.50	

To correct this duplication error the book-keeper needs to cancel out one of the entries in each account as follows:

- **Debit** – Austin Kitchenware Account £352.50
- **Credit** – Purchases Account £300.00
  – Value Added Tax Account £ 52.50

These adjusting entries are shown below in the 'T' accounts in bold type to distinguish them from the original entries:

WORKINGS

Dr			**Austin Kitchenware Account**			Cr
2009			2009			
3 Nov	**Purchases**	**352.50**	3 Nov	Purchases	352.50	
			3 Nov	Purchases	352.50	

Dr			**Purchases Account**			Cr
2009			2009			
3 Nov	Austin Kitchenware	300.00	**3 Nov**	**Austin Kitchenware**	**300.00**	
3 Nov	Austin Kitchenware	300.00				

Dr			**Value Added Tax Account**			Cr
2009			2009			
3 Nov	Austin Kitchenware	52.50	**3 Nov**	**Austin Kitchenware**	**52.50**	
3 Nov	Austin Kitchenware	52.50				

The journal entry is now shown to record the adjusting transactions:

Journal			
Date	**Details**	**Dr**	**Cr**
2009		£	£
3 Nov	Austin Kitchenware	352.50	
	Purchases		300.00
	Value Added Tax		52.50
	Correction of error – invoice posted twice.		

After the transaction has been entered in the journal it is normal practice to post the entries to the ledger accounts. As noted in the last chapter, this posting is not required in your OCR assessment.

credit note from supplier entered twice

Cucina Zone recently received a credit note from a supplier, Wong Yung & Co after returning goods which had been damaged in transit. The credit note from the suppliers, Wong Yung & Co, is shown below. Unfortunately it has been entered in the books of account twice by the book-keeper.

CREDIT NOTE

WONG YUNG & CO
Churchgate, Sheffield, S4 7WY
Tel 0114 923781

VAT Reg 231 3696 53

Cucina Zone
Dovedale Way
Derby
DE3 7EP

credit note number C/N 739

date   16 November 2009

quantity	description	unit price £	£
4	Citrus Juicers	20.00	80.00
	This credit note has been entered in the books twice		80.00
	VAT @ 17.5%		14.00
			94.00

reason for credit: Goods damaged in transit

You are required to correct the duplication error using a journal entry.

Think 'double-entry' and decide which accounts you will need to use to rectify the error and identify the debit and credit entries.

The damaged goods were returned to Wong Yung & Co, value £94.00 including VAT, therefore the credit note is from one of Cucina Zone's suppliers. The 'T' accounts needed to rectify this error are as follows:

- Wong Yung & Co Account
- Purchase Returns Account
- Value Added Tax Account

First of all draw up the 'T' accounts as part of your workings (on a separate piece of paper) and show the entries already made by the book-keeper as follows, remembering the credit note has been entered twice in error.

WORKINGS

Dr	**Wong Yung & Co Account**		Cr
2009		2009	
16 Nov Purchase Returns	94.00		
16 Nov Purchase Returns	94.00		

Dr	**Purchase Returns Account**		Cr
2009		2009	
		16 Nov Wong Yung & Co	80.00
		16 Nov Wong Yung & Co	80.00

Dr	**Value Added Tax Account**		Cr
2009		2009	
		16 Nov Wong Yung & Co	14.00
		16 Nov Wong Yung & Co	14.00

To correct this error the book-keeper needs to cancel one of the entries in each account and to do this the following entries are required:

- **Debit** – Purchase Returns Account   £ 80.00
  - Value Added Tax Account   £ 14.00
- **Credit** – Wong Yung & Co   £ 94.00

The adjusting entries are now shown on the 'T' accounts below in bold type to distinguish them from the original entries:

WORKINGS

Dr		Purchase Returns Account			Cr
2009			2009		
16 Nov	**Wong Yung & Co**	**80.00**	16 Nov	Wong Yung & Co	80.00
			16 Nov	Wong Yung & Co	80.00

Dr		Value Added Tax Account			Cr
2009			2009		
16 Nov	**Wong Yung & Co**	**14.00**	16 Nov	Wong Yung & Co	14.00
			16 Nov	Wong Yung & Co	14.00

Dr		Wong Yung & Co Account			Cr
2009			2009		
16 Nov	Purchase Returns	94.00	**16 Nov**	**Purchase Returns**	**94.00**
16 Nov	Purchase Returns	94.00			

The journal entry recording the above transactions is shown below. Note that the debits are entered first.

	Journal		
Date	**Details**	**Dr**	**Cr**
2009		£	£
16 Nov	Purchase Returns	80.00	
	Value Added Tax	14.00	
	Wong Yong & Co		94.00
	Correction of error: credit note entered twice.		

Also note that after the transaction has been entered in the journal it is normal practice to post the entries to the ledger accounts. Remember that this posting is not required by your OCR assessment.

sales invoice entered twice

The invoice shown below has been sent by Cucina Zone to one of its customers, Marlow Cookware. The book-keeper for Cucina Zone has entered the sales invoice in the accounting records twice by mistake. You are required to prepare a journal entry to correct the error.

Think 'double-entry' and work out which accounts you will need to use to rectify the error and what the debit and credit entries will be. These are shown on the next page.

INVOICE
Cucina Zone
Dovedale Way, Derby, DE3 7EP
Tel 01335 401278

VAT Reg 470 6352 81

Marlow Cookware
Grantham Road
Nottingham
NG7 3PN

invoice number   3016

date   8 July 2009

quantity	description	unit price £	£
2	Expresso Coffee Maker	50.00	100.00
6	Roasting tins	8.00	48.00
6	Classic flasks, 1 litre	17.00	102.00
			250.00
	VAT at 17.5%		43.75
			293.75

This invoice has been entered in the books twice

terms:
30 days

The goods were sold to Marlow Cookware for £293.75 including VAT, therefore, it is a 'sales invoice'. The following 'T' accounts will be needed to rectify this error are Sales Account, Value Added Tax Account and Marlow Cookware Account. They appear with the duplicated entry as follows:

Dr		Sales Account		Cr
		2009		
		8 Jul	Marlow Cookware	250.00
		8 Jul	Marlow Cookware	250.00

Dr		Value Added Tax Account		Cr
		2009		
		8 Jul	Marlow Cookware	43.75
		8 Jul	Marlow Cookware	43.75

Dr		Marlow Cookware Account		Cr
2009				
8 Jul	Sales	293.75		
8 Jul	Sales	293.75		

The following adjusting entries (shown in bold type) are required:

- **Debit** – Sales Account   £ 250.00
- – Value Added Tax Account   £43.75
- **Credit** – Marlow Cookware   £ 293.75

Dr		Sales Account				Cr
2009			2009			
8 Jul	**Marlow Cookware**	**250.00**	8 Jul	Marlow Cookware	250.00	
			8 Jul	Marlow Cookware	250.00	

Dr		Value Added Tax Account				Cr
2009			2009			
8 Jul	**Marlow Cookware**	**43.75**	8 Jul	Marlow Cookware	43.75	
			8 Jul	Marlow Cookware	43.75	

Dr		Marlow Cookware Account			Cr
2009			2009		
8 Jul	Sales	293.75	**8 Jul Sales**		**293.75**
8 Jul	Sales	293.75			

The journal entry is now made to record the above transactions:

	Journal		
Date	**Details**	**Dr**	**Cr**
2009		£	£
8 July	Sales	250.00	
	Value Added Tax	43.75	
	Marlow Cookware		293.75
	Correction of error – invoice entered twice.		

sales credit note entered twice

One of the items on the invoice to Marlow Cookware was damaged in transit and subsequently returned to Cucina Zone who issued Marlow Cookware with a credit note for £58.75:

CREDIT NOTE
Cucina Zone
Dovedale Way, Derby, DE3 7EP
Tel 01335 401278

VAT Reg 470 6352 81

Marlow Cookware
Grantham Road
Nottingham
NG7 3PN

credit note number   C752

date   23 July 2009

quantity	description	unit price £	£
1	Expresso Coffee Maker	50.00	50.00

> This credit note has been entered in the books twice

			£
			50.00
	VAT at 17.5%		8.75
			58.75

reason for credit: Goods damaged in transit

Unfortunately the book-keeper, who seems to be having major memory problems, entered the credit note in the accounting records twice. You are required to correct the error using a journal entry.

You should first identify the accounts you will need to use to rectify the error and then decide which to debit and which to credit. The faulty goods were returned by Marlow Cookware, one of Cucina Zone's customers, therefore, the 'T' accounts needed to rectify this error are as follows:

Dr	Marlow Cookware Account		Cr
		2009	
		23 Jul Sales Returns	58.75
		23 Jul Sales Returns	58.75

Dr	Sales Returns Account		Cr
2009			
23 Jul	Marlow Cookware	50.00	
23 Jul	Marlow Cookware	50.00	

Dr	Value Added Tax Account		Cr
2009			
23 Jul	Marlow Cookware	8.75	
23 Jul	Marlow Cookware	8.75	

The correcting entries made by the book-keeper are shown in bold type in the three accounts as follows:

Dr	Marlow Cookware Account		Cr
2009		2009	
23 Jul	**Sales Returns**	**58.75**	23 Jul Sales Returns	58.75
		23 Jul Sales Returns	58.75

Dr	Sales Returns Account		Cr
2009		2009	
23 Jul	Marlow Cookware	50.00	**23 Jul Marlow Cookware**	**50.00**
23 Jul	Marlow Cookware	50.00	

Dr	Value Added Tax Account		Cr
2009		2009	
23 Jul	Marlow Cookware	8.75	**23 Jul Marlow Cookware**	**8.75**
23 Jul	Marlow Cookware	8.75	

The journal entry will then be completed from the adjusting entries:

	Journal		
Date	**Details**	**Dr**	**Cr**
2009		£	£
23 July	Marlow Cookware	58.75	
	Sales Returns		50.00
	Value Added Tax		8.75
	Correction of error – credit note entered twice.		

As noted earlier, it is normal practice after writing up the journal to post the ledger accounts in line with your workings (shown on the previous page). This posting is not required in your OCR assessment.

Assessment Hints – dealing with invoices and credit notes entered twice in error

- When you are preparing journal entries for transactions that have been entered twice in error it is important to remember to identify which business you work for and highlight the name on your assessment.

- Identify whether the invoice is a 'purchase invoice' or a 'sales invoice'.

- If you are dealing with a credit note that has been entered twice in error, work out whether the credit note was issued by one of your suppliers– in which case it will be a 'purchase return' – or if the credit note was issued by your business, in which case it will be a 'sales return'.

- Next identify which 'T' accounts to use and using double-entry principles enter the document twice in the 'T' accounts in your 'Workings' on the assessment paper.

- In a different colour ink (if possible) enter in the 'T' accounts the adjusting entries required to correct the error.

- Use these adjusting entries to make the journal entry.

WRONG POSTINGS TO PERSONAL ACCOUNTS

purchase invoice – the wrong personal account

When book-keepers are posting transactions to ledger accounts they may post a transaction to the wrong ledger account by mistake. This sometimes happens if the name of the debtor or creditor is very similar for example 'T Johns' and 'T Johnson', or it may be purely just a careless error in posting.

For example, suppose Cucina Zone received an invoice from A J Harker & Son for £129.25 including VAT. The invoice was correctly posted to the nominal accounts but unfortunately posted to A Harker & Co's account instead of A J Harker & Son's account. You are required to correct the error using a journal entry.

Using the rules shown earlier and thinking 'double-entry' you will need to identify the accounts you will use to correct the error, and also decide which account is debited and which account is credited.

The ledger accounts affected in this transaction are:

- A Harker & Co Account
- A J Harker & Son Account

First of all draw up the 'T' accounts for the above two ledger accounts. Remember that the nominal account entries are correct so only the posting to the personal account is incorrect. In this example the invoice has been entered in error in A Harker & Co's account rather than the account of A J Harker & Son:

WORKINGS				
Dr	**A Harker & Co Account**			Cr
		2009		
		12 Aug	Purchases	129.25
Dr	**A J Harker & Son Account**			Cr

To correct this error the book-keeper needs to cancel the entry in the account of A Harker & Co and enter the invoice in the account of A J Harker & Son, which, as you can see above, does not yet have any entries recorded. This is carried out as follows:

- **Debit** – A Harker & Co Account £129.25

- **Credit** – A J Harker & Son Account £129.25

The ledger accounts then appear as follows (the adjusting entries are in bold type):

WORKINGS

Dr	**A Harker & Co Account**		Cr
2009		2009	
12 Aug A J Harker & Son 129.25		12 Aug Purchases	129.25

Dr	**A J Harker & Son Account**		Cr
		2009	
		12 Aug A Harker & Co 129.25	

The book-keeper will then write up the journal entry:

	Journal		
Date	**Details**	**Dr**	**Cr**
2009		£	£
12 Aug	A Harker & Son	129.25	
	A J Harker & Co		129.25
	Correction of error in posting.		

purchase credit note – the wrong personal account

In this example a credit note for £169.20 was issued by Oakes Ltd and sent to Cucina Zone. Since Cucina Zone purchased the goods initially from Oakes Ltd and have now returned the goods as unsuitable the credit note relates to a purchase return. The credit note was correctly posted to the nominal accounts but debited to Oldfield Ltd's account instead of Oakes Ltd's account. You are required to correct the error by preparing a journal entry.

Thinking 'double-entry' you should identify the accounts you will need to post to rectify the error and decide on the debit and credit entries.

The ledger accounts affected in this transaction are as follows:

- Oakes Ltd Account
- Oldfield Ltd Account

First of all draw up the 'T' accounts for the two ledger accounts and show the debit entry already made by the book-keeper in Oldfield Ltd's account. Remember that the nominal account entries are correct, so only the personal account posting is incorrect.

WORKINGS

Dr	Oakes Ltd Account	Cr

Dr	Oldfield Ltd Account	Cr
2009		
7 Oct Purchase Returns 169.20		

To correct this error the book-keeper needs to enter the credit note in the account of Oakes Ltd, which as you can see from the above workings, does not yet have any entries. You should cancel the entry in the account of Oldfield Ltd as follows:

- **Debit** – Oakes Ltd Account £169.20
- **Credit** – Oldfield Ltd Account £169.20

The ledger accounts then appear as follows (the adjusting entries are in bold type):

WORKINGS

Dr	Oakes Ltd Account	Cr
2009		
7 Oct Purchase Returns 169.20		

Dr	Oldfield Ltd Account	Cr
2009	2009
7 Oct Purchase Returns 169.20	**7 Oct Purchase Returns 169.20**

The book-keeper will then write up the journal entry:

Journal			
Date	**Details**	**Dr**	**Cr**
2009		£	£
7 Oct	Oakes Ltd	169.20	
	Oldfield Ltd		169.20
	Correction of error in posting.		

WRONG POSTINGS TO PERSONAL AND NOMINAL ACCOUNTS

cash received posted to a nominal account instead of a personal account

In this example Cucina Zone has received cash and issued a receipt for £147.24 in respect of payment of Invoice 3549 from a customer, Chang Kitchenware. The book-keeper entered the receipt of the cash correctly in the Cash Account but instead of posting the payment to the sales ledger account of Chang Kitchenware he incorrectly posted it to the Sales Account in the Nominal Ledger (see the Memo and receipt below). You are required to correct the error by preparing a journal entry.

MEMORANDUM

to: Book-keeper

from: Accountant   Date: 22 September 2009

The attached receipt was correctly entered in the Cash Book but incorrectly posted to Sales Account.

RECEIPT

Received from	Chang Kitchenware
The sum of	£147.24
	One hundred and forty seven pounds, twenty four pence.
	Trade debtor in cash settlement of Invoice 3549, account Chang Kitchenware.
Signed	J Barlow
Date	22 September 2009

The 'T' accounts to be used to amend the error in this example are:

- Sales Account
- Chang Kitchenware Account

First draw up the 'T' accounts for the two ledger accounts and show the credit entry made in error by the book-keeper in the Sales Account. The posting to the Cash Account for recording receipt of the cash is correct. The 'Balance b/d' refers to the balance that was being paid off by the cash.

WORKINGS

Dr	Sales Account		Cr
	2009		
	22 Sep	Cash	147.24

Dr	Chang Kitchenware Account		Cr
2009			
1 Sep	Balance b/d	147.24	

To correct this error the book-keeper needs to cancel the entry in the Sales Account and enter the receipt in the account of the debtor, Chang Kitchenware, which as you can see in the account shown above, does not yet have any cash entry recorded. The adjusting entries that need to be made are:

- **Debit** – Sales Account £147.24
- **Credit** – Chang Kitchenware Account £147.24

The above entries are now shown on the 'T' accounts in bold type to distinguish them from the original entries:

WORKINGS

Dr	Sales Account		Cr
2009		2009	
22 Sep Chang Kitchenware 147.24		22 Sep Cash	147.24

Dr	Chang Kitchenware Account		Cr
2009		2009	
1 Sep Balance b/d	147.24	**22 Sep Sales**	**147.24**

The journal entry is now shown to record the above transactions:

	Journal		
Date	**Details**	**Dr**	**Cr**
2009		£	£
22 Sep	Sales	147.24	
	Chang Kitchenware		147.24
	Correction of error in posting.		

invoice posted to the wrong nominal account

Another type of error that sometimes occurs is when an invoice or credit note is correctly posted to the personal account but posted to the wrong nominal account.

For example an invoice dated 16 September for £167.80 was received by Cucina Zone from Fosters Garages in respect of servicing one of the firm's vans. The invoice was correctly posted to Fosters Garages Account in the Purchase Ledger but the whole amount of £167.80 (which included VAT of £24.99) was incorrectly posted to Motor Vehicles Account in the Nominal Ledger instead of Motor Expenses Account.

You are required to correct the error using a journal entry.

Thinking 'double-entry' you should identify the accounts you will need to post to rectify the error and then decide on the debit and credit entries. The ledger accounts affected in this transaction are:

- Motor Vehicle Account (this records vehicles bought for the business)
- Motor Expenses Account (this records items such as fuel and insurance)
- Value Added Tax Account

To correct the error the book-keeper will need to enter the total of the invoice, before VAT is added, ie £142.81, to the Motor Expenses Account and enter the VAT amount, £24.99, in the Value Added Tax Account and then cancel the entry in the Motor Vehicle Account as follows:

- **Debit** – Motor Expenses Account £ 142.81
- **Debit** – Value Added Tax Account £ 24.99
- **Credit** – Motor Vehicle Account £ 167.80

Note that the personal account has been correctly posted, so only the nominal accounts will be affected. The adjusting entries are shown in bold type (see next page).

Dr	Motor Expenses Account		Cr
2009			
16 Sep	Motor Vehicle	142.81	

Dr	Value Added Tax Account		Cr
2009			
16 Sep	Motor Vehicle	24.99	

Dr		Motor Vehicle Account			Cr
2009			2009		
16 Sep	Fosters Garage	167.80	16 Sep	Motor Expenses	142.81
			16 Sep	Value Added Tax	24.99

The book-keeper will then make the appropriate entry in the journal:

Date	Journal Details	Dr	Cr
2009		£	£
16 Sep	Motor Expenses	142.81	
	Value Added Tax	24.99	
	Motor Vehicles		167.80
	Correction of error – invoice posted to Motor Vehicles instead of Motor Expenses and Value Added Tax Accounts		

JOURNAL ENTRIES FROM A MEMORANDUM ('MEMO')

There are occasions when certain types of errors are identified by the accountant which require correction in the accounting records and are notified to the book-keeper by **memorandum**, or more often these days by email. In these cases the memorandum (or email) will contain the details of the error and a request to the book-keeper to adjust the accounts accordingly.

Your assessment may ask you to carry out journal adjustment through a memorandum ('memo'). Examples of these are illustrated in the text that follows.

correction of nominal account posting – expenses

In this example of a memo adjustment an expense has been posted to the wrong nominal account and will need a journal adjustment.

MEMORANDUM

to: Book-keeper

from: Accountant   Date: 18 December 2009

The private motor expenses of Maria Fornara, the proprietor, have been correctly entered in the Cash Book but incorrectly posted to General Expenses. These amounted to £141.30. Please amend the records accordingly.

The ledger accounts affected in this transaction are:

• Drawings Account (used for private expenses paid by the business)

• General Expenses Account

Draw up 'T' accounts for the above ledger accounts. In this example the entry in the Cash Book is correct but the expenses have been posted to the wrong nominal account.

To correct this error the book-keeper will need to enter the expenses in Maria's Drawings Account (Nominal Ledger) since they are private motor expenses and then cancel the entry in the General Expenses Account as follows:

• **Debit**   – Drawings Account   £141.30

• **Credit** – General Expenses Account   £141.30

The entries will appear as follows in your workings; the adjusting entries are shown in bold type to distinguish them from the original(wrong) entry, which is in light type. Note that the date used is the date of the memo.

Dr	**Drawings Account**		Cr
2009			
18 Dec General Expenses 141.30			

Dr	**General Expenses Account**		Cr
2009		2009	
18 Dec Bank 141.30		**18 Dec Drawings 141.30**	

The journal entry will be as follows:

Journal		Dr	Cr
Date	**Details**	**Dr**	**Cr**
2009		£	£
18 Dec	Drawings	141.30	
	General Expenses		141.30
	Correction of error – private motor expenses posted to General Expenses instead of Drawings Account.		

correction of nominal account posting – sales

We will now look at a memo involving an office photocopier sold by Cucina Zone. In this case the transaction has been entered correctly in the Cash Book and also the Value Added Tax Account, but the net amount has been incorrectly posted to the Sales Account, which should only be used for the sale of kitchen equipment.

The memo reads as follows:

MEMORANDUM

to: Book-keeper

from: Accountant   Date: 3 August 2009

On 3 August 2009 the old office photocopier was sold for £150 cash plus VAT.

This transaction was correctly entered in the Cash Book and the Value Added Tax Account but the net amount was incorrectly posted to the Sales Account instead of the Office Equipment Account.

Please amend the records accordingly.

The 'T' accounts required to amend this error are as follows:

- Sales Account
- Office Equipment Account

To correct this error the book-keeper will only need to enter the net amount (ie the £150 before VAT) in the Sales Account to cancel the entry and then enter the net amount in the Office Equipment Account. The full amount and the VAT amount have already been correctly entered in the accounts and so will not need adjusting.

The entries are therefore:

- **Debit** – Sales Account £150.00
- **Credit** – Office Equipment Account £150.00

The entries will appear as follows in your workings; the adjusting entries are shown in bold type to distinguish them from the original(wrong) entry, which is in light type. Note that the date used is the date of the memo.

Dr	Sales Account			Cr
2009			2009	
3 Aug	**Office Equipment**	**150.00**	3 Aug Cash	150.00

Dr	Office Equipment Account		Cr
2009		2009	
		3 Aug Sales	**150.00**

The journal entry will be as follows:

	Journal			
Date	**Details**		**Dr**	**Cr**
2009			£	£
3 Aug	Sales		150.00	
	Office Equipment			150.00
	Correction of error – sale of old photocopier wrongly posted to Sales Account instead of Office Equipment Account.			

correction of bank and cash account postings

In the memo on the next page Cucina Zone receives a cheque from one of its debtors, N Patel Ltd for £340.00. The cheque was correctly entered in the account of N Patel Ltd in the Sales Ledger but incorrectly posted to the Cash Account instead of Bank Account.

In your assignment the actual cheque may be attached to the memo.

<table>
<tr><td colspan="2" align="center">MEMORANDUM</td></tr>
<tr><td>to:</td><td>Book-keeper</td></tr>
<tr><td>from:</td><td>Accountant   Date: 8 October 2009</td></tr>
</table>

A cheque for £340 was received from N Patel Ltd and was correctly entered in N Patel Ltd Account in the Sales Ledger, but incorrectly posted to the Cash Account.

Please make the necessary account adjustments to correct this error.

To correct this error the book-keeper will need to enter the cheque in the Bank Account and credit the Cash Account to cancel the error. the entries are as follows:

- **Debit**   – Bank Account   £340.00

- **Credit**   – Cash Account   £340.00

The entries will appear as follows in your workings; the adjusting entries are shown in bold type to distinguish them from the original(wrong) entry, which is in light type. Note that the date used is the date of the memo.

Dr		Bank Account			Cr
2009			2009		
8 Oct	**Cash - N Patel Ltd**	**340.00**			

Dr		Cash Account			Cr
2009			2009		
8 Oct	N Patel Ltd	340.00	8 Oct	Bank - N Patel Ltd	340.00

The journal entry will be as follows:

		Journal		
Date	**Details**		**Dr**	**Cr**
2009			£	£
8 Oct	Bank		340.00	
	Cash			340.00
	Correction of error – cheque received from N Patel Ltd wrongly posted to Cash Account.			

ACCOUNT TRANSFERS THROUGH THE JOURNAL

The accountant of a business normally decides the allocation of expenses to the various nominal accounts in the accounting records. There are occasions, however, when the accountant may want to vary the way the expenses are allocated. There are two main situations which can arise:

1 **splitting an account**

A single account which records different types of expense is split into new separate accounts. The old account can then be closed off. For example, stationery and postage may be charged to a 'Postage and Stationery Account' but then this may be split into two new accounts 'Postage Account' and 'Stationery Account'.

2 **creating a new account for one type of expense**

In this situation a new account is created but the old account is left open for the remaining expenses. For example, the accountant may have a 'General Expenses' account for all types of expense but then set up a new account for, say, insurance, and leave the old 'General Expenses' account still running.

Journal entries will be required for both these situations, which we will deal with in turn. These entries are normally communicated to the book-keeper by email or by memo. Your assignment is likely to use a memo for this purpose.

journal entries for splitting an account

In this example 'Postage and Stationery Account' is to be split into two new accounts 'Postage Account' and 'Stationery Account', leaving the old account to be closed off. The accountant sends the following memo:

MEMORANDUM	
to: Book-keeper	
from: Accountant	Date: 30 September 2009

Postage and stationery costs have previously been kept together in one account, the total costs incurred amount to £3,489.20. Due to the increased cost of postages these items are now to be allocated separate accounts.

Postage costs incurred have been calculated to be £1,223.90.

The 'T' accounts needed to make this transfer are Postage Account (a new account), Stationery Account (a new account) and Postage and Stationery Account (the existing account). Up until now all the costs of postage and stationery will have been debited to the Postage and Stationery Account (remember a debit is always an asset or expense). The accountant has now decided to charge the expenses to separate accounts, ie a Postage Account and a Stationery Account. To carry out this transfer it will be necessary to:

* **Debit** the postage costs of £1,223.90 to the Postage Account (an expense is a debit)
* **Debit** the stationery costs £2,265.30 (£3,489.20 − £1,223.90) to the Stationery Account (an expense is a debit)
* **Credit** £3,489.20 to the Postage and Stationery Account, bringing the balance of the account to nil

The account workings are as shown below. The adjusting entries are in bold type. Note that the abbreviation of 'transfer' is 'Tfr'.

Dr		**Postage Account**			Cr
2009			2009		
30 Sep	**Tfr: Postage and**				
	Stationery	**1,223.90**			

Dr		**Stationery Account**			Cr
2009			2009		
30 Sep	**Tfr: Postage and**				
	Stationery	**2,265.30**			

Dr		**Postage and Stationery Account**			Cr
2009			2009		
31 Aug	Balance b/d	3,489.20	**30 Sep**	**Tfr: Postage and**	
				Stationery	**3,489.20**

The journal entry will be as follows:

	Journal			
Date	**Details**		**Dr**	**Cr**
2009			£	£
30 Sep	Postage		1,223.90	
	Stationery		2,265.30	
	Postage and Stationery			3,489.20
	Postage and stationery costs to be recorded in separate accounts.			

journal entries for creating a single new account

In the memo shown below you will see that motor expenses have always been charged to General Expenses Account, but because the running costs of vehicles has risen, the accountant has decided to transfer them to a Motor Expenses Account, but keep the General Expenses Account going.

MEMORANDUM	
to: Book-keeper	
from: Accountant	Date: 30 September 2009

Motor expenses have previously been charged to the General Expenses Account.

As costs have increased recently it has been decided to open a new Motor Expenses Account and transfer the costs incurred so far this year to the new account. These costs amount to £1,867.00.

To carry out this transfer it will be necessary to:

- **Debit** Motor Expenses Account £1,867.00 (an expense is a debit)
- **Credit** General Expenses Account £1,867.00

The account workings and journal are shown below. The adjusting entries in the accounts are in bold type. Note that the abbreviation of 'transfer' is 'Tfr'.

Dr	**Motor Expenses Account**	Cr
2009		2009
30 Sep Tfr: General		
Expenses	**1,867.00**	

Dr	**General Expenses Account**	Cr
2009		2009
		30 Sep Tfr: Motor
		Expenses 1,867.00

	Journal			
Date	**Details**		**Dr**	**Cr**
2009			£	£
8 Oct	Motor Expenses		1,867.00	
	General Expenses			1,867.00
	Motor Expenses to be recorded in a separate account.			

Where now and where next?

chapter summary

In this chapter we have dealt with journal entries required as a result of internal errors and adjustments:

- documents entered twice in error, eg invoices and credit notes
- wrong postings to personal accounts and to nominal accounts
- memos requiring corrections in the accounts
- memos requiring adjustments and transfers in the nominal accounts
- memos requiring the creation of new accounts

what is in the next chapter?

The next chapter covers journal entries which are required as a result of **external** factors and further examples of **internal** adjustments, for example:

- bad debts written off where no payment has been received or where partial payment has been received
- returned cheques received 'Refer to Drawer' ('R/D')
- purchase and sale of fixed assets
- disallowed cash discounts
- errors corrected by 'reversal of entries'

Exam tips

- Assume the role of the book-keeper and identify from the question paper the name of the business where the book-keeper works.

- Identify the type of document – write on it what it is, ie a sales invoice, sales credit note, purchase invoice, credit note from supplier.

- Write out the 'T' accounts on your question paper marking them 'Workings' and decide on the debit and credit entries. Remember: debit entries are always assets or expenses and credit entries are liabilities, capital or income.

- If dealing with invoices and credit notes that have been entered twice then show the entries already made by the book-keeper. Then using a different colour pen make the entries required to correct the error.

- For other errors show the entry or entries already made into the account. Use a different colour pen to make the entries needed to correct the error.

- Finally prepare the journal entry to correct the error taking care to use the correct date and include an appropriate narrative.

In all the following exercises you should show your double-entry account workings on a separate piece of paper headed up 'Workings'.

13.1 (a)* The invoice shown below has just been received by Cucina Zone from a supplier, NGS Supplies. Unfortunately, Cucina Zone's book-keeper has entered the invoice twice by mistake.

You are required to prepare a journal entry, with suitable narrative, to correct the error.

INVOICE
NGS Supplies
Bank Street, Derby, DE4 8FN
Tel 01335 401700

VAT Reg 310 4652 10

Cucina Zone Dovedale Way Derby DE3 7EP	**invoice number** 73120 **date** 6 July 2009

quantity	description	unit price £	£
10	Chopping Boards	18.20	182.00
10	Tin openers	4.40	44.00
			226.00
	VAT at 17.5%		39.55
			265.55

terms:
30 days

> This invoice has been
> entered in the books
> twice

13.1 (b)* The tin openers supplied by NGS Supplies were different from those shown in the catalogue and were subsequently returned. NGS Supplies sent a credit note to Cucina Zone to rectify the situation. The book-keeper entered the credit note shown below in the books of account twice by mistake.

You are required to prepare a journal entry, with suitable narrative, to correct the error.

CREDIT NOTE

NGS Supplies

Bank Street, Derby, DE4 8FN

Tel 01335 401700

VAT Reg 310 4652 10

Cucina Zone Dovedale Way Derby DE3 7EP	**credit note number** 0937 **date** 30 July 2009

quantity	description	unit price £	£
10	Tin openers	4.40	44.00
			44.00
	VAT at 17.5%		7.70
			51.70

This credit note has been entered in the books twice

reason for credit:

Product design different from that ordered

13.2 (a) The sales invoice below was sent by Cucina Zone to one of its customers, Newton & Beech, on 11 May 2009. The book-keeper for Cucina Zone entered the sales invoice in the accounting records twice by mistake.

You are required to prepare a journal entry, with suitable narrative, to correct the error.

INVOICE
Cucina Zone
Dovedale Way, Derby, DE3 7EP
Tel 01335 401278

VAT Reg 470 6352 811

Newton & Beech
New Road
Matlock
ML23 7JT

invoice number   2977

date   11 May 2009

quantity	description	unit price £	£
6	Spice racks	34.00	204.00
6	Utensil sets	5.00	30.00
			234.00
		VAT at 17.5%	40.95
			274.95

This invoice has been entered in the books twice

terms:
30 days

13.2 (b)   Unfortunately two of the spice racks charged on the invoice to Newton & Beech were found to be faulty and the goods were returned to Cucina Zone who issued the credit note for £79.90 (including VAT) shown below. Unfortunately the book-keeper entered the credit note twice in the accounting records.

You are required to prepare a journal entry, with suitable narrative, to correct the error.

CREDIT NOTE
Cucina Zone
Dovedale Way, Derby, DE3 7EP
Tel 01335 401278

VAT Reg 470 6352 81

Newton & Beech
New Road
Matlock
ML23 7JT

credit note number   C471

date   21 May 2009

---

quantity	description	unit price £	£
2	Spice racks	34.00	68.00
		68.00
	VAT at 17.5%	11.90
		79.90

This credit note has been entered in the books twice

reason for credit:
damaged goods

13.3* Cucina Zone received an invoice from Gosling Ltd shown below for £199.75 including VAT. The invoice had been posted correctly to the nominal accounts but unfortunately posted to the account of Goggins Ltd instead of Gosling Ltd.

You are required to prepare a journal entry, with suitable narrative, to correct the error.

INVOICE
GOSLING LIMITED
Clayton Road, Burslem, Stoke-on-Trent ST7 3WT
Tel 01782 899760

UAT Reg 759 2173 41

Cucina Zone Dovedale Way Derby DE3 7EP	**invoice number** 67053 **date** 26 October 2009

quantity	description	unit price £	£
10	Flan dishes (small)	5.00	50.00
10	Flan dishes (large)	12.00	120.00
			170.00
		VAT at 17.5%	29.75
			199.75

This invoice has been posted to the account of Goggins Ltd in error

terms:
30 days

13.4 Cucina Zone received a credit note, shown below, from Robinson & Co for £75.20. The book-keeper correctly posted the credit note to the nominal accounts but unfortunately posted it to the account of Robertson & Co by mistake.

You are required to prepare a journal entry to rectify the error.

CREDIT NOTE
Robinson & Co
Smedley Street, Buxton, BX7 1NB
Tel 01298 673842

VAT Reg 651 5443 23

Cucina Zone Dovedale Way Derby DE3 7EP	**credit note number** CN439 **date** 15 May 2009

quantity	description	unit price £	£
2	Family Slow Cookers	32.00	64.00
			64.00
	VAT at 17.5%		11.20
			75.20

This credit note has posted to the account of Robertson & Co in error

reason for credit:
wrong size supplied

13.5* On 29 May 2009 Cucina Zone received cash of £27.00 from one of its customers, Shah Supplies. The book-keeper entered the receipt of the cash correctly in the cash book but instead of posting the payment to the personal account they posted it to the Sales Account. A memo from the accountant is shown below. It has the receipt attached to it.

You are required to prepare a journal entry, with suitable narrative, to amend the posting.

MEMORANDUM

to: Book-keeper

from: Accountant   Date: 29 May 2009

The attached receipt was correctly entered in the Cash Book but incorrectly posted to Sales Account. Please adjust the accounts accordingly.

RECEIPT

Cucina Zone
Dovedale Way, Derby, DE3 7EP
Tel 01335 401278

VAT Reg 470 6352 81

Received from   Shah Supplies

The sum of   £27.00
                   Twenty seven pounds only

Trade debtor in cash settlement of Invoice 49126

Signed   J Barlow
Date   29 May 2009

13.6 Cucina Zone recently had some repairs carried out on one of its vehicles by Smithy Garage and has received the invoice shown below. The invoice was correctly posted to Smithy Garage's Account but incorrectly posted, including the VAT, to Motor Vehicles Account instead of to Motor Expenses Account.

You are required to prepare a journal entry, with suitable narrative, to amend the posting.

INVOICE
Smithy Garage

High Street, Macclesfield, MC1 8TU

Tel 01625 750114

VAT Reg 882 4546 713

Cucina Zone
Dovedale Way
Derby
DE3 7EP

invoice number   10A/530

date   20 May 2009

---

quantity	description	unit price £	£
	Replacing 2 brake discs		
	Vehicle XF08 CNU		
	Parts and labour		120.00
			120.00
	VAT at 17.5%		21.00
			141.00

This invoice has been posted to Motor Vehicles Account in error, instead of to Motor Expenses Account

terms:
30 days

13.7* John works as book-keeper for Brough Services Ltd. It comes to his attention from a memo sent by the Accountant that the private motor expenses of the proprietor had been posted to the wrong nominal account. The memo is shown below:

MEMORANDUM

to: Book-keeper

from: Accountant   Date: 4 June 2009

The private motor expenses of Ben Brough, the proprietor, have been correctly

entered in the cash book but incorrectly posted to Sundry Expenses.

These amount to £168.22.

Please adjust the accounts accordingly.

You are required to prepare a journal entry, with suitable narrative, to correct the error.

13.8 You work as book-keeper for Far Destinations a local travel agency. The company accountant sends you the following memo:

MEMORANDUM

to: Book-keeper

from: Accountant   Date: 27 July 2009

On 27 July some of the old office furniture was sold for £100 cash plus VAT.

The transaction was correctly entered in the Cash Book and the Value Added Tax

Account but the net amount was incorrectly posted to Stationery Account instead

of Office Furniture Account.

Please adjust the accounts accordingly.

You are required to prepare a journal entry, with suitable narrative, to correct the error.

13.9 Ravi works as a book-keeper for Trasler Ltd. It comes to Ravi's attention from a memo sent by the accountant that a cheque received from one of their customers has not been dealt with properly. The memo from the Accountant is shown below.

MEMORANDUM

to: Book-keeper

from: Accountant   Date: 12 August 2009

The cheque below has been received from J Oliver & Co. It has been correctly posted to J Oliver & Co's Account but incorrectly posted to the Cash Account.

Please adjust the accounts accordingly.

SOUTHERN BANK PLC   date 6 August 2009   83-21-07
16 Broad Street, Mereford, MR1 7TR
Widnes L45 7GH

Pay   Trasler Limited   only

Three hundred and twenty eight pounds 52p ———   £ 328.52

                                                           J OLIVER & CO

                                                           J Oliver

528301   832107   33907102

You are required to prepare a journal entry, with suitable narrative, to correct the error.

13.10* Chloe works as a book-keeper for Bignell Ltd. The company Accountant has decided that the costs of hiring a delivery van which have previously been recorded in the General Expenses Account should now be charged to a separate Van Hire Account. The details are shown in the memo below:

MEMORANDUM

to: Book-keeper

from: Accountant   Date: 3 September 2009

The cost of van hire has previously been charged to the General Expenses Account. I have now decided, however, that these charges need to be recorded in a separate Van Hire Account. The delivery van hire costs have been calculated to be £2,283.30.

Please make the necessary transfer through the journal.

You are required to prepare a journal entry, with suitable narrative, to carry out the transfer.

13.11 Kate works as a book-keeper for the Parks Veterinary Practice. The cleaning and maintenance costs have until now been charged to a Cleaning and Maintenance Account. The practice Accountant has now decided to split the account and charge these costs to two separate accounts. The details are shown in the memo below:

MEMORANDUM

to: Book-keeper

from: Accountant   Date: 20 May 2009

Cleaning and maintenance costs have previously been kept together in one account, Cleaning and Maintenance Account. The total costs incurred so far on this account amount to £1,309.20. Due to the increased cost of cleaning these items are now to be allocated to separate accounts, Cleaning Account and Maintenance Account.

Cleaning costs incurred have been calculated to be £437.60.

Please make the necessary adjustments through the journal.

You are required to prepare a journal entry, with suitable narrative, to transfer the costs of cleaning to a separate Cleaning Account.

14 Journal entries – further examples

The last chapter described journal entries for errors and adjustments which were the result of internal factors such as:

- an invoice or credit note entered twice in error or being omitted altogether

- a transaction which had been posted to an incorrect nominal or personal account

- transferring balances from existing accounts into new accounts

This chapter describes further examples of journal entries, some of which have been brought about because of external factors outside the control of the business and some which relate to internal adjustments:

- bad debts written off – writing off the whole debt of a customer

- partial bad debts – where the customer pays off some of the debt and the rest is written off as bad

- bad debts recovered – where the debt has been completely written off and then the customer unexpectedly pays up and the debt is reinstated

- returned (Refer to Drawer) cheques – where there is not enough money in the customer's bank account to meet a cheque issued to the seller

- the purchase of fixed assets such as property, vehicles and computers

- the sale of fixed assets

- early settlement (cash) discount which has been taken by a customer but disallowed by the seller

- correction of errors, known as 'reversal of entries'

As in previous chapters, the case study Cucina Zone, a wholesaler in kitchen equipment and utensils, will be used to illustrate the journal entries.

JOURNAL ENTRIES FOR BAD DEBTS

By now you should be familiar with the process of dealing with a transaction involving a journal entry; however, if you need a reminder refer to pages 153-156.

Journal entries will be needed to record the actions taken in both the following areas:

- **Bad debts** - it may be that a customer is unable to pay his/her account and in this instance the whole outstanding amount will need to be written off as a bad debt.

- **Partial bad debt** - some customers may only be able to pay a proportion of the outstanding amount and therefore any unpaid balance will have to be written off as a 'partial' bad debt.

In both these cases journal entries will be needed to record the account entries made. We will deal with each of them in turn.

journal entry for writing off bad debts

The accountant of Cucina Zone, Sarah Blake, has just received notification that one of the firm's customers has been declared bankrupt. Sarah sends the following memo to the book-keeper giving instructions to write the debt off as a bad debt.

MEMORANDUM		
to:	Book-keeper	
from:	Accountant	Date: 4 August 2009

Stevens & Co who owe us £389.45 have been declared bankrupt. Since it looks most unlikely that the outstanding amount will be paid, please write off the whole of the outstanding balance as a bad debt.

Using double-entry rules, the following 'T' accounts will be needed to process the transaction:

- **Debit** Bad Debts Account £389.45 – this is an 'expense' account
- **Credit** Stevens & Co Account – this is the customer account which has to be written off: it already has a debit balance ('Balance b/d') of £389.45 and so the credit entry for £389.45 will reduce the balance to nil

The double-entry accounts are shown on the next page with the adjusting debit and credit entries in bold type.

Dr	**Bad Debts Account**		Cr
2009			
4 Aug	**Stevens & Co**	389.45	

Dr	**Stevens & Co Account**		Cr
2009			
1 Aug	Balance b/d	389.45	**4 Aug Bad Debts** 389.45

The journal entry to record this transaction is as follows:

	Journal			
Date	**Details**		**Dr**	**Cr**
2009			£	£
4 Aug	Bad Debts		389.45	
	Stevens & Co			389.45
	Account of Stevens & Co written off as bad			

The journal entry would then be posted to the ledger accounts as shown at the top of the page, but this is not required in your assignment.

journal entry for partial bad debt

Occasionally a debtor may be able to pay something towards an outstanding debt but not able to pay off the debt in full. This is called a **partial bad debt**.

In the following memo you will see that Strachan & Partners owe Cucina Zone £226.75 but are only able to pay part of the outstanding amount. The remainder will have to be written off as a partial bad debt.

MEMORANDUM

to: Book-keeper

from: Accountant   Date: 9 December 2009

Strachan & Partners, who owe us £226.75, have been declared bankrupt. A cheque for £126.75 has been received in part settlement of the debt. The remainder is to be written off as a bad debt.

No entries have been made in the books.

In this example a cheque for £126.75 has been received from Strachan & Partners in part payment and no entry has been made in the accounting records. The accounts that will be needed are:

- Bank Account – the cheque will have to be paid in
- Bad Debts Account – the partial bad debt will need to be written off
- Strachan & Partners Account – the balance will need to reduced to zero

Using double-entry rules, the following 'T' accounts will be needed to process the transaction:

- **Debit** Bank Account £126.75 (the cheque is paid into the bank; money *into* the bank account is a debit)

- **Debit** Bad Debts Account, an 'expense' account. The amount written off to this account is the total amount owed by Strachan & Partners *less* the amount of the cheque:

	Total amount owed by Strachan & Partners	£226.75
less	Amount of cheque received	£126.75
equals	Amount written off to Bad Debts Account	£100.00

- **Credit** Strachan & Partners Account – this is the customer account which has to be written off to a nil balance. There will be two credits totalling the debt of £226.75: £126.75 (Bank) and £100.00 (Bad Debts).

The double-entry accounts are shown below with the adjusting debit and credit entries in bold type. Note that the debit entry for £226.75 in light type in Strachan & Partners Account is the outstanding balance on 1 December.

Dr	Bank Account		Cr
2009			
9 Dec Strachan & Partners 126.75			

Dr	Bad Debts Account		Cr
2009			
9 Dec Strachan & Partners 100.00			

Dr	Strachan & Partners Account		Cr
2009		2009	
1 Dec Balance b/d 226.75		**9 Dec Bank**	**126.75**
		9 Dec Bad Debts	**100.00**

The journal entry is shown on the next page.

	Journal		
Date	**Details**	**Dr**	**Cr**
2009		£	£
9 Dec	Bank	126.75	
	Bad Debts	100.00	
	Strachan & Partners		226.75
	Part payment of debt; the remainder written		
	off as a bad debt.		

journal entry for bad debts recovered

There are occasions when a debt has been written off as bad but is subsequently recovered because the debtor is able to find the money and pay up. When this happens it will be necessary to reinstate the original debt in the debtor's account. When the payment is received from the debtor it is entered in the Bank Account and then posted to the debtors account to clear the amount outstanding.

Cucina Zone recently wrote off an amount of £94.50 which had been outstanding for over twelve months by one of their customers, Rogers Ltd. Quite unexpectedly a cheque arrived in the post for the total amount which Rogers Ltd had previously owed the firm. The accountant informs the book-keeper of the details in the following memo:

MEMORANDUM

to: Book-keeper

from: Accountant   Date: 9 July 2009

We have to-day received a cheque for £94.50 from one of our debtors, Rogers Ltd. The cheque is in payment of an old outstanding amount that was written off as a bad debt some time ago.

Please use the journal to reinstate the original debt and record receipt of the cheque.

The book-keeper will need to record the above transaction in two stages as follows:

1   Reinstate the original debt in the account of Rogers Ltd and transfer the bad debt recovered to a Bad Debts Recovered Account. This is illustrated in bold in the 'T' accounts shown on the next page:

Dr	Rogers Ltd Account		Cr
2009			
9 July	**Bad Debt Recovered**	**94.50**	

Dr	Bad Debts Recovered Account		Cr
		2009	
		9 July	**Rogers Ltd**	**94.50**

2. On receipt of the cheque from Rogers Ltd the book-keeper will need to record the cheque in the Bank Account; this is a debit entry because the cheque is going 'into' the bank. Then the cheque will be posted as a credit to Rogers Ltd Account to clear the outstanding balance (which was reinstated in [1] above). This second set of entries is illustrated in bold type in the 'T' accounts shown below:

Dr	Bank Account		Cr
2009			
9 July	**Rogers Ltd**	**94.50**	

Dr	Rogers Ltd Account		Cr
2009		2009	
9 July	Bad Debt Recovered 94.50	**9 July** **Bank**	**94.50**

The end-result of these entries is that the money is now in the bank and Rogers Ltd Account is back down to a nil balance. The two separate journal entries to record the above transactions are as shown below (note that the two entries are separated by a ruled line):

	Journal		
Date	**Details**	**Dr**	**Cr**
2009		£	£
9 July	Rogers Ltd	94.50	
	Bad Debts Recovered		94.50
	Reinstatement of bad debt now recovered.		
9 July	Bank	94.50	
	Rogers Ltd		94.50
	Cheque received in payment of outstanding debt previously written off.		

journal entry for returned (dishonoured) cheques

There are occasions when a business writes out a cheque but does not have sufficient funds in its bank account to meet the payment. When this happens the bank is unable to process the payment and returns the cheque marked '**Refer to drawer**' to the bank of the business which paid it in. This is known as a '**dishonoured cheque**' or '**returned cheque**'.

Cucina Zone received a cheque from one of its customers, Heath Ltd, in payment of an outstanding amount but unfortunately the cheque was returned by the customer's bank marked 'Refer to drawer' and then deducted by the bank from the bank account of Cucina Zone. This means that the debt remains unpaid, and an adjustment will have to be made to the account of Heath Ltd. The accountant informs the book-keeper of the situation in the following memo:

MEMORANDUM

to: Book-keeper

from: Accountant   Date: 23 November 2009

This cheque from Heath Ltd has been received from the bank unpaid and marked 'Refer to Drawer'.

Please adjust the accounts accordingly.

SOUTHERN BANK PLC   date 10 November 2009   83-77-03

Milsom Street, Bath **REFER TO DRAWER**

Pay   Cucina Zone   only

Account payee only

Five hundred and twenty one pounds 50p   £ 521.50

HEATH LIMITED

E Heath

842313   837703   70164033

Before this cheque was first paid in, Heath Ltd's account had an outstanding balance in Cucina Zone's Sales Ledger of £521.50. This is shown in the 'T' account 'workings' on the next page. On receipt of the cheque (on 17 November) the book-keeper entered it in the Bank Account (on the debit side – cheque paid into the bank) and posted the payment in the debtor's account (credit side). This is also illustrated in the 'T' accounts shown below. Heath Ltd's account at this point then has a nil balance with no debt outstanding. But then the bank returns the cheque to Cucina Zone as unpaid ('Refer to Drawer'). The book-keeper will then need to enter the returned cheque in the Bank Account on the credit side to cancel out the receipt and post the cheque to Heath's account to reinstate the amount originally owed.

This is illustrated in the following 'T' accounts. The original entries are in light type and the adjusting entries shown in bold.

Dr		Heath Ltd Account			Cr
2009			2009		
1 Nov	Balance b/d	521.50	17 Nov	Bank	521.50
23 Nov	**Bank**	**521.50**			

Dr		Bank Account			Cr
2009			2009		
17 Nov	Heath Ltd	521.50	**23 Nov**	**Heath Ltd (R/D)**	**521.50**

The journal entry to record the above transactions is as follows:

	Journal		
Date	**Details**	**Dr**	**Cr**
2009		£	£
23 Nov	Heath Ltd	521.50	
	Bank		521.50
	Bank returned customers cheque (Refer to Drawer)		

The amount £521.50 is shown above in Heath Ltd's account as outstanding and Cucina Zone will now have to find ways of recovering the debt.

FIXED ASSET JOURNAL ENTRIES

fixed assets

An **asset** is an item owned by a business and is recorded as a debit entry in the accounting system. A **fixed asset** is an item owned by a business for the long term (ie a year or more). Examples of fixed assets include property, vehicles and computers.

journal entry for purchase of fixed assets

The purchase of fixed assets by firms for use within the business is fairly infrequent and the purchase transactions are recorded in the journal as the book of prime (or original) entry.

Cucina Zone recently purchased two display units for use in the showroom from Gray & Grant. The invoice is shown below. The accountant, Sarah Blake, asks the book-keeper to record the transaction in the accounting records using a journal entry.

INVOICE

Gray and Grant

Trinity Square, Coventry, CV4 5DK
Tel 01245 861149

VAT Reg 229 3957 49

Cucina Zone Dovedale Way Derby DE3 7EP	**invoice number** 4378 **date** 27 July 2009

quantity	description	unit price £	£
2	RM61 Display Units	500.00	1,000.00
			1,000.00
		VAT at 17.5%	175.00
			1,175.00

terms:
30 days

Using the rules for dealing with journal entries and thinking 'double-entry', you need to identify the 'T' accounts required to record this transaction.

The display units are fixed assets and will need to be recorded in the Office Furniture Account. You will notice from the invoice that VAT is charged therefore, the Value Added Tax Account will also be needed.

The equipment is being bought on credit from Gray & Grant so an account for Gray & Grant, the supplier, will also be required.

The double-entry accounts entries required for your 'workings' are:

- **Debit** – Office Furniture Account £1,000.00
  The equipment is an asset of the business and an asset is always a debit entry.

- **Debit** – Value Added Tax Account £175.00 – this is a debit entry because it can be claimed back from the VAT authorities and so is an amount owed to Cucina Zone.

- **Credit** – Gray & Grant Account £1,175.00
  The amount due to be paid to the supplier is a liability which is always a credit entry.

These entries are shown in the 'T' accounts in bold type:

Dr		Office Furniture Account		Cr
2009				
27 July	**Gray & Grant**	**1,000.00**		

Dr		Value Added Tax Account		Cr
2009				
27 July	**Gray & Grant**	**175.00**		

Dr		Gray & Grant Account		Cr
		2009		
		27 July Office Furniture	**1,175.00**	

The journal entry to record the above transactions is as follows:

	Journal		
Date	**Details**	**Dr**	**Cr**
2009		£	£
27 July	Office Furniture	1,000.00	
	Value Added Tax	175.00	
	Gray and Grant		1,175.00
	Purchase of display equipment on credit		
	from Gray & Grant.		

journal entry for sale of fixed assets

If a business has no further use for some of its office furniture then one option available is to sell it.

Cucina Zone has purchased two new display units and decides to sell some old cabinets on credit to a new business Singh & Co for £300.00 plus VAT. The book-keeper sends Singh & Co an invoice for the equipment which is shown below.

	INVOICE **Cucina Zone** Dovedale Way, Derby, DE3 7EP Tel 01335 401278 VAT Reg 470 6352 81

Singh & Co Granby Row Leicester LE2 8BY	**invoice number** 56241 **date** 9 October 2009

quantity	description	unit price £	£
1 lot	Office furniture	300.00	300.00
			300.00
		VAT at 17.5%	52.50
			352.50

terms:
30 days

The invoice will require entry into the books of account as follows:

- **Debit** – Singh & Co. £352.50

  The old cabinets have been sold to Singh & Co on credit, so they are now Cucina Zone's debtors – a debit entry.

- **Credit** – Office Furniture £300.00

  The sale of the old cabinets reduces the amount of equipment owned by the company and the income from the sale is recorded in the Office Furniture Account. It is income to Cucina Zone and therefore a credit entry.

  Note that in later studies of accounting you will find that the sale of fixed assets is normally carried out through a 'Disposals Account' set up specifically for the purpose.

- **Credit** – Value Added Account £52.50

  The amount of VAT charged on the sale is a liability as it is due to be paid to the VAT authorities, it is therefore a credit entry.

These entries are shown in the 'T' accounts in bold:

Dr	Singh & Co Account			Cr
2009				
9 Oct	**Office Furniture**	**352.50**		

Dr	Office Furniture Account			Cr
		2009		
		9 Oct Singh & Co		**300.00**

Dr	Value Added Tax Account			Cr
		2009		
		9 Oct Singh & Co		**52.50**

The journal entry to record the above transactions is as follows:

	Journal		
Date	**Details**	**Dr**	**Cr**
2009		£	£
9 Oct	Singh & Co	352.50	
	Office Furniture		300.00
	Value Added Tax		52.50
	Sale of second-hand display equipment		
	on credit – no longer required.		

This entry would then normally be posted to the ledger accounts, but this procedure is not required in your assignment.

JOURNAL ENTRIES FOR DISALLOWED CASH DISCOUNTS

journal entry for discount received disallowed

Cash discount is a discount given to a debtor who pays an invoice within a specified period of time, for example 'Terms: 2.5% cash discount if paid within 14 days'. Occasionally a business will deduct the cash discount when making a payment but for various reasons, such as making a payment outside the terms stated, the cash discount is disallowed by the supplier. When this happens the cash discount deducted will then have to be paid to the supplier.

Recently Cucina Zone deducted £27.50 cash discount from a payment made to one of its suppliers, Carson Bros. Unfortunately the company has informed Cucina Zone that they are disallowing the discount because the payment was not received within the specified 14 days. The Cucina Zone accountant informed the book-keeper of this in the following memo:

MEMORANDUM

to: Book-keeper

from: Accountant   Date: 8 September 2009

On 27 August 2009 £27.50 cash discount was deducted from a payment to Carson Bros. We have been informed that the discount has been disallowed.

The discount was entered in the discount received account and the supplier's account.

Please use the journal to adjust the amount owing to Carson Bros.

In this example £27.50 cash discount was deducted from the amount owing to Carson Bros by Cucina Zone. You can see in the Carson Bros 'T' account on the next page that the amount originally owed to them (credit side) amounted to £1,100.00. In accordance with their payment terms, 2.5% could be deducted as cash discount if paid within 14 days. The cash discount amounted to £27.50 and was deducted from the £1,100.00 outstanding balance and a cheque sent to the supplier for £1,072.50.

This payment would have been recorded in the books of account as follows:

- **Debit** Carson Bros Account   – £1,072.50 cheque paid
                                      – £27.50 cash discount taken

- **Credit** Bank Account   – £1,072.50 cheque paid
                                      (money out of the bank)

- **Credit** Discount Received Account – £27.50 cash discount taken

This is shown in the 'T' accounts in your 'workings' as follows:

Dr	Carson Bros Account		Cr
2009		2009	
27 Aug Bank	1,072.50	1 Aug Balance b/d	1,100.00
27 Aug Discount Received	27.50		

this is the amount of the original invoice 'brought down' on 1 August

Dr	Bank Account		Cr
		2009	
		27 Aug Carson Bros	1,072.50

Dr	Discount Received Account		Cr
		2009	
		27 Aug Carson Bros	27.50

On 8 September 2009 Cucina Zone was informed that the £27.50 cash discount it had taken when paying its creditor, Carson Bros, had been disallowed – the payment has been received too late (see memo on the previous page). The double-entry requirements to record this transaction in your 'workings' are shown in the 'T' accounts below in bold. They are:

- **Debit** Discount Received Account £27.50
- **Credit** Carson Bros Account £27.50

Dr	Carson Bros Account		Cr
2009		2009	
27 Aug Bank	1,072.50	1 Aug Balance b/d	1,100.00
27 Aug Discount Received	27.50		
	1,100.0		1,100.00
		8 Sep Discount Received	**27.50**

Dr	Bank Account		Cr
		2009	
		27 Aug Carson Bros	1,072.50

Dr	Discount Received Account		Cr
2009		2009	
8 Sep	**Carson Bros**	**27.50**	27 Aug Carson Bros	27.50

The journal entry to record the disallowed discount is as follows:

Journal			Dr	Cr
Date	**Details**		**Dr**	**Cr**
2009			£	£
8 Sep	Discount Received		27.50	
	Carson Bros			27.50
	Cash discount disallowed by supplier.			

To summarise the above transaction: in this example cash discount of £27.50 has been taken by Cucina Zone when it made a payment to one of its suppliers, Carson Bros. Unfortunately, because Cucina Zone did not adhere to the terms of payment (it paid too late) the discount was disallowed by the supplier and the discount had to be 'added back' in the accounts to what Cucina Zone owed to Carson Bros.

In the next example, the discount disallowed situation is reversed and Cucina Zone disallows a customer's cash discount.

journal entry for discount allowed 'disallowed'

Cucina Zone allows its debtors to deduct cash discount of 2.5% from the amount owing provided the invoices are paid within 14 days.

Davies Cookshop, one of Cucina Zone's customers, recently paid its account having deducted cash discount; however, the payment was received after 14 days. As a result Cucina Zone has disallowed the discount. The accountant, Sarah Blake, informs the book-keeper of the details in the following memo:

MEMORANDUM

to: Book-keeper

from: Accountant   Date: 9 December 2009

I have to-day received a cheque from Davies Cookshop for £848.25 in payment of their outstanding account for £870.00. They have taken £21.75 cash discount to which they are not entitled because the account has been paid outside our terms of payment (14 days).

This transaction has already been entered in both the customer's account and the discount allowed account.

As we have disallowed the discount please make the necessary journal entry and adjust the accounts.

You will see from the memo that the original amount owed by Davies Cookshop was £870.00. This is shown in the accounts below as a 'brought down balance' entry on 1 November.

On 9 December 2009 Cucina Zone received a cheque for £848.25 from Davies Cookshop in settlement of the amount owing of £870.00. The difference of £21.75 (£870.00 – £848.25) is cash discount that has been deducted. Using double-entry rules, this payment would have been recorded in the accounts as follows:

- **Debit** Bank Account   – £848.25 cheque received
- **Debit** Discount Allowed Account   – £21.75 discount taken
- **Credit** Davies Cookshop Account   – £848.25 cheque paid
- **Credit** Davies Cookshop Account   – £21.75 discount allowed

The 'T' accounts in your 'workings' will appear as follows (including the original balance brought down of Davies Cookshop Account):

Dr	**Bank Account**		Cr
2009			
9 Dec	Davies Cookshop	848.25	

Dr	**Discount Allowed Account**		Cr
2009			
9 Dec	Davies Cookshop	21.75	

Dr	**Davies Cookshop Account**		Cr
2009			2009
1 Nov	Balance b/d	870.00	9 Dec Bank 848.25
			9 Dec Discount Allowed 21.75

this is the amount of the original invoice 'brought down' on 1 November

As you can see from the memo Davies Cookshop paid the invoice well after 14 days and Cucina Zone disallowed the discount. The following entries will be required to record the cash discount being disallowed:

- **Debit**   Davies Cookshop Account   £21.75

- **Credit**   Discount Allowed Account   £21.75

The double entry requirements to record this transaction in your 'workings' are shown in the 'T' accounts on the next page in bold.

Dr		Bank Account			Cr
2009					
9 Dec	Davies Cookshop	848.25			

Dr		Discount Allowed Account			Cr
2009			2009		
9 Dec	Davies Cookshop	21.75	**9 Dec Davies Cookshop**		**21.75**

Dr		Davies Cookshop Account			Cr
2009			2009		
1 Nov	Balance b/d	870.00	9 Dec Bank		848.25
			9 Dec Discount Allowed		21.75
		870.00			870.00
9 Dec	**Discount Allowed**	**21.75**			

The journal entry to record the above transactions is as follows

	Journal			
Date	**Details**		**Dr**	**Cr**
2009			£	£
9 Dec	Davies Cookshop		21.75	
	Discount Allowed			21.75
	Cash discount taken by customer disallowed			

To summarise the above transaction: in this example cash discount of £21.75 has been taken by Davies Cookshop when they made a payment to Cucina Zone. They did not adhere to the terms of payment (they paid too late) and so the discount was disallowed by Cucina Zone and had to be 'added back' by Cucina Zone to the account of Davies Cookshop as an amount still owing.

sorting out discount received and discount allowed

It is often difficult to distinguish between discount received and discount allowed, so you may find it useful to remember the following points:

- **Discount received**

    If you are a business paying the invoice of a supplier (creditor), the payment may be reduced by a set percentage, eg 2.5%, if you pay early, eg within 14 days. This is known as 'Discount Received' – because you receive it and that amount of money stays in your bank account. It is recorded in your Discount Received Account as a credit entry as it is effectively income received by you.

- **Discount allowed**

  If you are a business receiving payment from a customer (debtor), the payment may be reduced by a set percentage, eg 2.5%, if the customer pays early, eg within 14 days. This is known as 'Discount Allowed' – because you allow it and receive less money into your bank account. It is recorded in your Discount Allowed Account as a debit entry as it is effectively an expense to you.

'REVERSAL OF ENTRIES' ADJUSTMENTS

One of the errors that sometimes occurs within an accounting system is what is known as 'reversal of entries'. This is the situation where a transaction is entered on the wrong side of an account. The double-entry is complete in that both the debit and credit entries have been carried out but both entries have been entered on the wrong side of each account.

To correct an error such as this is different from any of the other corrections that we have looked at in Unit 3 because the error has to be corrected **twice**:

1 the incorrect entry has to be cancelled out

2 the transaction needs to be entered on the correct side of each account

This is explained in the examples shown below. We will first look at the situation where an entry is made on the wrong side of the Bank Account.

standing order on the wrong side of the Bank Account

The accountant from Cucina Zone has just noticed that an entry in the Bank Account has been entered on the wrong side and has sent the following memo to the book-keeper:

MEMORANDUM
to: Book-keeper
from: Accountant   Date: 21 July 2009
A standing order payment for Insurance of £168.00 has been entered on the debit side of the Bank Account and the credit side of the Insurance Account.   Please make the necessary entries to correct the error.

The entries mentioned in the memo are obviously wrong. The standing order payment for insurance £168.00 should have been entered on the credit side of the Bank Account (money out of bank = credit). The entry in the insurance account should have been on the debit side (expenses = debit). The error will need to be corrected in two stages:

1 First of all the original entry will have to be cancelled out as follows:

- **Debit** Insurance Account   £168.00
- **Credit** Bank Account   £168.00

The corrections are shown in bold type and the original entries in light type:

Dr		Bank Account			Cr
2009			2009		
21 Jul	S/O Insurance	168.00	**21 Jul**	**Insurance:**	
				error corrected	**168.00**

incorrect entry

Dr		Insurance Account			Cr
2009			2009		
21 Jul	**Bank:**		21 Jul	Bank	168.00
	error corrected	**168.00**			

incorrect entry

2 The transaction has then to be entered correctly as follows, **on the same side** of the account as the first correcting entry:

- **Debit** Insurance Account   £168.00
- **Credit** Bank Account   £168.00

This second correction is shown in the 'T' accounts below in bold type:

Dr		Bank Account			Cr
2009			2009		
21 Jul	S/O Insurance	168.00	21 Jul	Insurance:	
				error corrected	168.00
			21 Jul	**S/O Insurance**	**168.00**

incorrect entry

Dr		Insurance Account			Cr
2009			2009		
21 Jul	Bank:		21 Jul	Bank	168.00
	error corrected	168.00			
21 Jul	**Bank**	**168.00**			

incorrect entry

In summary: to correct this error it has been necessary to enter each of the transactions twice, first to cancel the wrong entry and secondly to enter the payment correctly. The journal entries are as shown below. Note that in this case there is a single narrative to cover both sets of account entries and there is no line drawn between the two sets of entries.

	Journal		
Date	**Details**	**Dr**	**Cr**
2009		£	£
21 Jul	Insurance	168.00	
	Bank		168.00
	Insurance	168.00	
	Bank		168.00
	Correction of reversal of entries:		
	S/O Insurance entered in the Bank Account		
	on the wrong side in error.		

debtor's cheque on the wrong side of the Bank Account

In this example Cucina Zone has received a cheque for £421.40 from one of its debtors, P Webb. Unfortunately the cheque has been entered on the wrong side in both the Bank Account and the debtor's account. The accountant informs the book-keeper of the error in the memo shown below:

MEMORANDUM
to: Book-keeper
from: Accountant   Date: 29 May 2009
A cheque for £421.40 received from P Webb, a debtor, in settlement of her account, has been entered on the debit side of P Webb's account and the credit side of the Bank Account.
Please amend the accounting records.

Again this is an error where there has been a 'reversal of entries' which will need to be amended in your 'workings' in two stages. Firstly, the incorrect entry has to be cancelled and secondly the transaction needs to be entered on the correct side of each account (see the next page).

The balance outstanding on 1 May is shown in P Webb's account as 'Balance b/d £421.40' on the debit side of the account because P Webb is a debtor.

The entries in the account are clearly incorrect. The cheque received from P Webb should have been entered on the debit side of the Bank Account. P Webb has paid the balance owing of £421.40 in full. This entry should have been on the credit side of the account so leaving a nil balance.

The error will need to be corrected in two stages:

1 First of all the original entry will have to be cancelled out as follows:

- **Debit** Bank Account   £421.40
- **Credit** P Webb Account   £421.40

The correcting entries are shown in the 'T' accounts below in bold type. The original incorrect entries are shown in lighter type and are labelled.

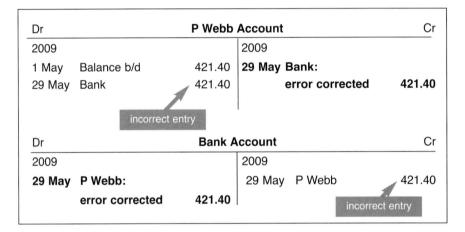

Dr	P Webb Account				Cr
2009			2009		
1 May	Balance b/d	421.40	**29 May Bank:**		
29 May	Bank	421.40		**error corrected**	**421.40**

incorrect entry

Dr	Bank Account				Cr
2009			2009		
29 May	**P Webb:**		29 May	P Webb	421.40
	error corrected	**421.40**			

incorrect entry

2 The transaction then needs to be entered correctly **on the same side** of the account as the first correcting entry:

- **Debit** Bank Account   £421.40
- **Credit** P Webb Account   £421.40

This second correction is shown in the 'T' accounts below in bold type:

Dr	P Webb Account				Cr
2009			2009		
1 May	Balance b/d	421.40	29 May	Bank:	
29 May	Bank	421.40		error corrected	421.40
			29 May	**Bank**	**421.40**

incorrect entry

Dr	Bank Account				Cr
2009			2009		
29 May	P Webb:		29 May	P Webb	421.40
	error corrected	421.40			
29 May	**P Webb**	**421.40**			

incorrect entry

In summary: to correct this error it has been necessary to enter each of the transactions twice, first to cancel the wrong entry and secondly to enter the payment correctly. The journal entries are as shown below. Note that in this case there is a single narrative to cover both sets of account entries and no line drawn between the two sets of entries.

Journal				
Date	**Details**		**Dr**	**Cr**
2009			£	£
29 May	Bank		421.40	
	P Webb			421.40
	Bank		421.40	
	P Webb			421.40
	Correction of reversal of entries:			
	Cheque received entered in the Bank			
	Account on the credit side in error.			

Where now and where next?

chapter summary

In this chapter we have explained account and journal entries relating to:

● bad and partial bad debts written off

● bad debts recovered – the situation where the customer unexpectedly pays up and the debt is reinstated

● returned (Refer to Drawer) cheques – where there is not enough money in the customer's bank account to meet a cheque issued to the seller

● the purchase and sale of fixed assets such as office equipment

● cash discount (allowed and received) which has been disallowed

● correction of errors, known as 'reversal of entries'

what is in the next chapter?

The next chapter deals with:

● ledger accounts and adjustments resulting from journal entries

● the creation of new ledger accounts resulting from journal entries

● the format of the trial balance, using correct headings, account balances, adjustments, and then preparing a simple revised trial balance

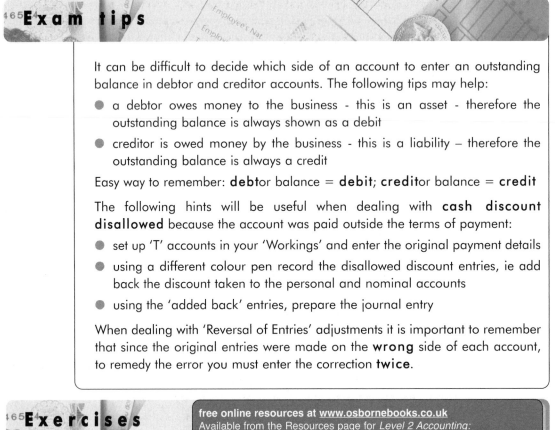

It can be difficult to decide which side of an account to enter an outstanding balance in debtor and creditor accounts. The following tips may help:

● a debtor owes money to the business - this is an asset - therefore the outstanding balance is always shown as a debit

● creditor is owed money by the business - this is a liability – therefore the outstanding balance is always a credit

Easy way to remember: **deb**tor balance = **debit**; **credit**or balance = **credit**

The following hints will be useful when dealing with **cash discount disallowed** because the account was paid outside the terms of payment:

● set up 'T' accounts in your 'Workings' and enter the original payment details

● using a different colour pen record the disallowed discount entries, ie add back the discount taken to the personal and nominal accounts

● using the 'added back' entries, prepare the journal entry

When dealing with 'Reversal of Entries' adjustments it is important to remember that since the original entries were made on the **wrong** side of each account, to remedy the error you must enter the correction **twice**.

465**Exercises**

free online resources at www.osbornebooks.co.uk
Available from the Resources page for *Level 2 Accounting:*
• blank journals for use in these exercises
• answers for the exercises in this book marked with an asterisk (*)

In all the following exercises you should show your workings on a separate piece of paper headed up 'Workings'. Be sure to carry out the journal entries required in your answer including the date, accounts to be debited/credited and a suitable narrative.

14.1* Antonio works as book-keeper for Woodburn Products. The accountant sends the following memo to Antonio informing him that one of the company's debtors has just been declared bankrupt. You are required to prepare a journal entry, with suitable narrative, to write off the debt.

MEMORANDUM	
to: Book-keeper	
from: Accountant	Date: 17 November 2009
Kitchen Designs who owe us £430.00 have been declared bankrupt. Please write the debt off as a bad debt.	

14.2 Harry is the book-keeper for Jones & Co, and has just received the following memo from the firm's accountant informing him that a customer has just been declared bankrupt.

MEMORANDUM

to: Book-keeper

from: Accountant

Date: 30 September 2009

B Arber who owes us £312.78 has been declared bankrupt. Please write the debt off as bad.

You are required to prepare a journal entry, with suitable narrative, to write off the debt.

14.3* Bertie works as a book-keeper for Hunt & Nanadra Ltd. The company accountant sends Bertie the following memo:

MEMORANDUM

to: Book-keeper

from: Accountant

Date: 28 July 2009

Topson & Sons who owe the company £344.80 have been declared bankrupt. The attached cheque has been received in full and final settlement of the debt. The remainder is to be written off as a bad debt. No entries have been made yet in the books.

NORTHERN BANK PLC
Princes Street, Bolton

date 20 July 2009

97-76-54

Pay Hunt & Nanadra Ltd

only

One hundred and seventy two pounds 40p

£ 172-40

Account payee only

TOPSON & SONS

J Topson

710473 977654 98427031

You are required to prepare a journal entry, including a suitable narrative, to record the necessary adjustments.

14.4 Ying works as an accounts clerk for Murray Printers, a small printing company. On 21 October 2009 the company accountant informs Ying that a customer has been declared bankrupt. The accountant sends the following memo to Ying outlining the details:

MEMORANDUM

to: Accounts clerk

from: Accountant   Date: 21 October 2009

Edward Carr Ltd, who owed the business £452.10 has been declared bankrupt. A cheque for £224.90 has been received in full settlement of the debt. The remainder is to be written off as a bad debt.

No entries have been made in the books.

You are required to prepare a journal entry, including a suitable narrative, to record the above.

14.5* Morgan Supplies recently wrote off an outstanding account owed by Kemal Ltd. The debt of £182.00 had been outstanding for the previous six months and the accountant of Morgan Supplies considered it unlikely to ever be paid. However, quite unexpectedly a cheque for the total outstanding amount arrived in the post. The accountant informs the book-keeper of the details in the following memo:

MEMORANDUM

to: Book-keeper

from: Accountant   Date: 8 December 2009

I have today received a cheque for £182.00 from one of our debtors, Kemal Ltd. The cheque is in full payment of our invoice no. K7865 which was recently written off as a bad debt.

No entries have been made in the books.

You are required to prepare journal entries, including suitable narratives, to record the above.

14.6   Fred works in the accounts department for Berry Bros a company which sells photographic equipment. The accountant informs Fred that a cheque from one of the company's debtors, Robert Black & Co, has just been returned from the bank marked 'Refer to drawer'.

The accountant sends Fred the following memo attaching the returned cheque and asks him to carry out the necessary entries to record the transaction:

MEMORANDUM

to: Book-keeper

from: Accountant   Date: 16 June 2009

The bank has returned this credit customer's cheque unpaid.

No entries have been made in the books. Please make the necessary adjustments.

SOUTHERN BANK PLC
Milsom Street, Bath   date 28 May 2009   83-77-03

Pay   Berry Bros   only

Sixty four pounds and ten pence only   £ 64.10

Account payee only

REFER TO DRAWER

ROBERT BLACK & CO

R Black

401752   837703   60424381

You are required to prepare a journal entry, with suitable narrative, to record the necessary adjustments to the accounts.

14.7*   Negus & Co recently purchased a new photocopier on credit for use in the office from Yates Ltd. The accountant asks Charles, the book-keeper, to record the transaction in the accounting records via a journal entry.

The details of the invoice for the photocopier from Yates Ltd are as follows: date 9 October, total before VAT £280.00, VAT £49.00 and invoice total £329.00.

You are required to prepare the journal entries, together with a suitable narrative, to record this transaction.

14.8   Guan & Sons have recently replaced some of their office equipment and decided to sell off their old office equipment to Burns & Co on credit. Mark is the book-keeper for Guan & Sons and the accountant asks him to record the sale of the second-hand office equipment in the books of account using a journal entry.

The details of the invoice for the sale of the old office equipment are as follows: date 7 October, total before VAT £120.00, VAT £21.00 and invoice total £141.00.

You are required to prepare the journal entry, using a suitable narrative, to record the above transaction.

14.9*   Richard is the book-keeper for SW Supplies and has just received the following memo from the company's accountant:

MEMORANDUM
to: Book-keeper
from: Accountant   Date: 30 November 2009
On 16 November 2009 £7.00 cash discount was deducted from a payment to Palmer & Co. We have been informed that the discount has been disallowed.
The discount was entered in the discount account and the supplier's account.
Please amend the accounting records.

You are required to enter the above transaction in the journal together with a suitable narrative.

14.10   Michael is employed by Baldwin Bros as their accounts clerk and has just received the following memo from the company's accountant:

MEMORANDUM
to: Book-keeper
from: Accountant   Date: 9 July 2009
Casby Curtains Ltd have taken £22.50 cash discount to which they are not entitled; this has been entered in both the customer's account and the discount account. We have disallowed the discount.
Please amend the records accordingly.

You are required to prepare the journal entry, with a suitable narrative, to record this transaction.

14.11* Shamir works as book-keeper for Charlie Cope Ltd. The accountant sends the following memo to Shamir pointing out that an error has been made in one of the entries in the company's Bank Account:

MEMORANDUM

to: Book-keeper

from: Accountant   Date: 19 November 2009

A standing order payment for rates of £212.00 has been entered on the debit side of the Bank Account and on the credit side of the Rates Account.

Please make the necessary entries to correct the error.

You are required to prepare the journal entries, with suitable narrative, to correct the error.

14.12 George works as an accounts clerk for Moore Motors Ltd. The accountant sends the following memo to George informing him that a cheque received from one of the company's debtors has been entered on the wrong side of the Bank Account.

MEMORANDUM

to: Book-keeper

from: Accountant   Date: 29 May 2009

This cheque has been entered on the debit side of J Fielding's account and the credit side of the Bank Account. Please amend the accounting records, making the necessary adjustments.

SOUTHERN BANK PLC
Milsom Street, Bath

date 28 May 2009   83-76-54

Pay   Moore Motors Ltd   only

Ninety seven pounds and thirty pence only   £ 97.30

J FIELDING

J Fielding

900348   837654   01599102

You are required to prepare journal entries, with suitable narrative, to correct the error.

15 The trial balance and journal adjustments

what this chapter covers . . .

The previous chapters covering the requirements of Unit 3 'Make Journal Entries and Adjustments and Produce a Trial Balance' have dealt with the procedures for the construction of journal entries arising from different situations. This chapter considers the effect of the journal entries on the ledger accounts and the adjustments required when transferring the balances to the trial balance.

This chapter firstly provides:

● an introduction to the trial balance and a definition of the trial balance

it then goes on to describe:

● the structure of the trial balance

● how to deal with debit and credit entries

● the effect of the journal entries on the trial balance (using Case Study worked examples)

The diagram below is a reminder of how this all fits in with the accounting process explained so far in this book.

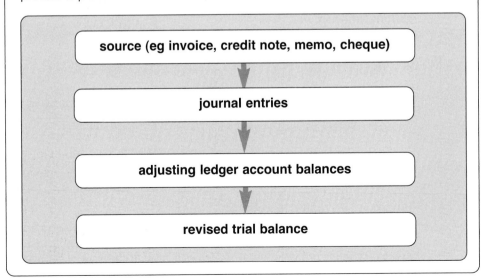

source (eg invoice, credit note, memo, cheque)
journal entries
adjusting ledger account balances
revised trial balance

THE TRIAL BALANCE - HOW IT WORKS

The topic of the **trial balance** was introduced in 'Chapter 5 'Balancing the Trial Balance' and features in basic form in the Unit 1 Examination.

In this chapter we will explain the adjustments made to a trial balance using the journal entries and the effect the journal entries have on the trial balance.

definition

A trial balance is a list of balances taken from the accounting ledgers: sales (debtors) ledger, purchase (creditors) ledger, nominal ledger.

The balances are shown in either the debit or credit columns of the trial balance and, provided no errors have occurred in the book-keeping entries, the totals of the two columns should agree. The trial balance not only provides a check on the accuracy of the book-keeping entries, it also provides information to enable the business to produce financial statements for the owners and other interested parties.

the structure of the trial balance

The case study Cucina Zone, a wholesaler in kitchen equipment and utensils, will again be used in this chapter.

Study the trial balance layout shown below and read the notes that follow.

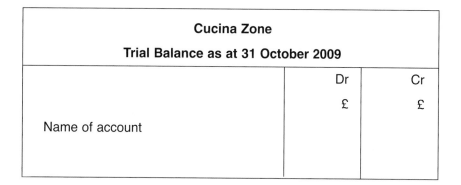

Cucina Zone		
Trial Balance as at 31 October 2009		
	Dr	Cr
	£	£
Name of account		

The trial balance has three columns: one for the name of the account and two money columns, one for debit entries and one for credit entries. The totals of the two money columns should balance, ie they should be the same.

It is important to write in the correct heading at the top of the trial balance: the full name of the business is entered, ie Cucina Zone, together with the date the trial balance was drawn up, ie 31 October 2009.

trial balance – debit column or credit column?

The following table shows in which money column – debit or credit – the various account balances should be entered. In order to avoid unnecessary errors these entries should always be made carefully, legibly and accurately. You will see that the entries follow the double-entry rules used when posting accounts and making journal entries:

- **debits** = assets (items owned) and expenses to the business
- **credits** = capital, liabilities (items owed) and income to the business

---

TRIAL BALANCE ENTRIES

debit balances include:	**credit balances include:**
Assets	**Capital and liabilities**
Premises	Capital invested by the owner(s)
Machinery	Loans
Office Equipment	-
Office Furniture	-
Motor Vehicles	-
Stock	-
Debtors	Creditors
Bank (money in the bank)	Bank Overdraft
Cash held	Value Added Tax
Expenses	**Income**
Purchases	Sales
Sales Returns	Purchase Returns
Discount Allowed	Discount Received
Rent and Rates	Rent Received
Advertising	-
Bad Debts	-
General Expenses	-
Insurance	-
Motor Expenses	-
Postage and Stationery	-
Wages and Salaries	-
Drawings	-

Note the following situations where a balance can appear **on either side**:

* The **Value Added Tax Account** is shown on the credit side, indicating that there is a net VAT **liability,** ie the business owes VAT to HM Revenue and Customs. Businesses which sell non VAT-able goods (eg food at supermarkets) are able to claim back VAT they themselves pay on what they spend and so may show a **debit** balance in Value Added Tax Account, representing **money owed** by HM Revenue & Customs.

* The **Bank Account** can appear as either a debit or a credit: a debit balance means that there is money in the bank account (an asset) but a credit balance means that there is a bank overdraft (a liability).

CUCINA ZONE TRIAL BALANCE: A WORKED EXAMPLE

The following list of balances was extracted from Cucina Zone's books at 31 October 2009. Note that the list shows whether each entry is a debit or a credit.

Cucina Zone: list of balances as at 31 October 2009		
	£	
Purchases	33,970	Dr
Sales	60,320	Cr
Office Furniture	3,448	Dr
Motor Vehicles	18,540	Dr
Purchase Returns	450	Cr
Sales Returns	300	Dr
General Expenses	1,310	Dr
Motor Expenses	1,853	Dr
Discount Allowed	468	Dr
Discount Received	1,208	Cr
Stationery	241	Dr
Wages	16,690	Dr
Debtors	6,550	Dr
Creditors	4,680	Cr
Rent & Rates	3,200	Dr
Insurance	600	Dr
Bank	2,500	Dr
Cash	498	Dr
Value Added Tax	2,510	Cr
Capital	21,000	Cr

The trial balance is then prepared by the book-keeper. The completed trial balance is shown below. This is in traditional format with each account balance on a separate line.

Note the following rules are illustrated:

- **debit** balances – are assets or expenses
- **credit** balances – are capital, liabilities or income

Notice also that the total of the debit column equals the total of the credit side. In other words the trial balance balances (agrees).

Cucina Zone
Trial Balance as at 31 October 2009

	Dr £	Cr £
Purchases	33,970	
Sales		60,320
Office Furniture	3,448	
Motor Vehicles	18,540	
Purchase Returns		450
Sales Returns	300	
General Expenses	1,310	
Motor Expenses	1,853	
Discount Allowed	468	
Discount Received		1,208
Stationery	241	
Wages	16,690	
Debtors	6,550	
Creditors		4,680
Rent & Rates	3,200	
Insurance	600	
Bank	2,500	
Cash	498	
Value Added Tax		2,510
Capital		21,000
	90,168	90,168

This trial balance is presented in a commonly found format, but, as we will explain on the next page, there are alternative formats.

alternative trial balance format

You will see from the trial balance shown on the previous page that each item is on a separate line for example 'purchases' are shown on one line, 'sales' on another line and so on. In your assignment you may find that two accounts appear **on one line**, for example 'purchases and sales'. There are several accounts that often appear together. To illustrate this we will draw up the trial balance again in this alternative format. Balances shown in bold type indicate where there are two balances on one line. The arrows have been added here for illustrative purposes only – they will not appear in the trial balance.

Cucina Zone

Trial Balance as at 31 October 2009

	Dr £	Cr £
Purchases and Sales	**33,970**	**60,320**
Office Furniture	3,448	
Motor Vehicles	18,540	
Sales and Purchase Returns	**300**	**450**
General Expenses	1,310	
Motor Expenses	1,853	
Discounts Allowed and Received	**468**	**1,208**
Stationery	241	
Wages	16,690	
Debtors and Creditors	**6,550**	**4,680**
Rent & Rates	3,200	
Insurance	600	
Bank	2,500	
Cash	498	
Value Added Tax		2,510
Capital		21,000
	90,168	90,168

two accounts on one line – which figure is which?

When two accounts are shown together on one line, as above, it is important that you know which figure relates to which account. The answer is very simple: the figure on the left (the debit) relates to the account referred to on the left, ie the first account mentioned. Therefore 'Purchases' (on the left of 'Purchases and Sales') is the debit (on the left) figure, £33,970. Similarly 'Creditors' (on the right) is the credit entry (on the right), ie £4,680.

THE EFFECT OF JOURNAL ENTRIES ON THE TRIAL BALANCE

the accounting process so far

You will appreciate from your study of the double-entry bookkeeping system that provided that all entries to the ledger accounts have been recorded twice, once on the debit side and once on the credit side of an account and no errors have been made, the trial balance should balance. If it does not balance a mistake (or mistakes) will have been made and will need to be corrected.

In Chapters 12 to 14 we dealt with journal entries which corrected errors and made other account adjustments such as writing off bad debts. In this and the next chapter we will explain the effect of these journal entries on the trial balance. These include:

- making adjustments to existing account balances in the trial balance
- setting up new accounts to enter in the trial balance

the accounting process – the revised trial balance

The process you will be carrying out from now on is shown in the diagram below. This follows the process required by your assessment.

To summarise: you start with an initial trial balance, which is correct; then you make the journal debit and credit entries and make adjustments and add any new accounts to the initial trial balance. Then, if you have been accurate in your workings, the revised trial balance should balance.

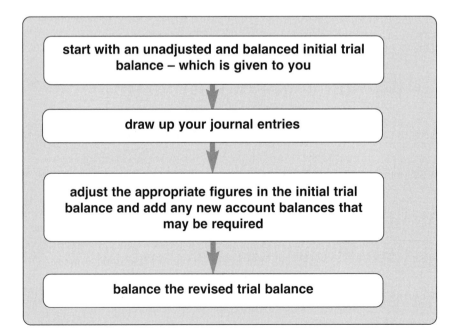

start with an unadjusted and balanced initial trial balance – which is given to you

draw up your journal entries

adjust the appropriate figures in the initial trial balance and add any new account balances that may be required

balance the revised trial balance

WORKED EXAMPLE – FROM JOURNAL TO TRIAL BALANCE

Using the trial balance of Cucina Zone shown on page 247 and entries to the journal, we will describe a number of adjustments to the trial balance figures.

errors of omission

If there has been an error of omission where an invoice or credit note has not been entered in the accounting records, then this error will need to be corrected by the use of a journal entry. In normal circumstances the journal entry would then be posted to the appropriate ledger account. In your assignment, however, you are not required to carry out this posting, but you are, however, required to make the adjustment in the trial balance.

error of omission – purchase invoice

Let us assume that after completing the trial balance the book-keeper finds a purchase invoice, dated 6 October 2009, for £80.00 plus VAT £14.00 from Austin Kitchenware that had not been entered in the accounts. The book-keeper will prepare a journal entry as follows:

	Journal		
Date	**Details**	**Dr**	**Cr**
2009		£	£
6 Oct	Purchases	80.00	
	Value Added Tax	14.00	
	Austin Kitchenware		94.00
	Correction of error – purchase invoice not entered.		

Adjustments are then entered on the trial balance as shown below in bold type. Study this and then read the notes on the next page.

Cucina Zone

Trial Balance as at 31 October 2009 (extract)

	Dr	Cr
	£	£
Purchases **(33,970 + 80)**	34,050	
Creditors **(4,680 + 94)**		4,774
Value Added Tax **(2,510 – 14)**		2,496

notes

- you should write down the adjustments on the initial trial balance
- show your workings next to the specific account
- you will need to take care when there are two accounts on one line
- start with the original figure and add or subtract the adjustment figure
- write the adjusted total in the appropriate column in the trial balance
- the journal entry shows the name of the creditor (Austin Kitchenware) but in the trial balance all the creditors are added together and shown as one figure 'Creditors . . . £4,680'; you will need to add the £94 to this figure.

The workings for the omitted purchase invoice adjustment on the previous page are as follows:

- **Purchases** originally amounted to £33,970 to which we have added the net price of the goods (before VAT) £80.00 = £34,050. This new figure for purchases is entered in the debit column of the trial balance.
- **Creditors** originally amounted to £4,680. This figure needs increasing by the total of the invoice £94.00 which is owed to Austin Kitchenware, a creditor. The new figure for creditors now amounts to £4,680 + £94.00 = £4,774. This is entered in the credit column in the trial balance.
- **Value Added Tax** was originally shown as a credit balance of £2,510, being the amount owed to HM Revenue & Customs (HMRC). Since Cucina Zone has purchased goods from the supplier, Austin Kitchenware, the £14.00 VAT charged on the purchase invoice (which can be claimed back from HMRC) can therefore be deducted from the amount owed to HMRC, ie £2,510 − £14 = £2,496. This figure is then entered in the credit column of the trial balance.

error of omission – sales invoice

In this example a sales invoice, dated 9 October 2009, has been sent to one of Cucina Zone's customers, Marlow Cookware, but unfortunately the copy invoice has not been entered into the accounting records. The journal entry detailing the sale of goods to Marlow Cookware is as follows:

	Journal		
Date	**Details**	**Dr**	**Cr**
2009		£	£
9 Oct	Marlow Cookware	188.00	
	Sales		160.00
	Value Added Tax		28.00
	Correction of error – sales invoice not entered.		

Cucina Zone

Trial Balance as at 31 October 2009 (extract)

	Dr	Cr
	£	£
Sales **(60,320 + 160)**		60,480
Value Added Tax **(2,510 – 14 + 28)**		2,524
Debtors **(6,550 + 188)**	6,738	

Working through the example above we will now look at each account where adjustments are needed:

- **Sales** originally amounted to £60,320 to which we have added the net price of the goods sold (before VAT) £160 = £60,480. The new figure of sales has been entered in the credit column of the trial balance.

- **Value Added Tax**: in the trial balance there is a credit balance £2,510 – £14 = £2,496. To this figure we need to add £28 VAT charged on the invoice to Marlow Cookware making a total of £2,496 + £28 = £2,524, which requires entering in the credit column of the trial balance.

- **Debtors** originally amounted to £6,550 and to this figure we need to add the amount owed by Marlow Cookware. The total debtors outstanding now becomes £6,550 + £188 = £6,738 this figure being entered in the debit column of the trial balance. You will notice that the journal entry gives the name of the debtor (Marlow Cookware) whereas in the trial balance the debtors are added together and shown as one total.

error of omission – credit note (purchase returns)

In the following example Cucina Zone has returned goods to a supplier, Fosters Ltd, in respect of goods which had been damaged in transit. A credit note, dated 14 October, 2009, was received from Fosters Ltd but unfortunately had not been entered in the accounting records.

	Journal		
Date	**Details**	**Dr**	**Cr**
2009		£	£
14 Oct	Fosters Ltd	47.00	
	Purchase Returns		40.00
	Value Added Tax		7.00
	Correction of error – credit note not entered.		

Cucina Zone		
Trial Balance as at 31 October 2009 (extract)		
	Dr	**Cr**
	£	£
Purchase Returns (**450 + 40**)		490
Value Added Tax (**2,510 – 14 + 28 + 7**)		2,531
Creditors (**4,680 + 94 – 47**)		4,727

Working through the example above we will now look at each account where adjustments are needed. You will see that as we work through the various adjustments, some accounts are accumulating a sizeable series of figures.

- **Purchase Returns** originally amounted to £450, to which we have added the net price of the goods returned (before VAT) £40 = £490. The new figure of purchase returns has been entered in the credit column of the revised trial balance.

- **Value Added Tax**: in the trial balance shown above there is a credit balance £2,510 – £14 + £28 = £2,524. To this figure we need to add £7 VAT shown on the credit note from Fosters Ltd. The workings now show £2,510 – £14 + £28 + £7 = £2,531. This figure requires entering in the credit column in the trial balance.

- **Creditors**: in the trial balance shown above there is a credit balance of £4,680 + £94 – £47 = £4,727. Notice that £47 in respect of the credit note from Fosters Ltd has been deducted. This revised figure is now entered in the credit column of the trial balance.

error of omission – credit note (sales returns)

Some of the goods sold to Marlow Cookware were unsuitable and returned to Cucina Zone who issued a credit note on 15 October 2009. The credit note was sent to Marlow Cookware but unfortunately the Cucina Zone office copy was mislaid and not entered into the accounting records until recently via a journal entry as shown below:

Journal			
Date	**Details**	**Dr**	**Cr**
2009		£	£
15 Oct	Sales Returns	120.00	
	Value Added Tax	21.00	
	Marlow Cookware		141.00
	Correction of error – credit note not entered.		

This adjustment would then have to be noted on the trial balance as shown below. Note again that as we work through the various adjustments, a number of accounts are accumulating a long string of figures.

Cucina Zone		
Trial Balance as at 31 October 2009 (extract)		
	Dr	**Cr**
	£	**£**
Sales Returns **(300 + 120)**	420	
Value Added Tax **(2,510 – 14 + 28 + 7 – 21)**		2,510
Debtors **(6,550 + 188 – 141)**	6,597	

Working through the above example we will now look at each account where adjustments are needed:

- **Sales Returns** originally amounted to £300, to which we have added the net price of the goods returned (before VAT) £120 = £420. The new figure of sales returns has been entered in the debit column of the revised trial balance.

- **Value Added Tax**: in the trial balance extract shown above there is a credit balance £2,510 – £14 + £28 + £7 = £2,531. To this figure we need to deduct £21 VAT shown on the credit note to Marlow Cookware: £2,510 – £14 + £28 + £7 – £21 = £2,510. This figure requires entering in the credit column in the trial balance.

- **Debtors**: in the trial balance extract shown above there is a debit balance of £6,550 + £188 = £6,738. To this figure we need to deduct £141 in respect of the credit note issued to Marlow Cookware: £6,550 + 188 – £141 = £6,597. This revised figure is now entered in the debit column in the trial balance.

Now study the trial balance shown on the next page, paying special attention to the entries in bold type and making sure that you know where the figures come from. Then read the exam tips which follow.

Note that this trial balance, for sake of clarity, shows the following accounts on separate lines:
- purchases and sales
- sales returns and purchase returns
- discounts allowed and discounts received
- debtors and creditors

Note that in your assignment you may be required to list these pairs of accounts on a single line, for example 'Purchases and Sales'.

Cucina Zone

Trial Balance as at 31 October 2009

	Dr £	Cr £
Purchases **(33,970 + 80)**	34,050	
Sales **(60,320 + 160)**		60,480
Office Furniture	3,448	
Motor Vehicles	18,540	
Sales Returns **(300 + 120)**	420	
Purchase Returns **(450 + 40)**		490
General Expenses	1,310	
Motor Expenses	1,853	
Discounts Allowed	468	
Discounts Received		1,208
Stationery	241	
Wages	16,690	
Debtors **(6,550 + 188 – 141)**	6,597	
Creditors **(4,680 + 94 – 47)**		4,727
Rent & Rates	3,200	
Insurance	600	
Bank	2,500	
Cash	498	
Value Added Tax **(2,510 – 14 + 28 + 7 – 21)**		2,510
Capital		21,000
	90,415	90,415

Exam tips

When tackling your assignment you may find the following tips useful:

● Prepare the journal entries first of all.

● Write out the format for the trial balance on your answer paper ensuring that you use the correct title, the revised date of the trial balance and the correct column headings.

● On your question paper it is a good idea to rule lines under each item of the trial balance across both amount columns. This ensures that you select the right figure for each specific account.

continued from previous page

- Enter the account names on your answer paper. If two account names appear on one line, for example, 'Purchases and Sales,' enter each account on a separate line (as in the trial balance on the previous page). This will allow you sufficient room to make any adjustments.

- Deal with the journal entries first, starting off with the balance of the account from the trial balance in the question and then make any adjustments necessary before entering the final balance in the appropriate debit or credit column.

- Remember that if the journal entry involves a named debtor or creditor account, the 'debtors' or 'creditors' entry in the trial balance will have to be adjusted accordingly.

- Remember also to leave a couple of extra lines at the bottom of your trial balance before totalling it up in case you have omitted an account or if you need to add a new account (see next chapter).

- When you have finished all the journal adjustments, enter the remaining balances from the initial trial balance and then add up each column. If you have been accurate in your workings, the trial balance should agree.

Where now and where next?

chapter summary

In this chapter we have:

- introduced, defined and considered the uses and advantages of the trial balance

- illustrated how journal adjustments are written in the trial balance

- completed a revised trial balance after taking into account journal entry adjustments

what is in the next chapter?

The next chapter continues the use of worked examples and deals with:

- further journal entry adjustments and the effect they have on the trial balance

- the creation of new account balances

- the drawing up of a revised trial balance

Exercises

15.1 Daniel has just been appointed accounts clerk for a small company, Brough Bros Ltd. The accountant has passed the following list of balances to Daniel and asks him to prepare a trial balance as at 30 June 2009.

	£
Computer Equipment	32,000
Office Furniture and Fittings	10,625
Premises	200,000
Salaries and Wages	112,100
Purchases	299,640
Sales	457,760
Motor Vehicles	65,000
Telephone, Printing and Stationery	5,445
Heating and Lighting	7,400
Motor Expenses	9,455
Creditors	68,000
Debtors	76,100
Bank Overdraft	5,540
Capital	317,125
Drawings	26,700
General Expenses	3,960

You are required to draw up a trial balance for Brough Bros Ltd as at 30 June 2009.

15.2* Louise is the accounts clerk for Super Garages Ltd. One of her tasks is to prepare a trial balance at the end of each month to check that the books of account balance. After preparing the trial balance at the end of July 2009 Louise realises that she has omitted to enter a purchase invoice.

Details of the invoice and the extract from the trial balance are shown below:

Purchase Invoice

From:	Wearwell Tyres Ltd
Date:	10 July 2009
Amount:	£320 plus VAT £56 = £376

Trial Balance Extract from Super Garages Ltd as at 31 July 2009

	Dr	Cr
	£	£
Purchases and Sales	87,264	174,770
Value Added Tax		7,006
Debtors and Creditors	62,224	41,232

You are required to:

(a)   prepare a journal entry with a suitable narrative to record the purchase invoice

(b)   calculate your adjustments and correct the appropriate ledger account balance

(c)   prepare a revised trial balance extract as at 31 July 2009.

15.3   Sam, the book-keeper for Silverdale Services, has prepared the trial balance as at 31 August 2009 for the accountant. However, on tidying his desk at the end of the day he finds a sales invoice that has not been entered. Details of the invoice and the trial balance extract are as follows:

Sales Invoice

To:	Lowe & Moss
Date:	19 August 2009
Amount:	£280 plus VAT £49 = £329

Trial Balance Extract of Silverdale Service as at 31 August 2009

	Dr	Cr
	£	£
Purchases and Sales	74,379	156,739
Value Added Tax		4,296
Debtors and Creditors	30,906	24,672

You are required to:

(a)   prepare a journal entry with a suitable narrative to record the sales invoice

(b)   calculate your adjustments and correct the appropriate ledger account balance

(c)   prepare a revised trial balance extract as at 31 August 2009.

15.4*   Shamir works as book-keeper for Unwins Ltd a small engineering company. After preparing the trial balance at the end of September 2009, Shamir finds a credit note that has not been entered in the books of account. The credit note is from Chang and Lau, one of Unwins Ltd suppliers and is in respect of goods that were faulty and had to be returned. Details of the credit note and the trial balance extract are as follows:

Credit Note

From:	Chang & Lau
Date:	23 September 2009
Amount:	£720 plus VAT £126 = £846

Trial Balance Extract of Unwins Ltd as at 30 September 2009

	Dr	Cr
	£	£
Sales and Purchase Returns	2,597	1,878
Value Added Tax		3,252
Debtors and Creditors	23,379	25,370

You are required to:

(a)   prepare a journal entry with a suitable narrative to record the credit note

(b)   calculate your adjustments and correct the appropriate ledger account balance

(c)   prepare a revised trial balance extract as at 30 September 2009.

15.5 Anya is the book-keeper for Wild's Catering Services and has prepared the trial balance as at 31 October 2009 for the accountant. Unfortunately when tidying her desk she finds the office copy of a credit note that has not been entered. The credit note was issued to Joyce Inman in respect of an overcharge by the company. Details of the credit note and the trial balance extract are as follows:

Credit Note

To: Joyce Inman

Date: 8 October 2009

Amount: £480 plus VAT £84 = £564

Trial Balance Extract of Wild's Catering Service as at 31 October 2009

	Dr £	Cr £
Sales and Purchase Returns	1,557	1,878
Value Added Tax		1,514
Debtors and Creditors	15,076	9,190

You are required to:

(a)   prepare a journal entry with a suitable narrative to record the credit note

(b)   calculate your adjustments and correct the appropriate ledger account balance

(c)   prepare a revised trial balance extract as at 31 October 2009

15.6 The following trial balance has been prepared by John, the book-keeper, for Hartdale Supplies for the year ended 30 September 2009.

Hartdale Supplies

Trial Balance as at 30 September 2009

	Dr £	Cr £
Purchases and Sales	13,784	29,599
Computer Equipment	12,786	
Machinery	5,978	
Vehicle	19,280	
Sales and Purchase Returns	736	1,033
Debtors and Creditors	7,842	3,824

	Dr	Cr
	£	£
Drawings	4,426	
General Expenses	2,496	
Motor Expenses	1,154	
Discount Allowed and Discount Received	706	1,113
Bad Debts	402	
Wages	10,618	
Rent and Rates	3,185	
Postage and Stationery	1,287	
Bank	3,923	
Cash	719	
Value Added Tax		1,166
Capital		52,587
	89,322	89,322

After preparing the above trial balance the book-keeper discovers some invoices and credit notes on his desk that have not been entered in the accounting records. The details are as follows:

- **Purchase Invoice** from AJ Services dated 7 September 2009 for £640 plus £112 VAT, making an outstanding total of £752.

- **Sales Invoice**, dated 17 September 2009, in respect of goods supplied to Wong and Shah £235 including VAT.

- **Credit Note**, dated 21 September 2009, received from a supplier, Parkin, Peck & Co, for £240 plus VAT of £42 making a total of £282. This was in respect of goods which had been damaged in transit and returned by Hartdale Supplies.

- **Credit Note**, dated 24 September 2009, sent to one of Hartdale's customers, Reg McFarlin, for £423, including VAT. The credit note was in respect of the supply of faulty goods which were returned.

You are required to:

(a)   prepare journal entries with suitable narratives for each of the above

(b)   calculate adjustments

(c)   adjust or correct ledger balances

(d)   enter the correct title and date of the revised trial balance

(e)   enter correct column headings

(f)   enter balances into correct columns

(g)   total the revised trial balance

16 The trial balance – creation of new accounts

what this chapter covers . . . .

This chapter will describe further adjustments made to the trial balance as a result of journal entries which create new accounts, for example:

- the purchase of a fixed asset
- a bad debt written off
- when part of an outstanding debt is paid and the remainder written off
- bad debts recovered after they have been written off
- transfers involving new expenses accounts

This chapter will explain:

- how a new account is created following a journal entry
- the adjustments that will be needed to the ledger account balances
- the way in which these adjustments will affect the figures in the trial balance
- the preparation of a revised trial balance

These processes are illustrated in the diagram shown below.

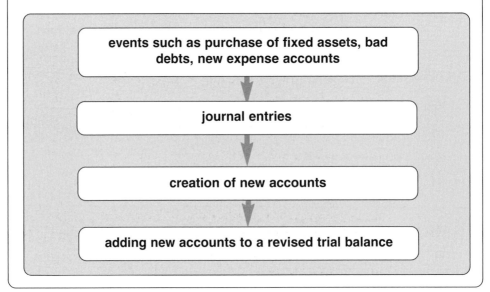

events such as purchase of fixed assets, bad debts, new expense accounts

↓

journal entries

↓

creation of new accounts

↓

adding new accounts to a revised trial balance

REASONS FOR THE CREATION OF NEW ACCOUNTS

purchase and sale of fixed assets

Sometimes a business transaction requires the creation of a new ledger account; this could be when a new fixed asset is purchased. For example the business may decide to purchase computer equipment for the first time; in this case a new account for 'Computer Equipment' would be needed.

bad debts written off

Another example where a new account may be needed is where there is a debtor who is unable to pay an outstanding account. If, for example, a debt had to be completely written off, a 'Bad Debts Account' would be required. If this was the first occasion the business had written off a bad debt, a new account would need to be opened.

This Bad Debts Account could also be used if a debtor was only able to pay part of the outstanding balance, the remainder being written off. This topic was covered fully in Chapter 14 (pages 216-217).

recovery of bad debts

A similar situation would arise if a debt that had previously been written off was then paid by the debtor. Here a 'Bad Debts Recovered Account' would need to be created, if it did not already exist.

CREATING NEW ACCOUNTS – WORKED EXAMPLE

We will use our Case Study of Cucina Zone to illustrate the creation of new accounts and other adjustments through the journal and describe the effect this has on the trial balance.

The trial balance of Cucina Zone is shown on the next page. Note that this relates to the month of November, a month later than the Case Study in the last chapter.

Note also that the trial balance uses separate lines for accounts such as Purchases Account and Sales Account which are sometimes shown on the same line.

In your assignment, however, you may be required to list these pairs of accounts on a single line, for example 'Debtors and Creditors'.

Cucina Zone
Trial Balance as at 30 November 2009

	Dr	Cr
	£	£
Purchases	48,413	
Sales		90,480
Office Furniture	5,172	
Motor Vehicles	18,540	
Purchase Returns		675
Sales Returns	450	
General Expenses	1,965	
Motor Expenses	2,779	
Discount Allowed	702	
Discount Received		1,812
Wages	26,847	
Debtors	9,825	
Creditors		7,020
Rent & Rates	4,800	
Stationery	300	
Insurance	600	
Bank	3,825	
Cash	534	
Value Added Tax		3,765
Capital		21,000
	124,752	124,752

PURCHASE OF FIXED ASSETS – NEW ACCOUNT

Let us assume that Cucina Zone, which is VAT registered, purchases some new exhibition equipment for use at trade fairs. The details are as follows:

Purchase Invoice
From: Gray and Grant
Date: 3 November 2009
Amount: £3,600 plus VAT £630 = £4,230

The journal entry would be as follows:

	Journal		
Date	**Details**	**Dr**	**Cr**
2009		£	£
3 Nov	Exhibition Equipment (new account)	3,600	
	Value Added Tax	630	
	Gray & Grant		4,230
	Purchase of exhibition equipment on credit from Gray & Grant.		

Adjustments are then entered on the trial balance as shown below in bold. Note that Exhibition Equipment Account is a new account which will have to be created in the Nominal Ledger. You will not have to set up this account in your assignment.

Cucina Zone

Trial Balance as at 30 November 2009 (extract)

	Dr	Cr
	£	£
Exhibition Equipment **(new account)**	**3,600**	
Creditors **(7,020 + 4,230)**		**11,250**
Value Added Tax **(3,765 – 630)**		**3,135**

Note that Gray & Grant are creditors and their names are shown in the journal entry. In the trial balance, however, all the creditors' outstanding balances are added together and the total entered as 'Creditors'. See the account explanations below:

- **Exhibition Equipment** is a **new account** which is debited with £3,600, the net price of the new equipment (an asset) and therefore a debit entry in the trial balance.

- **Value Added Tax**: in the trial balance the original figure is £3,765; from this figure £630 is deducted in respect of the VAT charged on the purchase of the exhibition equipment. In the trial balance the difference (£3,765 – £630 = £3,135) is entered in the credit column as this is a liability and owed to HMRC.

- **Creditors**: here the original trial balance figure is £7,020, to which is added £4,230, the amount owed to Gray & Grant, making a new creditors total of £11,250.

BAD DEBTS WRITTEN OFF – NEW ACCOUNT

When a business experiences difficulty in getting payment from a debtor it may try various options to secure payment such as sending out statements, writing letters and so on. However, on occasions if it is unlikely that payment will be received then the business has no option but to write the debt off as bad. If this is the first time that the business has to take this action it will have to open up a new Bad Debts Account in the Nominal Ledger.

Assume Cucina Zone has a debt of £152 that has been outstanding since 15 January 2009 on the account of Shaw & Sons. After trying unsuccessfully to obtain payment on 30 November 2009 it was decided to write the debt off as bad. The journal entries would be as follows:

	Journal		Dr	Cr
Date	**Details**		**Dr**	**Cr**
2009			£	£
30 Nov	Bad debts (new account)		152	
	Shaw & Sons			152
	Account of Shaw & Sons written off as a bad debt.			

Adjustments are then entered on the trial balance as shown below in bold:

Cucina Zone
Trial Balance as at 30 November 2009 (extract)

	Dr	Cr
	£	£
Bad debts **(new account)**	152	
Debtors **(9,825 – 152)**	9,673	

Note that Shaw & Sons are debtors. In the trial balance all the debtors' outstanding balances are added together and the total entered as 'Debtors'. The account balance of Shaw & Sons is deducted from this total.

The accounts involved in this transaction are as follows:

- **Bad Debts:** this is a new account which has been opened to record the bad debt of £152 that has been written off. This is entered on the debit side of the trial balance since it is treated as an expense of the business.

- **Debtors:** the original figure from the trial balance £9,825 is entered first and then the £152 representing the bad debt written off is deducted to give a new figure of debtors' outstanding of £9,673. This figure is entered in the debit column of the trial balance. The £152 is deducted from the debtors' figure because this account is no longer outstanding.

partial bad debt

A partial bad debt is the situation where a debtor has been able to pay part of an outstanding debt but the remainder would have to be written off as bad.

In the Case Study, Peak Designs Ltd owe Cucina Zone £422 in respect of an invoice dated 24 March 2009. On 30 November 2009 Peak Designs sent a cheque for £250 on account and informed Cucina Zone that it is unable to pay the full amount since it is possible that they are going into liquidation. The journal entry to record this transaction is shown below:

	Journal		
Date	**Details**	**Dr**	**Cr**
2009		£	£
30 Nov	Bank	250	
	Bad Debts	172	
	Peak Designs Ltd		422
	Part payment of debt, remainder written off as bad debt.		

Adjustments are then entered on the trial balance as shown below in bold:

Cucina Zone		
Trial Balance as at 30 November 2009 (extract)		
	Dr	**Cr**
	£	£
Bank **(3,825 + 250)**	**4,075**	
Bad Debts **(152 + 172)**	**324**	
Debtors **(9,825 – 152 – 422)**	**9,251**	

These account workings can be explained as follows:

- **Bank**: the original figure of £3,825 is taken from the trial balance and the cheque received from Peak Designs for £250 is added giving a new bank balance of £4,075.

- **Bad Debts**: since this new account was created in the previous example the account can be used again for this transaction. So far Cucina Zone has written off £152 in respect of the amount owed by Shaw & Sons. A further £172 needs to be added to this amount making a total of £324 written off as bad debts. This figure is entered in the debit column since it is treated as an expense.

- **Debtors** outstanding originally amounted to £9,825 from which £152 was deducted in respect of the bad debt written off in the previous example. A further £422 now has to be deducted in respect of the payment of £250 received and partial bad debt written off of £172. The new figure for debtors (£9,825 - £152 - £422 = £9,251) is entered in the debit column of the trial balance.

Reminder: in the trial balance the Debtors are always entered on the debit side and creditors are always entered on the credit side.

bad debts recovered

A bad debt recovered is the rare situation where the debtor is able to pay off the debt after it has already been written off as bad by a business. If this has not happened to a business before, it may not have an account in which to make the book-keeping entries. It will need to set up a new account, 'Bad Debts Recovered Account'.

Using our Case Study, let us assume that a bad debt that had been written off over a year ago was unexpectedly repaid in full. On 30 November 2009 Cucina Zone received a cheque for £248 from BB Services Ltd in full payment of this amount previously written off as bad.

Remember from Chapter 14 (see pages 218-219) that this process is carried out in two stages, using journal entries:

1 Reinstate the original debt in the debtor's account (BB Services Ltd)

Journal			
Date	**Details**	**Dr**	**Cr**
2009		£	£
30 Nov	BB Services Ltd	248	
	Bad Debts Recovered (new account)		248
	Reinstatement of a debt previously written off, but now recovered.		

2 Record the receipt of the cheque in the Bank Account and credit the debtor's account (BB Services Ltd)

Journal			
Date	**Details**	**Dr**	**Cr**
2009		£	£
30 Nov	Bank	248	
	BB Services Ltd		248
	Cheque received in payment of debt previously written off.		

Adjustments are then entered on the trial balance as shown below in bold:

Cucina Zone

Trial Balance as at 30 November 2009 (extract)

	Dr	Cr
	£	£
Debtors (9,825 – 152 – 422 + 248 – 248)	9,251	
Bad Debts recovered **(new account)**		248
Bank **(3,825 + 250 + 248)**	4,323	

The account workings are as follows:

- **Debtors**: there is effectively no change to this figure in the trial balance. Following the reinstatement of the debt, £248 was added to the debtor's figure, on receipt of the cheque the total debtors' figure is then reduced by £248. Thus the figure of outstanding debtors' remains as shown above ie £9,251.

- **Bad Debts Recovered**: here a new account is opened and the amount of the debt now recovered is shown on the credit side of the trial balance. The balance of this account is a credit entry because it is treated like income.

- **Bank**: the cheque received from BB Services Ltd is put into the business bank account thereby increasing the bank balance by £248.

TRANSFERS INVOLVING NEW EXPENSE ACCOUNTS

Sometimes a business may have nominal accounts that record more than one type of expense. For example various types of running expenses may be charged, to a 'General Expenses Account'.

Circumstances may change, however, and the business may decide to create a new expense account if a particular type of expense increases and needs to be recorded separately, leaving the 'General Expenses Account' still running.

Cucina Zone, for example, has a General Expenses Account to which it charges various types of expenses, including printing costs. It has now decided that due to increased charges, printing costs are to be kept in a separate account. Printing costs have been calculated to be £612 and need to be transferred from the General Expenses Account to a Printing Account. The journal entries for the transfer would be as follows:

	Journal		Dr	Cr
Date	**Details**		**Dr**	**Cr**
2009			£	£
30 Nov	Printing (new account)		612	
	General Expenses			612
	Creation of a separate Printing Account.			

Adjustments are then entered on the trial balance as shown below in bold:

Cucina Zone		
Trial Balance as at 30 November 2009 (extract)		
	Dr	**Cr**
	£	£
General Expenses (1,965 – 612)	1,353	
Printing (new account)	612	

Working through this example we will now explain the adjustments to each account.

- **General Expenses**: in the trial balance the amount charged to general expenses is shown as £1,965. Printing costs of £612 are deducted, making a total of £1,353, to be entered in the debit column of the trial balance, as it is an expense.

- **Printing**: this is a new account showing the transfer of £612 from the General Expenses Account. Since it is an expense account it is entered in the debit column of the trial balance.

REVISED TRIAL BALANCE

After adjusting for the journal entries, the revised trial balance for Cucina Zone as at 30 November 2009 will appear as shown below. Note that the workings are shown in bold type. The four new accounts opened are listed at the bottom of the trial balance and are also shown in bold type.

Cucina Zone
Trial Balance as at 30 November 2009

	Dr	Cr
	£	£
Purchases	48,413	
Sales		90,480
Office Furniture	5,172	
Motor Vehicles	18,540	
Purchase Returns		675
Sales Returns	450	
General Expenses **(1,965 – 612)**	**1,353**	
Motor Expenses	2,779	
Discount Allowed	702	
Discount Received		1,812
Wages	26,847	
Debtors **(9,825 – 152 – 422 + 248 – 248)**	**9,251**	
Creditors **(7,020 + 4,230)**		**11,250**
Rent & Rates	4,800	
Stationery	300	
Insurance	600	
Bank **(3,825 + 250 + 248)**	**4,323**	
Cash	534	
Value Added Tax **(3,765 - 630)**		**3,135**
Capital		21,000
Exhibition Equipment	**3,600**	
Bad Debts (152 + 172)	**324**	
Bad Debts Recovered		**248**
Printing	**612**	
	128,600	128,600

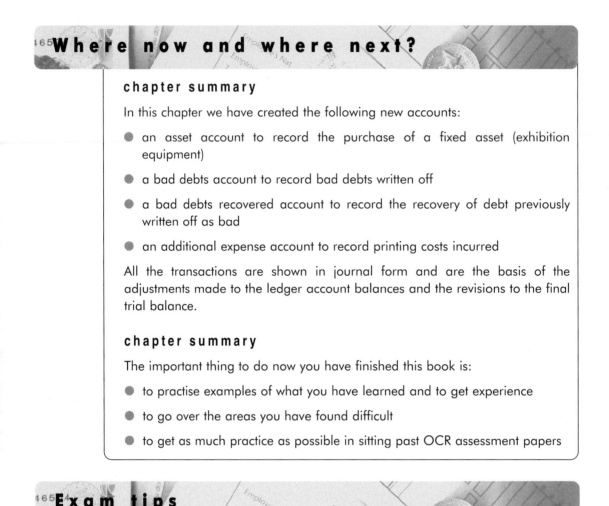

Where now and where next?

chapter summary

In this chapter we have created the following new accounts:

- an asset account to record the purchase of a fixed asset (exhibition equipment)
- a bad debts account to record bad debts written off
- a bad debts recovered account to record the recovery of debt previously written off as bad
- an additional expense account to record printing costs incurred

All the transactions are shown in journal form and are the basis of the adjustments made to the ledger account balances and the revisions to the final trial balance.

chapter summary

The important thing to do now you have finished this book is:

- to practise examples of what you have learned and to get experience
- to go over the areas you have found difficult
- to get as much practice as possible in sitting past OCR assessment papers

Exam tips

- Read again the exam tips at the end of the previous chapter (pages 254-255) taking particular care with the trial balance headings.

- Following on from the journal entries ensure you make all the necessary adjustments to the ledger balances by showing your workings alongside the specific ledger balance in the trial balance.

- When making adjustments to the Value Added Tax Account extra care is needed. Usually this account is a credit balance, indicating that the balance is a liability, ie a payment needs to be made to HMRC at the end of the VAT period. Therefore, when making an adjustment consider if the transaction means additional VAT has to be paid to HMRC, for example, if the company has made extra sales. Alternatively, if the transaction involves the purchase of goods then the VAT paid on the purchase can be claimed from the HMRC and is offset against the VAT balance.

continued from previous page

- Transfer the ledger balance to either the debit or credit column in the trial balance. Remember debit balances are assets or expenses and credit balances are capital, liabilities or income.

- In the trial balance use the full name of the ledger account – do not abbreviate the account names.

- When first preparing the revised trial balance it is a good idea to leave a few extra lines before totalling the trial balance. This will provide space to include any new accounts that have been created.

- Add up the columns of the trial balance which, provided all the adjustments have been carried out correctly, should agree. If, however, the totals do not agree then, although you may not have much time in an examination, it may be worthwhile checking your additions:

  - If you added the figures from the bottom of the trial balance when checking your addition, start from the top and work down (or vice versa).

  - Find the difference between the two sides and look for that amount.

  - Halve the difference and look for that amount.

  - Further hints on what to do if the trial balance does not agree can be found in Chapter 5 'Balancing the Trial Balance' (pages 67-68).

Exercises

free online resources at www.osbornebooks.co.uk
Available from the Resources page for *Level 2 Accounting:*
- blank journals and trial balances for use in these exercises
- answers for the exercises in this book marked with an asterisk (*)

16.1 Moore & Moss Ltd, which is VAT registered, has recently been expanding their business and have decided to purchase some display equipment for their new showroom. The equipment was purchased on credit from Bell's (Display Equipment) Ltd on 21 September 2009 for £4,800 plus VAT £840 making a total of £5,640. No entry has been made in the accounting records for this purchase and there is currently no account set up for display equipment.

An extract from the company's trial balance is shown below:

Trial Balance Extract from Moore & Moss Ltd as at 30 September 2009		
	Dr	Cr
	£	£
Value Added Tax		2,788.00
Creditors		25,900.00

You are required to:

(a)   prepare a journal entry with a suitable narrative to record the purchase invoice

(b)   calculate adjustments

(c)   adjust and correct ledger balances and create any new account balances that may be required

(d)   prepare a revised trial balance extract as at 30 September 2009

16.2   Jane is the book-keeper for Lester & Sons, a small printing business. The accountant has just received notification that one of the business's debtors has just been declared bankrupt and will be unable to pay their outstanding account. Jane receives the following memo:

MEMORANDUM

to: Book-keeper

from: Accountant   Date: 31 August 2009

Inman & Co, who owe us £533.67, have been declared bankrupt. Since it looks most unlikely that this outstanding amount will be paid, please write the whole of the debt off as bad and make adjustments to the trial balance.

The trial balance extract is shown below:

Trial Balance Extract from Lester & Sons as at 31 August 2009		
	Dr	Cr
	£	£
Debtors	45,912.89	

You are required to:

(a)   prepare a journal entry with a suitable narrative to write off the debt as bad

(b)   calculate adjustments

(c)   adjust and correct ledger balances and create any new account balances that may be required

(d)   prepare a revised trial balance extract as at 31 August 2009

16.3   Spark Electrics owes £632.60 to KS Supplies Ltd. Unfortunately, due to financial difficulties they are unable to pay their account in full. On 30 June 2009 the accountant of KS Supplies Ltd receives a letter from Spark Electrics informing him that the company has just been declared bankrupt and a cheque for £400.00 is enclosed in settlement.

The accountant asks the book-keeper, Sam, to record the receipt of the cheque and write the remaining balance off as bad.

The trial balance extract is shown below:

Trial Balance Extract from KS Supplies Ltd as at 30 June 2009

	Dr	Cr
	£	£
Bank	12,956.40	
Debtors	28,123.90	

You are required to:

(a)   prepare journal entries, with suitable narratives, to record receipt of the cheque and writing off the remaining balance

(b)   calculate adjustments

(c)   adjust and correct ledger balances and create any new account balances that may be required

(d)   prepare a revised trial balance extract as at 30 June 2009.

16.4   Estela is the book-keeper for Lomax Services and has just received the following memo from the accountant, John Hughes.

MEMORANDUM

to: Estela Stavic, Book-keeper

from: John Hughes, Accountant   Date: 31 December 2009

You may remember that some time ago we wrote off £602.50 which was owed to us by Heath & Son. Today I have received a cheque for this amount from the company.

Could you please reinstate the original debt and record receipt of the cheque.

The trial balance extracts are shown below:

Trial Balance Extract from Lomax Services as at 31 December 2009

	Dr	Cr
	£	£
Bank	34,501.87	
Debtors	29,776.72	

You are required to:

(a) prepare journal entries, with suitable narratives, to record reinstatement of the debt and receipt of the cheque

(b) calculate adjustments

(c) adjust and correct ledger balances and create any new account balances that may be required

(d) prepare a revised trial balance extract as at 31 December 2009

16.5 Singh & Co is a well established company which imports goods from India. Recently the costs of carriage and freight have increased considerably and Mr Singh has decided to transfer these costs, currently £6,345.00 from the General Expenses Account to a new Carriage & Freight Charges Account. No entry has yet been made in the accounting records.

The trial balance extracts are shown below:

Trial Balance Extract from Singh & Co as at 30 November 2009		
	Dr	Cr
	£	£
General Expenses	23,784.00	

You are required to:

(a) prepare a journal entry with suitable narrative to record the transfer of the carriage and freight charges from the General Expenses Account to the new Carriage & Freight Charges Account

(b) calculate adjustments

(c) adjust and correct ledger balances and create any new accounts that may be required

(d) prepare a revised trial balance extract as at 30 November 2009

16.6 Albert is the book-keeper for Anderson Engineering Ltd and has recently completed all the book-keeping entries for the company and produced a trial balance as at 30 September 2009. He presents the trial balance to the accountant, Bill, who informs Albert that the following additional transactions require journal entries and adjustments to the trial balance.

(a) Casby & Co, who owe the company £723.90, are unable to pay their outstanding balance in full owing to financial difficulties. They have sent a cheque for £500 in settlement. The balance will have to be written off.

(b) The General Expenses Account includes the company's printing costs, currently £2,175.60 to date. The printing costs should be transfered from the General Expenses Account to a new Printing Account.

(c)   J Peterson Ltd which owes the company £410.56, has gone into liquidation. As a consequence, the debt will have to be written off.

(d)   Purchase of new photo-copier for use in the office on credit from Burn's (Office Supplies) Ltd. The photocopier cost £520.00 plus VAT £91.00, making a total of £611.00.

Extracts from the Trial Balance are shown below:

Trial Balance Extract of Anderson Engineering Co as at 30 September 2009		
	Dr	Cr
	£	£
Office Equipment	1,200.00	
Bank Overdraft		4,138.00
Value Added Tax		2,117.30
General Expenses	6,329.40	
Debtors	31,520.82	
Creditors		29,642.55

You are required to:

(a)   prepare journal entries, with suitable narratives, to record the transactions listed above

(b)   calculate adjustments

(c)   adjust and correct ledger balances and create any new account balances that may be required

(d)   prepare a revised trial balance extract as at 30 September 2009

16.7   Louise is the book-keeper in the accounts department of Paterson & Co and has recently completed all the book-keeping entries for the company and produced a trial balance as at 31 December 2009 (see next page). Louise presents the trial balance to the company accountant who informs her in an email that a number of transactions require journal entries and the trial balance adjusting accordingly. This is an extract from the email:

Louise,

(a)   Togwell & Sons Ltd who owe us £245.00 have written informing us that they are having financial difficulties and are going into liquidation. Unfortunately they are unable to pay this outstanding account therefore would you please write the debt off as bad.

(b)   We have purchased a computer and printer for use in the accounts department on credit from Data Supplies Ltd. The cost of the computer and printer is £600.00 plus VAT £105.00 making a total of £705.00. This is the first time the business has purchased computer equipment and so a new account will be needed to record the transaction.

(c) The General Expenses Account includes the company's insurance costs, currently £921.00. Could you please transfer these insurance costs from the General Expenses Account to a new Insurance Account.

(d) John Roberts who owes the company £856.00 has just sent us a cheque for £422.00 in settlement of the outstanding account. In his letter he states that he has recently been declared bankrupt and will not be able to pay the remaining balance. Could you please record receipt of the cheque and write off the remaining balance as a bad debt.

(e) You may recall that some time ago we wrote off £1,043.00 which was owed to us by GX Control Services. To-day I have received a cheque for the full amount from the firm. Could you please reinstate the original debt and record receipt of the cheque. You may need to create a new account for bad debts recovered.

The following trial balance was extracted from the books of Paterson & Co on 31 December 2009:

Paterson & Co

Trial Balance as at 31 December 2009

	Dr	Cr
	£	£
Purchases and Sales	46,968	80,615
Office Equipment	4,895	
Motor Vehicle	9,325	
General Expenses	4,029	
Motor Expenses	2,318	
Wages	14,920	
Stationery & Postage	603	
Rent & Rates	2,950	
Debtors and Creditors	5,800	4,461
Value Added Tax		1,688
Cash	122	
Bank	4,017	
Capital		9,183
	95,947	95,947

You are required to:

(a) prepare journal entries, with suitable narratives, to record the transactions listed in the email

(b) calculate adjustments

(c) adjust and correct ledger balances and create any new account balances that may be required

(d) prepare a revised trial balance as at 31 December 2009 (remember to leave extra lines in the trial balance before totalling to allow for any new accounts that may need to be created)

notes

index

*Note:
This book follows the OCR assessment requirements in the differing presentation of the Trial Balance in Units 1 and 3.
If you are studying Unit 1, use the Trial balance '(Unit 1)' references in this index; if you are studying Unit 3, use the Trial balance '(Unit 3)' index references.